THE
ORDER OF
RITUALS

THE
ORDER OF
RITUALS

THE INTERPRETATION OF EVERYDAY LIFE

HANS-GEORG
SOEFFNER

TRANSLATED BY MARA LUCKMANN

TRANSACTION PUBLISHERS
NEW BRUNSWICK (U.S.A.) AND LONDON (U.K.)

Library of Congress Catalog Number: 96-41532
ISBN: 1-56000-184-4
Printed in the United States of America

Library of Congress Cataloging-in-Publication Data

Soeffner, Hans-Georg.
    [Ordnung der Rituale. English]
    The order of rituals : the interpretation of everyday life / Hans-Georg Soeffner ; translated by Mara Luckmann.
        p. cm.
    Includes bibliographical references and index.
    ISBN 1-56000-184-4 (cloth : alk. paper)
    1. Social structure. 2. Social norms. 3. Rites and ceremonies. 4. Individualism. I. Title.
HM131.S617813 1996
306—dc20   96-41532
                                                                      CIP

Contents

Prologue

How Rituals are Ordered and the Order of Rituals

The "question of the subject" is woven into the network of contemporary social theory's themes whose concepts and contents shine brightly—system and lifeworld; constructivism and deconstruction; discourse, code, and difference—as central line of inquiry, general theme, and leitmotif at the same time. It is the inquiry into the here and beyond of systems, codes, and discourses; into the names of the "authors"; into the concrete, materially incarnate "place" in which "it" thinks, writes, acts, and "processes"; into the agency that makes and must make a distinction between an "I" and an "other."

The implicit and explicit ubiquitousness of this question is a reason, in the market of theories and schemes, why the "deconstruction of the subject" finds itself in immediate proximity to a simultaneously asserted, inflationary individualism (individualization of lifestyles, life situations, life stories, etc.). Moreover, as a result of the emphasis on a "de-subjectivization of the theory," the subject who is supposed to have disappeared is theorized upon more fervently than ever. Finally, the observer of markets can enjoy the perfect presentations in which the theoreticians of subject-free concepts stage themselves as a decorated empty space for their theories: as bodily performatory existence of that which is not supposed to exist.

Turning to the "order of symbols and rituals" in the face of this situation could easily be mistaken for an attempt to enrich the "deconstruction of the subject" by yet another variant or by the analyses of "discourse codifications." Yet nothing could be further from my intentions in the following chapters. Instead, my aim is, on the one hand, to pursue selected tracks on the paths to the contemporary belief or hope in an autonomous social subject. On the other hand, I shall also search for partial answers to the question of what efforts of order and orientation hold individualistically organized (purportedly atomized) societies together.

In doing so, I shall focus on those symbolic forms of (self-)presentation which at present permit us to bring enough order and clarity into the "new lack of clarity" conjured up by social critics (e.g. Habermas) that we feel quite comfortable in it.

Our society presents itself as unclear and unmanageable to all those who were (or are) still accustomed to seeing social order depicted in classes, strata, "central" groups or institutions, and who measure and classify the social world(s) according to "centers" and "margins." But human societies get caught up time and again in situations in which the traditional grids of order and stratifications lose their value and no longer serve as orientation for the individual. Situations like those can be found in the sixteenth and at the close of the eighteenth centuries in Central Europe, in which old orders give way to new ones, the social balance of power shifts, traditional hierarchies crumble and are replaced or destroyed by others.

Our times are not so very different *structurally* from those predecessors. Thus, in the United States, one has been able to observe for a long time now the development of a social structure pattern that is increasingly gaining importance in Western Europe, too: The social rise and fall of individuals is regulated less and less by stable, "hereditary" membership in classes or groups. The elevators of "vertical mobility" can no longer be rented beforehand and used exclusively by specific social groups. Drop-ins and drop-outs now belong to other and very various groups. They are evaluated more according to their future than according to their provenance. In addition, the "homemade mixture" of Western societies through global migrations receives a further, only temporarily "external" component: Mobility and variety, opposing interests and conflicts, dissimilarity and inequality, mass concentration and isolation, mechanisms of merging and exclusion are characteristic of these societies. The individual has to perform his own self-classification since the existing relations are losing their value. He has to make himself so recognizable by actions and external presentation as a member "of something" and as belonging "to something" that, tendentially, anyone can "classify" him without having ever seen him and without knowing him personally.

The combination of other and self-observation, of social presentation and self-staging, gains importance in these societies: They are, more than others, societies of observation and staging. The repertoires and styles of presentation become insignia of lifestyles. These for their part signal not only consumer habits, but also membership in collective attitudes in terms of conduct and value systems. Forms of presentation as elements and instruments of orientation put their special mark on the "mixed" societies.

As in historical situations of social re-formation, those guarantors of social orientation now appear in which social order becomes *visible* as a social product that is constantly to be renewed, and as an act of presentation by *each* individual member of society. Thus, frequent council decrees regulating clothing enjoyed their zenith precisely in those times in which the estate system collapsed: The willed ("new") self-classification replaced the matter-of-course that was traditional and anchored in routines.

Emblems, fashions, styles in staging, and the search for "new" symbols for a while replaced the corporative social order just as they later, time and again, were to replace the orders of classes or strata. The attempt to replace privilege, class, or strata-specific formations of demeanor with the help of ritualized or "ritualizable" rules of conduct stems from the same source, from Castiglione to Knigge and Pappritz, all the way to contemporary "how-to"s for "stylish" conduct.

This gives rise to the suspicion that economically, culturally, and ethnically "mixed" societies not only replace an old order through their return to specific, visible forms of presentation, but that they present themselves and their world views in them: as a public stage of lifestyles, attitudes, and demeanor, interests and worldviews, generally available to all. This stage hardly knows permanently distinguishable—through office or origin—"performers" any more. The stage is at the same time medium, market, and arena: the place in which every social formation, in fact everyone, must appear and present itself, himself, herself—insofar as they wish to hold their own in the face of the competition. Success on stage, however, comes only to those who are able to let their presentation become an element of a collectively recognized and all-embracing order.

My interest, then, is in social order as a permanently to-be-enacted achievement. It is in those admixtures that accompany all social acting. It is in the elementary devices we use when we orient ourselves according to one another and thereby also according to our conjectures about the expectations (and expectations of expectations) others have of us. My focus is on the incessant work on the social form and on the presentation patterns, arrangements, and staging practices to which social forms of expression themselves are indebted.

These forms of presentation have to constantly be converted through acting. They are bound to their realization in the acting, but in turn bind the action to pre-existing, traditional, and learned patterns. They subject the action to their "self-meaning" (*Eigen-Sinn*). Since the actors are frequently enough not conscious of this "self-meaning," a foreign will is just as often imposed upon them by the forms of presentation: the "frozen" and set knowledge, and the often barely recognizable intentions of past generations.[1]

Our knowledge of the origins, of the accomplishments of order, and of the original meaning of the presentational forms that we return to in acting is not very great. It is not knowledge *about* the acting, but rather knowledge *in* acting: There is no explicit knowledge of the form that relates to the forms of knowledge represented in the acting.

Thus, we tend to separate "form" from "content." Discussions of the supposedly "empty" rituals or of the "simply dead" ritualized action stems from this tendency. We thereby ignore the fact that, in customs and rituals, we are forming the cult of everyday life. We forget or overlook the fact that the "choice" of a form—along with many other things—lets us make this identification: The form *is* itself "content," which forms the expressions of action in a specific composition and tunes into the key and harmonies or disharmonies typical for those expressions. Just as one cannot call the Odyssey a novella or "Wanderers Nachtlied" a short novel, one can not either exchange at will rituals of greeting and parting, of burial and courtship. Action has its "genres," the same as literature.

So it can easily be misunderstood when the new, wondrously increasing, antiresearch handbooks and recipe collections for "qualitative" methods in the social sciences talk of "pattern analyses" (or suchlike) and invite social scientists—in a misunderstood application of conjectures drawn from speech-act theory and ethnomethodological conversation analysis—to act as taxonomists and archivists of forms and patterns "with whose help," this is the implication, social order is created. The attentive observer cannot help but notice that the patterns and forms of presentation he or she examines do not lead to a specific order, but that they *are* that specific order.

Realizing a form of presentation means creating an order, concretely and practically. Pattern collections can thus be no more than anthologies of exemplarily documented and reconstructed forms of presentation, to which one can justifiably assign a genre designation.[2] Consequently, it is useless to compile a guide for rituals and forms of presentation in acting. The way acting is ordered is not a result of laboratory desk work. It is created and perpetuated in its traditions and variations by those who act, who in turn shape the individual elements of action into ever new mosaics within the framework of familiar genres—or else create new genres.

As unique as the concrete realization of a ritual or form of presentation is on the one hand, as uniform on the other hand seem the sequences of routines, "habits of conduct," and rituals in the "everyday" of constantly recurring duties and work. In the cycle of routines, time seems to become viscous or even to stand still. The impression arises that nothing "really" happens. But in order to arrive at a partial answer to the question of the nature of social order, precisely what occurs when nothing (seemingly) takes place is also decisive: What is taking place here is the handing-down and settling-in of the forms. Here, the large and small rituals and "patterns" acquire their indestructibility. But here, too, is the source for their "insufficient" explicitness, for the no-longer-articulated, literally "tacit" knowledge: What we do constantly and as a matter of course over and over again requires no further elucidation in everyday action.

In the repetition, clues as to time and "reasons" for the emergence of specific forms are lost. The "everyday actors" would, if asked why they "use" certain routines, forms, and rituals, respond with new, often ad hoc "practical explanations" (Scott/Lyman). But even the most tenacious observers of everyday rituals can discover no more than a few clues and traces, unless they engage in a detailed reconstruction of individual cases. That, however, will offer them insight into the process that lets order and repetition turn into compulsory repetition and compulsory use of a specific order and specific form.

The observers will see how the forms create their own realities, destroy the new as such, or remove it, as something "new," from perception, and shape it according to "old" patterns. They will recognize the consequences of the "self-meaning" (stubbornness) of rituals and forms, and will discover that they figure as patterns of articulation for a certain view of reality, and *simultaneously* as triggering patterns for a largely pre-determined action sequence, in which that view is manifest as real action. And finally, they will understand that certain continuously handed-down rituals and forms of action can be preserved as specific symbolic forms by a society over a long period of time—in a sense, as action triggers at rest.

Such—for the time being—deactivated ignition devices are on call and at the disposal, in various constellations, of every society and its members as a kind of repertoire of conduct for the purpose of mastering future events. They [the devices] react to specific social problem-situations "assigned" to them as it were, conditioned by preceding experiences like contact fuses; they dictate to us a specific, preformed way of conduct. Whoever is at home in such symbolic forms (and who isn't, at least partially?!) is ignited in a predetermined, handed-down form by seemingly new but in fact already preinterpreted events. These become stimuli to him, which he responds to in a chain of reactions which in turn are often already determined and acquired by frequent practice in the past, down to the ignition order: they are, in fact, learned.

The Reconstruction of the Social Construction of Order

The reconstruction of the structure and effect of rituals, a small part of the total of symbolic forms in which we bed our social order, is not feasible except by analyzing individual cases: Only thus can structure and effect be "read" from a documented, concrete action sequence, and be presented both as qualities of the acting itself and also as processes of the reconstruction of order and reality. Such a structural-analytical reconstruction and presentation of individual cases attains its sociological explanatory value when it leads to the construction of a historical-genetic "ideal type." One should be able to distinguish this ideal type's model-like and consciously constructed distance from reality from concrete, historical action, thereby seeing it as meaningful and explaining the origins of its course, effects, and consequences.[3] This procedure of constructive reconstruction is that used by historical-reconstructive hermeneutics.[4]

Now, a prologue is the wrong place to face the periodically recurring debates on the already achieved or imminent "demise of hermeneutics." Nonetheless, I shall be so bold as to make some brief observations on hermeneutics' use of the concepts of "subject-bound" and "subject-centered" and the misunderstandings that result from these concepts.

Just as every worldview and every "truth," every theory, methodology, and method has its history, so, too, does hermeneutics. It has undergone changes and expansions, and, as a self-reflexive style of cognition, has through criticism contributed substantially to its own transformation. In historical-systematic terms, it is bound to *the principle* of the written word, first to the recording of language (texts), but then—a logical consequence—to *the quality of the being recorded of "data" in gen-*

eral, to the fixedness and, thus, tendentially infinite "recallibility" (discursiveness) of documents, now nonlinguistic as well as linguistic ones: human signs, actions, productions, and man-made "objects" of any kind.

In the—primarily but not exclusively Western—history of hermeneutics, the specific type of theological exegesis by many interpreters of the one Holy Scripture left its mark conspicuously on the schools of thought and interpretation. It was the search for the one subject represented in the text and the search for the subject's will. At the same time, though, philosophy and jurisprudence, two very ancient hermeneutic disciplines, have long tended to deal with quite other than the "one" subject and "meaning." Through this very other relation to their subjects and objects they placed the plural of the many (possible) truths and probabilities side by side with the singular of the one truth: side by side with the discovery of the "one" meaning, the "one" sense, they placed the development of the *potential* of meaning and sense.

The self-reflection inherent in the hermeneutic style of cognition led (from Spinoza through Schleiermacher, Dilthey and Gadamer, up to the present discussion) to the discovery and problematization of the reader and the interpreter as "co-author of texts."[5] By his interpretative action, this implicit co-creator fills the interpreted "text" (in the above, general sense of "document") with his own meanings and ranges of meaning. Where in our myths and Holy Scriptures the "one" holy subject itself already often used a human voice (via a prophet or even, splitting the authority, of a legislator *and* another voice by his side: Moses and Aaron), thus now, the interpreted ("represented" in the text) subject (or the document as subject) acquires an opposite: the interpreting subject. Both enter—already for Schleiermacher—a relationship of tension to each other that requires constant rebalancing.

With this redoubling of the subjects the dissolution of the (also theological!) subject centrism becomes *structurally* possible, and with it the dissolution of the axiom of the "one meaning" (text truth, meaning, sense, etc.). The potential of interpreters, of their stories, and of their histories systematically and historically "opens" the interpretee's potential meaning. In the course of all this, both on the side of the interpreter and that of the specific document, the transformation is made from absolute to historical semantics. The potential of context and reference grows to unmanageable proportions on both sides: The decomposition of (the interpreting and interpreted) subject and the "one" meaning had commenced—long before "decomposition" and "deconstruction" as drop-dead-arguments celebrated their boom.

As a logical consequence, the search for the "one" meaning lost some of its significance. At the same time, the insight into our imprisonment ("interwovenness") in sense and meaning increased: the insight into the fact that we are always interpreting, have to interpret, move in an always preinterpreted world and in seemingly hardly controllable surplusses of meaning.

This insight complemented and changed the formulation of the question in hermeneutics. Whereas earlier, it was exclusively the "what" of understanding, it now became, more and more, the "how": understanding itself as well as devices, "rules," "patterns," implicit premisses, socially conveyed ways of appropriating, "training," and handing down interpretation and understanding. Without knowledge of structure and method of understanding, this much was evident, founded statements about the "adequateness" of interpretations were and are hardly to be made any more: One comes close to understanding a concretely understood thing (an interpretation or explication) only if one can reconstruct, while understanding, how an "understood thing" is constructed in—and through—interpreting and understanding, and at what concrete, historical places subjects let their interpretations and constructions coagulate into texts as they write and interpret.

So here they are again, the subjects that were deemed lost. They step forward from the theater of the world and the scenery of signs, rows of citations, and figures of meaning, at two structurally significant places: (1) as historical-concrete actors (producers of documents) at a concrete historical place; and (2) as historical-concrete interpreters with specific historical ranges of interpretation. Moreover, both producers of documents and interpreters (the producers of documents of the second degree) *embody* the concrete, living authority of experience and decision which decides on adequateness, rightness, and plausibility of the product in question (i.e. the document or interpretation).

This decision is made in the course of the subject's "inner conversation" of the subject with himself, in the comparison of "interior" images. In this respect, both the producing and the interpreting subject remain the undeceivable authority of experience, perception, and decision. However, none of this internal communication as inner-subject-experience can be disposed of—except the choice, visible in the document, of a specific action and its product. The cycle of interpreting and understanding starts all over again.

Sociological Novellas

The lover of sociological "macro-theories," especially system theories, takes pleasure in the arithmetics of the world. If, in addition, he succeeds in translating the arithmetics of the world into a world of arithmetics, then his fondest desires are fulfilled. Whatever comes up against him is sucked in by the gears of theory, fed into the machinery of concepts, translated and processed serially until it rolls off the production line conspicuously marked with the linguistic and quality stamp of its producer: the new serial number for a prefabricated encyclopedia. As sociologist, the macro-theoretician now is rid of all problems, he merely continues himself to be one for his colleagues: predominantly for those colleagues whose aim it is to describe and comprehend concrete social phenomena as such and to explain these phenomena causally both in their specificity and in their societal "generalizability."

Material sociology as a science of reality has a far harder time than system theories: It must first get to know the phenomenon thoroughly before speaking about it. Its questions and answers are "open" insofar as they have to adapt to the peculiar traits of the phenomenon. And finally, the formation of such a sociological theory is perpetuated by analyzing individual cases. Where it loses its grounding in empiricism and can neither be verified nor falsified by the latter, such theory formation loses its claim of being sociology. Consequently, the case study is the King's highway of theory-guided and theory-perpetuating sociology.

The object of the case study can be anything that hits the eye of the observer, that seems to contradict former theoretical insights—or simply anything that arouses curiosity. The "case" is delineated by the explicitly to-be-stated interest of the observer and the subsequent theoretical definition of what is to be the "case" and its demarcations, wherein lie the hopes for insights resulting from the case analysis that can then be generalized.

The case study does not, unfortunately, share the language of that literary genre, the novella, but it does share its proximity to the individual, delineable and yet exemplary phenomenon. However, in the case study the interest—or at least my sociological interest—is not in what Goethe called "an unheard-of event that has taken place."[6] Instead, my interest is in the reasons for the exigency of every single detail in order to construct meaning in an action. The unheard of is the detail and its specific location, the individual element which in *its* specific location contributes to the meaning (a potential of meaning) of the whole in its enactment, and which later makes this potential of meaning accessible to interpreters.

It is the unique form (*Gestalt*) and position of each individual element of the social order that engenders the case analyst's fascination with detail, his or her love for the seemingly secondary, his or her attention to the network of motives and symbols. They all are the expression of a certain enchantment on the part of the interpreter by the interplay of coincidence and logical consistency, wherein forms of acting *and* interpreting are created out of the sequence and combination of individual elements. It is true that this magic loses some of its sheen when the interpretation decodes how a general phenomenon is articulated and presented in the specific, the concrete historical phenomenon. Nonetheless, the fascination with the singular is not lost: It is the concrete location where society lives and is kept alive.

Before Boccaccio lets his heroes begin narrating their "novellas," he recounts, in the form of a frame story, where his narrators are and why they are narrating: They have retreated to a castle on their flight from the plague. So great "was the virulence of the plague in communicating itself from one person to another, that not only did it affect human beings, but, what is more strange, it very often proceeded in an extraordinary way. If an article belonging to one sick of the plague or one who had died of it was touched by an animal outside of the human species, the creature was not only infected, but in a very short time it died of the disease."[7] In short, everything in the outside world is contaminated. The narrators, though, are, or at least deem themselves, safe.

The sociological "novella writer" as case analyst requires his or her own field. He may love castles, but he doesn't live in one. Unlike some of his colleagues who push nothing but theories, he does not fear "his" field in the "outside world" like the plague. He doesn't necessarily love it, either, although he is not dealing with victims of the plague, but rather, to a large extent with "his own kind." If at all, the contagiousness is mutual. To create and maintain a certain distance is important for both sides, for those who observe and explain something, and for the others who want to remain anonymous as they act. The observer is not primarily responsible for what he doesn't see and thus doesn't make accessible, in terms of possibilities, to himself and others. This distance has nothing to do with flight, just as little as with submerging oneself "in the field" without re-emerging.

For this kind of observer, sickness or health, pathology or normality—this is where the range of images borrowed from Boccaccio ends—are neither measurements of degree for the conduct of others nor categories of a social theory. He likes to be spared these classifications just as do his compatriots. His focus is on the comprehending reconstruction of what he finds as a given, on explaining the causes of what he observes, and on developing the realm of possibilities before the background of historically grown "facticity."

As an hermeneutic analyst, he hands over the deduction of and responsibility for that which could and should be—not exclusively but primarily—to himself, but also to his readers.

Notes

1. The connection frequently made between such presentation patterns and "everyday rituals" to customs, conventions, behavioral norms, and traditions is anything but coincidental. The concrete origins of these patterns of conduct can no longer be clearly determined, however. The reasons for their creation are lost in the dark and/or are no longer accessible to the actor's consciousness. See also Benedict, Ruth (1955), *Urformen der Kultur,* Hamburg.
2. Concerning the concept of "communicative genres" see Luckmann, Thomas (1989), *Kultur und Kommunikation,* in *Kultur und Gesellschaft,* Verhandlungen des 24. Deutschen Soziologentages, des II. Österreichischen Soziologentages und des 8. Kongresses der Schweizerischen Gesellschaft für Soziologie in Zürich 1989, ed. by M. Haller, H.-J. Hoffmann-Nowotny, and W. Zapf: 33–45.
3. See Weber, Max [(5) 1972], *Wirtschaft und Gesellschaft,* Tübingen: 1–11.
4. In this context, see Soeffner, Hans-Georg (1989), *Auslegung des Alltags—Der Alltag der Auslegung,* Frankfurt.
5. See Iser, Wolfgang (1972), *Der implizite Leser, Kommunikationsformen des Romans von Bunyan bis Beckett,* Munich.
6. Goethe to Eckermann, 25. 1. 1827.
7. Boccaccio, Giovanni [(1492) 1930, 1955], *The Decameron,* transl. by Frances Winwar, New York.

Martin Luther before The Diet of Worms

1

Luther—From the Collectivity of Faith to a Lutheran-Protestant Type of Individuality

"Why don't you come by sometime and tell me your story?"

—Citizen Kane

There is a long history, at least in Central Europe, to the present fact that practically everyone can tell their story, practically everyone offers, at all times and places and with great virtuosity, self-thematization, either openly declared or else dressed up as "relationship problems"; that practically every kind of social action, from defense pleas via political legitimations to explanations of "private" decisions, is not only autobiographically tinged, but also deemed explicable by autobiography itself. It is the history of a form of knowledge and representation which was and is clearly marked by the interpretation of reality, world and self in the modern world and the present—it is the history of the social type of presentation of "accentuated subjectivity."

Some of the conditions for successful, collectively accepted self-thematization are: (1) knowing the techniques of self-observation; (2) the collectively known and societally trained "guidelines" [including "guidelines for suffering," which supply points of orientation for self-perception (see Hahn, 1982: 407ff.; Hahn, 1984: 229ff.)]; (3) the *structural* isolation of a "self" that is perceiving itself (Hildebrandt, 1985) and securing the significance of self-perception; (4) historically embedding *and* preparing the "newly" developing forms of representation and knowledge through existing, institutionally secured and collectively recognized forms of presentation; and (5) social structural and economic changes that present or represent[1] themselves through the "new" form of

1

knowledge in everyday consciousness, and are legitimized "ideologically" by them (see Luckmann, 1980).

Such conditions are neither created by one individual, nor do they emerge "suddenly," unexpectedly, or—as some seem to find desirable— at a precise historical moment in time. Rather, they tend to be the result of a long development, heralded by "traces" and "isolated tendencies" long before they become collectively accepted. And they point the subsequent interpreter to earlier social structures that only later take on a recognizable form. These structures are but rarely visible to the consciousness of those who live within their confines. And frequently, the quality of these structures and, even more, the ensuing social consequences and effects, are actually in opposition to the intentions and interests of those who, in fact and objectively, helped create those structures. In the following I shall attempt to show this, taking Luther as an example.

Some of these "great individuals," whose stories to this day illustrate and constitute the everyday, living consciousness of "history," neither invent new structures nor effect the implementation of the current ones, let alone new ones through their implicit, at times also explicit use of the new structures for political, scientific, or artistic action. Others—among them Martin Luther—are able to find a collective language for already existing social phenomena, which have not and could not formerly be articulated. They supply the intentions, actions, and plans with a representative means of expression, with their own linguistic system of symbols. They combine the collectively existing repertoire of symbols, having listened to the way ordinary people speak, *through* and *into* a great defining text, beside which all other texts, everything else, including one's own life, become no more than background text.

Therefore, apart from their historical meaning, the central significance of the "great articulators" lies in the way they prepare, in an exemplary fashion, the "data" that the later interpreter requires in order to understand fragments and excerpts of the historical developments by analyzing the historical preconditions that brought them about. The following discussion will be about the path that Luther paved structurally, even if not intentionally, and which he in part took himself, from the collectivity of faith and life style to isolation in faith and lifestyle, from collective curriculum vitae to (auto)biography, from observation of the other to observation of the self, from the individual in the world to the world within the individual.

The Old in the New and the New in the Old—
Luther and His Name[2]

Originally, Luther's family was called "Luder" (Loewenich, 1983: 36). He entered the University of Erfurt under the name "Martinus Ludher Mansfeldt." In 1517, he changed his name from *Luder* to Luther, and included his parents in this undertaking. All this is common knowledge. What has been a matter of argument, however, are the reasons he might have had for changing his name. There are two interpretations that refer to language use and polemics in connection with Luther's name during the Reformation. His opponents, as opponents playing by the rules of proper opposition were compelled to, brought the name "Luder" in connection to *lotter* ("sloven"), *Luderleben* ("debauched life"), and *Lockerspeise,* or *Aas* ("carrion"), and the odors associated with the latter. In other words, they quoted linguistic usage that was possible at the time and that one finds intact to this day in words like *Luder* ("scoundrel") and *Lude* ("pimp"). The other camp of interpreters, philologically educated as it was, knew the rules of sound change and semantic change, and defended an opposite position. According to their theory, *Luder* is connected to the word *lauter,* or "honest."

What we can deduce from these opposing interpretations is the irritating fact that, as so often, quasi-scientific—in this case, philological—arguments are wielded in a rhetorical tournament jostling for the correct worldview. Contradicting the above, it has recently been proven with great philological accuracy (Moeller and Stackmann, 1981) that the change from *Luder* to "Luther" referred neither to *lotter* ("sloven") nor to *lauter* ("honest"), but rather, that the change came about because at the time he changed his name, Luther was signing letters he wrote to his friends (e.g. Spalatin, Melanchton, and Lang), with the name *Eleutherius* (i.e., "the liberated one", "the one who feels free"). This "derivation" from the Greek is symptomatic of that mixture of allusion and interpretation, using etymologies, which was commonly used in the Humanistic Circle (*Humanistischer Kreis*). Luther applied the same stylistic devices weighed down with self-interpretation.

Luther used the signature *Eleutherius* only between 1517 and 1519. There is a definite chronological correspondence between his use of the Greek epithet and the changing of his German name. The Greek epithet appears shortly before his *Theses,* that is, before their publication. In

1519, it disappears abruptly. Moeller and Stackmann put forth the theory that the connection between the name change and the epithet *Eleutherius* expresses latently in 1517 what later becomes manifest in the idea: Luther's new conviction that he had become free from other human beings through his servitude to God. Luther's new self-concept—"freedom through servitude"—was first symbolized in the Greek epithet and finally confirmed in the symbolic/pragmatic name change. Luther's writings develop and explicate theoretically in retrospective what had already been accomplished symbolically in the act of representing a conviction.

If one interprets this biographical detail in the life of the translator, theologian, and truth seeker more exactingly, then one sees a characteristic image become manifest in the symbolic act of Luther's name change. That is, the new name "Luther"—retaining the "old," the family, and religious tradition except for the one letter, which he replaces by two others—symbolically joins the past with the new conviction expressed in an "old" language. The name thus is more reformed in the symbolic new formation than it is actually newly formulated.

The contradictory unity of "liberty and servitude," symbolically implied in the name change, refers, through Luther's seemingly magic use of linguistic symbolism, to an encompassing symbolic pattern of world and self-interpretation, to the allusion or re-evaluation of his own life as well as of the world via symbolic acts. At the same time, the symbolic act or symbolic context lends all the individual elements and individual experiences a consistent, uniform meaning. This becomes visible in the issue of mind-body or soul-flesh. Flesh, or body—material housing of the soul and/or mind in our culture usually suffers a bad reputation—gains its meaning and worth, if any, through its visible or suspected symbolic connection to its tenants, who are considered superior to the lodging (i.e., through the soul and the mind, which in their turn represent a superior or *the* Supreme Being of whom they partake). If soul and mind are free, then so is the whole person. In short: Along with his name change, Luther has not only pulled a new spiritual cloak around his old Adam; the old Adam becomes a whole new person. The symbolic conversion becomes a real one.

Christian tradition knows many precursors to this conversion figure. Luther chose one of the most prominent, albeit not as *exemplum vitae,* but rather as a form of existence. He chose that inquisitive rager Saul, on whom suddenly, on his way to Damascus (Acts 9) "a light shone from heaven," who heard a voice saying "Saul, Saul, why are you persecuting me?"[3], who was the only one among his companions to understand the voice, who became blind and finally regained his sight from out of the blindness—who turned from a Saul into a Paul.

Almost 1500 years later, this story can be told in a different way. It is given a different context and a different milieu, but remains perfectly recognizable. Saul's journey to Damascus becomes Luther's return from Gotha to Erfurt. The fledgling law student—Luther's father wants his son to make his career in this field—has bought the necessary books in Gotha. On his return, he experiences a "frightening apparition from heaven."[4] He secretly sells all his law books, gives a goodbye dinner for his friends in Erfurt, and goes "immediately to the Augustinian monastery in Erfurt that same night. For that was what He had ordered, and became a monk." In the Erfurt monastery of the Augustinian hermits, he first is named Augustinus[5] after the saint of his order, another conversion story. But already shortly thereafter, he is called "Martinus" again. And then the revived Acts of the Apostles and Luther's own self-interpretation permanently gain the upper hand. Professor Nathin, one of Luther's theological superiors, recommends him to the nuns in the convent of Mühlhausen as a "second Paul," who "was miraculously converted, just like the apostle" (Friedenthal, 1983: 59ff.).

Saul/Paul is more than a mythical pendant to Martin Luther. Paul became not only an "identification figure" for him, but also the crown witness of the "Holy Scripture"—a crown witness, however, who never saw Jesus, but only knows Him from the acolytes' stories and sermons. A crown witness, in other words, who possesses authority not through his presence or participation in the event, but rather through his convincing *interpretation* of what he has heard. And, conversely, the reported stories attain their meaning and authorization not through the eyewitness, but rather, through the *interpreter.* Consequently, in Luther's prologue to his Romans theology, he says, "This Epistle is the true central piece of the New Testament and the truest Gospel" (Luther, 1983b). Accordingly, it is here, in Romans 3:28, that we find the focal point for the development of Luther's theology: "Therefore we conclude that a man is justified by faith apart from the deeds of the law." This "alone"—*sola fide*—Luther adds to the "old" faith, the "old" text, the same as he added the "th" to his name. Here, too, he is following the example of his model, who signalled his conversion by changing one letter of his name, albeit the first one. He changes the old interpretatively—only seemingly in a minimal way—by centering it in *one* specific meaning.

But stories and myths would not exist, or continue to exist, if they weren't capable of rejuvenation while maintaining their structure. They connect predecessor and successor, make visible the repetition and, at the same time, vary the material, actualize it, revitalize it.[6] Thus, the "second Paul" from Erfurt has Saul/Paul as his model. The Saul from the New Testament for his part refers to a Saul from the Old Testament who also tenaciously pursues a just man. The Saul from the New Testament and his successor were able to convert "to redemption"; the Old Testament Saul, on the other hand, unwillingly performed a negative conversion "away from redemption," an act from which he never recovered, all his efforts notwithstanding. Saul/Paul are here—prior to the works of Jesus, "David's son"—still split into two actors: Saul and David.

The former becomes disobedient to his God. God loses "interest" in him (I Samuel 15). The other, David, is selected in order to replace the former. Saul tries to appease his Lord through visible deeds and sacrifices. His attempts are to no avail. David, the newly elect, has no works to show (yet), but still is preferred, "For the Lord does not see as man sees; for man looks at the outward appearance, but the LORD looks at the heart" (I Samuel 16:7). The *leitmotif* of Lutheran theology is sounded here in no uncertain terms. Not the works, but faith alone; not that which is visible from the outside, but the "interior" that is invisible to others, the heart decides on the path toward attaining "justice before God." Already here, Lutherism and Calvinism become recognizable in their structural opposition.

But in Luther's real existence, too, this interesting—not only for sociologists—approximation of life to theology and vice versa take place. The Old Testament Saul is not only "rejected" by his God, he is also punished with the "distressing spirit" (I Samuel 16:16) or, in modern parlance, with melancholy and despair. When that "distressing spirit" comes over him, the only thing that can help him is harp music. David is a virtuoso on the harp and thus Saul's therapist: "And so it was, whenever the spirit from God was upon Saul, that David would take a harp and play it with his hand. Then Saul would become refreshed and well, and the distressing spirit would depart from him" (I Samuel 16:23).

For Luther, who suffered bouts of deep depression all his life, it was music more than anything that helped soothe sadness and despair—to be exact, helped against "Satan, the spirit of melancholy." When he was suffering from those attacks, friends would bring him his lute. And Luther—reportedly a master of this difficult instrument—would begin to play. Luther himself expressed his understanding of music by quoting the old patterns, as "prologue to all good breviaries" (1538).[7]

His state improves. The evil spirit leaves him.[8] David-Martinus-Paul II (let us remain in the terminology of myth and legend) hold their own against Saul I-Saul II and their evil spirit, a spirit that can completely besiege a human being, overpower him, and drive him to suicide.[9]

What is divided up between two people in the Old Testament, between the one rejected and the one elected (Cain/Abel, Saul/David), between two antipodal *Doppelgänger,* in the New Testament is transferred, especially through Paul's writings, onto the individual. The double structure becomes the characteristic of the individual, his essential and by the same token antipodal possibilities. *The conversion is the visible realization of this double structure within one person, made manifest through action.* Conversion is a specific form of presentation and self-interpretation, which we have inherited from our Judeo-Christian tradition and which seems to persist, albeit with new contents.

Luther's way of dealing with his own name and the concomitant acceptance and "lived appreciation" of examples passed down through a "holy text," no matter how marginal they may have appeared initially, connote a thoroughly symbolic self-perception that marked Luther's perception of his life. They connote the contradictory unity of "being free in respect to others and in respect to the world" on the one hand, and "servitude to God" on the other. In this context, "servitude to God" conceals the fact that Luther, when he uses the term "freedom" in general, goes much further: It is his conviction that humans without God are fundamentally unfree. God alone is free and in possession of a free will, the only subject entitled to freedom in general and, thus, also freedom concerning His will. "Human will" on the other hand, according to Luther, "is set down in the middle. Like a beast of burden, if God sits on it, then his will and direction are as God's, like in the Psalm, 'I have become a beast of burden and I am always with You.' If Satan sits on it, then his will and direction are as Satan's. And it is not in the realm of his free choice to run to one of the two riders nor to seek out one or the other; for the riders themselves fight in order to keep him or claim him."[10]

Upon closer inspection, this much-quoted simile of the human will as beast of burden—one should, in general, quote less ritualistically and interpret more carefully instead—makes Luther's specific treatment of tradition, its reception and reformation clear. What I first noticed while examining the Psalm Luther quotes (Ps. 73:22–24) was that Luther, the Bible translator, can hardly have taken from this Psalm the image of the beast of burden as a beast to be ridden, or at any rate not from *his* translation of the Psalm. "I was so foolish and ignorant; I was like a beast before You. Nevertheless I am continually with You. You hold me by my right hand. You will guide me with Your counsel, and afterward receive me to glory." Luther's interpretation of the (unfree) will—which, if one takes the image of the beast seriously, is not a rationally founded will, but much more impulse and affect—is covered by this part of the text: without God who takes him by the hand and guides him with his counsel, man is a fool or a beast (i.e., not master of his own decisions).

But where does the image of the mount come from and that of the two riders fighting for it? Literary criticism gives us some information on the subject (Adam, 1962): The man who has now become a "reformer" and bible translator, the former member of the order of the Augustinian hermits, combines the text of the Psalm with an image from the pseudo-Augustinian Hypomnesticon.[11]

This combination seems to suggest a comparison of Augustine's and Luther's manner of argumentation and their central themes. In the course of such a comparison, we discover a narrowing and centering of themes that is specific to Luther. Augustine's thought processes are schooled according to Plato and his image of mankind, which sees an originally free will (i.e., in Adam), blessed with rational thought, as the core of man's personality. This is according to Augustine's "De libero arbitrio," from the year 395. Luther takes up this topic antithetically, but "cleansed" of all classical philosophical tradition and blind faith in rational thought, oriented instead toward a Judeo-Christian image of mankind.

At the same time, and this is decisive, the world becomes narrower with Luther. Augustine's *civitates,* the divine or satanic commonalities, filled with human beings, are reduced to the individual. No longer is the *civitas* the battlefield upon which the armies of God and Satan meet. Accordingly, the war with "Satan" is no longer to be waged by the polis or community. This war "rages" within the individual. The war for the human being takes place *within* the human being. And at the same time he is (usually the sole) witness of this merciless event. Two subjects, God and Satan, fight for a third, who is denied the free will and status of subject. Where, then, does this third subject stand? What is his status? How is he determined? Luther's answer: the subject exists and acts "*ex alterius arbitrio,*" or is, in "modern" terms, determined by exterior forces. Incidentally, *alterius* could also be, grammatically speaking, of neutral gender, a determining "id" such as later times invented. External determination on the one hand, strict individualization of the battle on the other, now characterize the image of mankind.

This has many consequences, and one of my theses derives from this Lutheran linking of individualization of the battlefield on the one hand with the doctrine of irrational will, or instinct and affect, on the other. The thesis is that Luther's and Freud's Christian-Judaic and Judeo-Christian positions, metaphors, and concepts of reality are in many ways closely related to each other. But more importantly, Freud has Luther to thank not only for the preparation of certain views of the world, mankind, and reality as well as vital preliminary work on the construction of a certain kind of subjectivity. Psychoanalysis also has Luther to thank for its own effect on "modern" individuals, as well as on German Protestantism and its concept of pastoral care and care for the human being, which of late includes assorted methods of psychotherapy.

Luther spent his formative years in a monastery. At the age of twenty-one, he entered the "Black Monastery" in Erfurt, and he lived in the Wittenberger monastery to the end of his days. He began his monastic life as an Augustinian hermit—and died, husband and father, still in a monastery. He was and remained during all this time a scholar and interpreter of texts. His worldview was shaped not by his journey to Rome, not by his appearance at the Parliament (*Reichstag*) of Worms, nor his "excursion" to the Wartburg. His segment of the world is the study room, a cell. His world originates from the text, and he in turn influences the world through texts.

Once again, he illustrates the "metaphor" in his lifestyle, the metaphor he lives and represents. It is the double structure, consisting of retrospection to the "old," the "original" given, and variation of the "old" through interpretation; of conversion in life and in text interpretation, of collectively existing tradition and individualization of experience: of acceptance and simultaneous destruction of tradition, which he robs of its collective, "external" security by making it prove itself on an "inner" battlefield—in individual experience and in the isolation of the individual.

From "Collective" Curriculum Vitae to (Auto)Biography

Although we cannot compete with "those two men" (Socrates and Plato) and their "perfect humanity," we can still attempt to emulate, "as much as we are able, their exemplary actions and follow their tracks" (Plutarch, 1947: 51). With this brief characterization of his paedagogical goals, Plutarch formulated a fundamental conviction of ancient Greece and a premiss for its image of mankind. It is that human life gains the quality of "complete humanity" through participating in rational thought and through insight into the "essence of the spirit" or of the "ideas." The focus is not on individuality or on the story of the individual's development, but rather on the forming of complete humanity, of the general, the universal—of reason and mind—which define the essence of the human being. Accordingly, life is subordinate to "the point of view of *paideia*, of upbringing in the sense of education...to the thought of self-improvement as borne by Eros" (Bultmann, 1956: 110). Upbringing in the sense of "education" is, however, "a term alien to the biblical world" (Bultmann, 1956: 110). In place of the development of man to a "harmonious," "well-ordered," and "balanced" life, biblical man encounters God and His interference in human life as the center both of the image of mankind and of life orientation. The categories that the biblical-Christian lifestyle applies are "being called," "being selected," "being rejected." The encounter with God that makes recognizable which of these directions one's life is to take occurs within the "concrete, historical events"—the place where "God is encountered as the demanding, judging, or pardoning One" (Bultmann, 1956, 110). As ancient Greece oriented itself—*structurally*—according to ideal curricula vitae, thus in Christianity, the historically very gradually developing autobiography emerges—also *structurally*—"as a description of the individual life, guided by God" (Bultmann, 1956, 110). Upbringing as—and toward—education, toward perfection, the ancient Greek ideal, in the eyes of Christendom quickly assumed the aftertaste of "superbia," or arrogance; that means it is seen not only as dispensable, but basically even as dangerous.

Bultmann's historical-structural comparison of the image of man from Greek antiquity and that of "biblical man" enables us to differentiate between, on the one hand, the orientation of life according to ideal biographies and, on the other, the orientation according to individualized autobiographies, tendencies that come together in Christendom, in Christian churches, as well as in Christian lifestyle "types." The historical shift from one to the other can thus be observed with greater precision. What becomes evident is that the medieval church, with its living admonition to the faithful to take the saints as role models for their lives according to the traditional hagiography, reverts to the patterns of upbringing and education from ancient pedagogy not in terms of content,[12] but very much in terms of structure. How did this come about?

Human life is rendered nearly intolerable by the idea of a transparent, arbitrarily interfering God standing directly opposite man who is at God's mercy without defense in the "concrete historical encounter," and further rendered intolerable by the immense threat emanating from this image. Structurally contained in this concept is the invitation to flee from the situation. This is historically realized both in the protective, ritual ordering of one's day and one's life in orthodox Judaism, and in the exemplary middlemen who insert themselves between the directly interfering God and the individual who is so threatened by Him—visibly successful *receivers* of mercy whom, because of their success, the Church makes into *mediators* of mercy.

Luther grew up in this situation of the wish fulfilled—in a ritual distance to God created by the Church and secured by exemplary mediators. Outside of his parents' house, in which father and mother tried to adhere to the then highly common and to them valid Christian concept of child rearing by staging a kind of competition in beating their children,[13] Luther encountered religion "as a whole" for the first time when he entered Latin School at the age of five: not as a religion of revelation, but rather, as a system of convictions and rules of conduct. These were literally beaten into Luther and his co-students, as was common practice at the time (see Paulsen, 1919: 3ff.), the Saints' Calendar in hand. Latin and religious instruction thus merged into one impressive and easy-to-memorize didactic unity.

The Saints' Calendar's succession of days and years repeats the timeless saints' names and their exemplary lives—the finite chronology of the Calendar suspended in the repetition of the "eternally valid." At the same time, parents tend to bind their children, their children's names, and orientation in life—via the "name-day"—to an ever-valid model of action and type of curriculum vitae.[14] The individual's life moves to a specific position within a given context of order.

This already barely surmountable grid of rules and regulations on how to lead one's life is further reinforced by a ritually secured system of holy actions, in other words, by the sacraments. Much has been written and said about the "effect," "function," "symbolic form," and symbolic contents of the sacraments. What has scarcely been touched upon is the *organizing and forming of the individual Christian life into stations,* which the sacraments attempt to do. If the reader will bear with me in considering the number seven of the sacraments, which was only established in the twelfth century,[15] and from a different point of view, then it will become apparent how that number, among other things, also serves to firmly structure the individual's life into stations.

Birth, the end of childhood, marriage, and death are not only depicted in the sacraments of passage, that is, christening, confirmation, marriage,[16] and extreme unction, but also sanctified as eternal stations in life which link all generations. But more: they link the generations among each other into families and communities of manageable size. Parents and godparents accompany the growing-up and the first phases of the child's life with his christening and confirmation—symbolically reminding the adults of their own childhood. In a symbolic preparation of their own end, the parents and godparents experience, together with the following generation, the "extreme unction," the final passage of the older generation. All generations stand within a life cycle that faces both forward and backward—a cycle they share that is rendered orderly and eternal by the sacraments.

It is the, shall we say, *confirmative sacraments* of Eucharist and penitence that guarantee the believer continual reminders of this life cycle. They bring order to the weeks and years—recalling the larger continuity—and connect everyday life with the order of the life cycle. This leaves little or no room for individual autobiography. Life-cycle and everyday conduct are subject to the same system of rules and regulations—from the "weighty" stations in the life cycle all the way to the ramifications of everyday actions.

The institutional guarantor of the lasting realization and repetition of this symbolic pattern of order, the religious specialist, expert, and administrator of rituals (see Douglas, 1974) himself is visibly included in this order through the participation in a sacrament: he secures this order and is in turn secured by it in the sacrament of "ordo"—ordination—in a *sacrament of guarantee*, which sanctifies the institution itself. The institutional repetition of the rite in Christian mythology thus turns into—as in other myths, too—the faith in the magical character of repetition: the repetition of myth becomes the myth of repetition (see Lévi-Strauss, 1967). Already in his time as Augustinian hermit, Luther destroys—initially for himself alone—these ritual networks of rules and regulations and thereby too, the protective distance which the network lays between the faithful and the immediacy of the "sanctified." Luther aims his entire attention at "the God revealed in the Word," at the "holy text" itself, not at the tradition of exegesis by the church fathers, a tradition which, in his view, comes between the faithful and the "bright, naked truth," the immediacy of God. As one of the learned padres and future docents of theology, he receives a complete Bible edition bound in red leather (see Friedenthal 1983: 65): the prescribed Latin translation by Hieronymus. He thereby enjoys a privilege not accorded the lesser brothers. They never behold the Holy Scripture; they are merely read aloud select passages. Luther so visibly concentrates on reading the Bible that, according to reports, his teacher Usingen sees fit to warn him: "Eh, Brother Martin, what is the Bible? One should read the old teachers, they distilled the juice of truth from the Bible, the Bible causes all turmoil" (quoted according to Friedenthal, 1983: 67).

Luther was convinced of the opposite: tradition is little or nothing, the immediacy of the "manifest word" or the immediacy of God Himself is everything. As he, at first only for himself in his perusal of the Bible, later for others in his translation of the Bible, pushes aside tradition's distancing element and establishes "genuine" access to the "only true word," to the immediacy of "God's given word," he also destroys, by reducing the sacraments to baptism and Eucharist, the cycle of ritually ordered and sanctified stations of life. The attention of the faithful is focused on faith, penitence, and mercy, on the individual's immediacy to God. *The cyclically and ritually ordered time is dissolved, by concentrating on the immediate encounter with God, into a chain of moments of decision and testing, while the cyclical succession of generations is dissolved into one person's individualization before God. The smallest unit of society—the individual—becomes, tendentially, the sole and thus the highest authority by way of the postulate of immediacy.*

With Luther, Protestantism turns back to what Bultmann later termed "biblical man," to that human being who encounters his God as a "demanding, judging and merciful" God in a "concrete historical context," who sees himself rather than the world as the stage for his trials, who can reach the point of considering his surroundings and the external world as secondary, seen in the light of his immediacy to God. Luther's man, radically oriented toward the individual's immediacy to God, as well as Bultmann's biblical man belong "to the world" as though they did not belong to it. They belong to "those who have wives [should be] as though they had none, those who weep as though they did not weep, those who rejoice as though they did not rejoice, those who buy as though they did not possess, and those who use this world as not misusing it. For the form of this world is passing away"(I Corinthians 7: 30ff.).[17] Luther's performance at the Diet at Worms was thus exemplary for the realization of this image of man. This performance is not the symbol of a new collective and merely "reformed" practicing of religion. Rather, it is an exquisite demonstration of how *individualization* is the central quality of this religious type who firmly places *himself,* his own conscience, against the collective authorities. "Thus I cannot and will not retract anything, because it is neither salutary nor safe to do anything against *one's conscience* (emphasis added). So help me God." (Quoted according to Friedenthal, 1983: 338; Loewenich, 1983: 185.) In these final words from his defense speech (on the second day of his questioning), what resounds is not only the individualization of the human being who answers to God alone through his conscience, but by their structure they also articulate, in referring to the conscience, that historically much later construct for legitimation and judgment, the "ego," which has its secure place in the store of knowledge of modern "Western" cultures as a rarely questioned explicatory pattern. Here, the individual becomes immediate to himself or rather to that part of himself which represents, as a "result of socialization," "society," and not "God." In concrete terms, though, the individual refers reflectively to his "ego," not society, that alliance of his fellow human beings. He remains within himself in "communication" with his "ego" and, if he does justice to his "higher," or "upper" self, then he is at peace with himself. Regardless of the external dangers, he can shout out, like Luther at the conclusion of the Parliament, "I have come through, I have come through." (Quoted according to Friedenthal, 1983: 338; see Loewenich, 1983: 185.)

What also belongs to the structural effects of this turning (back) from participation in the general (including the social) and toward individualization, and to the consequences of the escape and departure from the cyclically ordered time of exemplary stations and stories into historical chains of moments and events, is the development of autobiography as a description of the individual encounter, the development of the history of the individual with God: the recounted recapitulation of a life guided by God.[18]

But whoever wants to describe needs to know what is important to himself and to others. He requires points of orientation for the observation and recollection of events. He cannot do without criteria that enable him to differentiate between what is "relevant" and what is "irrelevant." In short, he who has a story to tell not only must have the "contents" of the story, but must also have knowledge of the structure and form of presentation for the story that is to be told. Accordingly, a specific pattern of observation and a specific system of relevance belong to the structure of an autobiography; and the autobiographer must be practiced in them, must have had "training" in them.

From Other-Observation to Self-Observation

In Luther's day, the monasteries in Germany and elsewhere were not, generally speaking, all that they should have been. It was with good cause that those who lived under the rules of the order—the "regulated ones"—did not enjoy the best of reputations, according to contemporary documents (see Bohler, 1921; Lohse, 1962). The European medieval literature, especially that of the late Middle Ages and the Renaissance, treats the whole arsenal of the degenerate "saints" in farces and novellas, with a combination of pleasure, sarcasm, derision, and also bitterness. This arsenal includes both the lecherous and drunken/gluttonous monk and the corrupt, intriguing, financially insatiable and dissolute prelate, the amorous nun and the depraved abbess. In Luther's day, those who entered a monastery out of religious conviction had to take their cues from a radical monastic minority that still took its faith and the rules of the order seriously.

As mentioned above, Luther chooses the order of the Augustinian hermits in Erfurt.[19] The "Black Monastery," which he enters, belonged to the congregation of the Augustinian-Observants,[20] an unusually strict minority even within the order of the Augustinians. There he learns the rules and inner guidelines of a collective other-observation and self-observation according to the so-called chapter on offenses (*Schuldkapitel*), which is held every Friday. The prior speaks the opening formula "Let us deal with sin!," the question "What do you say?," and the communal answer is "Our sin!" Thus, the account listing the offenses is revealed to the collective revisor once a week, but in addition, the behavior prerequisite for this kind of bookkeeping is practiced—the regulated self- and other-observation.

Individually, the brothers rise and confess those offenses concerning the breaking of rules and regulations of the order (see Balthasar, 1961: 135 ff.). The confession of all other sins was the object of the confessional. As a consequence, it is not only the "practice in societalness" (see Friedenthal, 1983: 56) that is decisive in the regular practice of the "offence chapter," but also the concomitant training in observation according to a given guideline—precursor of and pattern for certain techniques in empirical social research. The "offence chapter" was based on the obligation and training of each brother to observe the other, to control and to publicize his shortcomings, albeit anonymously. The name of the accused was not named; the person in question was expected to admit to his offenses himself.

The observation of another person, and the description of his offenses in such a way that that other would recognize himself, demands of the observer, to an extreme, the combination of "external" observation and internalized "appropriation of the perspective" of the observed person. Thus, the monastic society becomes a self-observation society, the contemplative or "active" shared life is interrupted by observation. A community of action or meditation becomes an association of observed observers. The focus is no longer on the acting person, but rather, on observing the action; no longer on the success of action, but rather, on its failure. If one reads the rules of the orders and considers them in connection with a strict observance of the "divine" commandments, then one knows that by those standards, not a day, barely an hour passes in human life without offenses being committed. Under this aspect and through the trained observation that uses it as its measure, life becomes an endless chain of trespasses. And the chain becomes heavier with each passing day. All else loses its meaning, all else recedes into the background.

Luther places his life under this new sign and, as a consequence, has much to report and to confess to. He loses his measure of proportion. Details and small matters take on disproportionate importance. Staupitz is reported to have responded to Luther's complaints about his (Luther's) immeasurable sinfulness that all those things he accused himself of were "no kind of righteous sin," that he, Luther, should not "deal with such bungling stuff and doll sins and make a sin of every fart" (Friedenthal, 1983: 57 ff.). His novitiate master is theologically more direct, he responds to Luther's confessions of trivial sins, along with his fear of God's wrath, with the words "You are a fool, God is not angry with you, it is you who are angry with God" (Loewenich 1983: 77).

What we can see in the reactions of Staupitz and Luther's novitiate master is that this "new Paul" has taken a path that is removed from the goals of monastic life and those of the rules of the order. Luther focuses alone and solely on his own relationship to God—expressed initially in his negative relationship to himself and his offenses—and not on the strictly methodical, timelessly collective control over the way one leads his life within a community. In the midst of a much-regulated communal tradition, Luther has broken through precisely that tradition of communality, applying the to him only valid writings. To him, the rules of other-observation become exclusively the rules of self-observation. The monastic community recedes into the background: the "hermitism" of external isolation turns into an internal hermitism. The offenses of the others become as nothing, one's own offenses are everything. In short, the social partner disappears—the only partner is God. Once again, the isolation of the individual before "his God" is exemplarily demonstrated.

Luther's treatment of his own name, the new variation of the mythical Saul/Paul pattern, the "reformation" of "biblical man" and his "cleansing" of the ancient ways of thinking, the establishment of the lonely reader and interpreter of *the* Script, and finally, the isolation of the individual before his God—they all form the same configuration of meaning by which Luther lived and interpreted his life, or rather, lived his life while interpreting it. *Isolation before the totality—the historically later isolation as totality becomes, in modern terminology, "authenticity," "fulfilled subjectivity," and the like.*

But these "isolations," like so many others, would have remained without consequence if that "second Paul" and reformer had not simultaneously created the *institutional* conditions for making sure his experience of isolation would not remain singular, but instead turn into a collective pattern. Here, too, he remained faithful to the thus far developed configuration of meaning. At the decisive juncture, he varies a pattern that already contains a structure "receptive" to this change: he who to the end of his days retained and defended the confession at the same time radicalizes it and abolishes it in its ritualized, distanced, and protective form for the later realm of Protestant influence. Nor does the "Catholic" form of confession remain unaffected by these changes.[21]

Already at the IV Lateran Council (1215), where confession became obligatory for Christians of both genders (see Forevill, 1970: 265 ff.), the point of reference is less the Holy Scripture than the necessity to defend the "unity of faith" against heresy. Both the obligation to go to confession and the unification of the teachings of the sacraments (see above) are aimed toward institutionally securing the ministerial offices of the Church's pastoral care and of the Church as a whole.[22] The point is not only a vindication of the works, but also control over what constitutes the true faith.[23]

Many—although not all—religions share the magical belief that the spoken word or confession, combined with the also verbal expression of repentance, can itself cleanse the soul of sin or misdemeanor. This belief contradicts the image of an omniscient, planning God, even in the Old Testament, as clearly evidenced in the "cross-examination" of Adam and Eve by that omniscient God. That God gives in neither to the word nor the repentance, nor does He require a mediator between Himself and the human beings. He punishes or pardons directly, giving no indication of how He might be swayed. What is abundantly clear, however, is that "biblical man's" chance lies in the immediate approach to God, not a mediated approach, just as His approach to man is direct and not mediated. Luther and with him the entire Protestant theology once again emphasize this "basic worldview of the Bible," Luther initially in a strangely ambiguous way as regards the sacrament of confession.

In keeping with his specific configuration of meaning, Luther retains the tradition of the confession, but changes it in a central way. It is common knowledge that Luther remained faithful to the sacrament of confession to the end of his days, to wit his characteristic behavior that led him to go to confession even during the Diet at Worms. His father confessor was the archbishop of Trier; once again Luther makes use of, for his confession, an institution that accused him and doubted the legitimacy of his faith. Yet, both father confessor and child confessor adhere to their duties: The confession is accomplished according to the rules, and the confessional secret is kept in spite of repeated efforts to induce the father confessor to break it (see Friedenthal, 1983: 56).

Nonetheless, it is presumably already at this time—although there is proof for it only somewhat later at the Wartburg—that the "lonely Bible reader's (Luther's) partner" in confession has changed. Although he confesses before a priest in the monastery, before a representative of the Church, he addresses his confession directly to Christ. For him, it is Christ who listens, who will answer and is able to bestow forgiveness—not man. The priest, or whichever person listens to the confession—later on, Luther designated friends as the "involved" persons—is not the *addressee,* but rather the *witness* of the confession. That person is a representative of the community, and not of the institution to which alone one is accountable and from which alone one can expect an answer.

While in the teachings of the Catholic Church the Church itself as sacred institution and "sacrament"[24] and, during the confession, in the guise of the priest, approaches the individual believer with immediacy and concreteness, the individual believer who reveals and entrusts himself to the Church, who lets himself be protected and represented by it, in Luther's belief and practice of confession it is the individual believer who appears before God Himself. According to the teachings of the Catholic Church, the believer is not only God's child, but also the Church's. Luther dissolves these family ties to the "Mother Church"—the believer becomes "directly subordinate" to God in his faith, in his practice of confession and prayer.

Thus the "external" Church as a sacred institution is, in the Protestant view, relieved not only of legitimation and power, but also - far more significantly - of its influence on daily life, in which it formerly had been included in a pastoral, protective, and advisory role. The Protestant parish, in which on the one hand each individual develops his unique relationship to God and in which, on the other hand, the community as a whole shows its tendency to control the individual members of the parish,[25] is utterly different from the ritual and ritualized, institutionally organized, traditional community of the Catholic Church and its basically "rational-systematic form" (Weber, 1972a: 283) of pastoral care.

Systematized and ritualized pastoral care—"the priests' actual sphere of power as regards everyday life"[26]—not only influences the believers' lifestyle through collective systematization and measuring of life stories and landscapes of the soul, it also protects the believer from the abyss of isolation that is connected to the thesis of the individual's immediacy to God. Pastoral care represents a collective orientation, while Luther makes each individual find his or her own path by dealing with "their" God. It "represents" the individual when he "fails," whereas Luther's—and Calvin's—believer is accountable directly to God and must negotiate his "failures" directly with God. Luther not only destroyed the *cordon sanitaire* which the Church had erected between believer and God, he also dissolved a previously valid collective system of orientation. Formerly, the Church had observed and advised its believers; now the individuals had to observe themselves and seek counsel from "their" God.

With the contradictory yet, for the confession constitutive unit of self-revelation by the believer and concealment of the revelation based on the priest's vow of silence, yet another ritually secured safe haven for the individual is destroyed. During confession before "lay witnesses," the ritually protective, mutual relationship between believer and institution (i.e., a fairly impersonal control) turns into a means of public control. But if the believer remains alone with his God during confession and self-revelation, then on the one hand he reveals to an omniscient God what that God already knows; on the other hand he is forced—in self-observation and interchange with his God, particularly in the face of an omniscient God—to refine and perfect his knowledge of his own offenses and misdemeanors, and to come closer to equaling the omniscient God in that respect. For he may not keep anything concealed—that, too, would be sinful. In short, the believer must search his soul deep into its furthest reaches. *The confession before lay witnesses destroys the distance to the "outside," that is, between the individual and the public—the "lonely" self-revelation destroys the distance to the "inside," that is, between self-observation, self-judgment, and justification.* The latter merge into an infinite process. The "outer world" tends to dissolve. The subject now becomes so extensively self-engrossed that it would lose itself, were it not for that absolute *"outside"* which it still finds *within* itself: God.[27]

However, Luther didn't leave the individual completely without orientational guidelines. On the one hand, he pointed to that one—and only—guideline that "God Himself" gave man, that "book of books." On the other hand, he didn't hesitate to add a little postscript to that book for further orientation—the "big" and the "little catechism."[28] They, too, are manuals for action and observation, in which Luther, through the manifestly applied "inner perspective" in daily life, makes an observation guideline out of the action guideline in the recapitulation of the day just ended. This is where the individual stages his own "offence chapter" with himself.

To the extent that Luther's teachings are lived, and his instructions for leading a Christian life are perceived and implemented in everyday life, a new type of lifestyle emerges (see Weber, 1972b) as does a new type of sociality: *isolation within the community.*

This isolation is pervasive even in the "primary" human "relationships" in the family, which had hitherto offered protection from isolation. Luther and his Katharina von Bora and their children, in their active, often excessively sociable (by the standards of their times) and altogether "normal" life, did not yet live what those whose teacher Luther became through his writings reshaped into a new type of family life. Protestant marriage and family, characteristically referring to the "strictness" practiced in them, became, on the whole, a community of self-observation and confession—even more, a controlling and disciplinary institution, where the equally Protestant requirement to be a "happy Christian" left nothing but a thin-lipped frozen smile on the couples' ascetic faces (see Douglas, 1974: 167 ff.).

Refining self-observation and expanding the reflective ego's knowledge of self creates other, novel objects of observation. To bring it to a point: Those who are permanently occupied with observing and reflecting upon themselves become incapable of producing any kind of "works" that would be worthy of their attention. At the very least these "works," if they do come about, lose their fascination. What becomes more important are the intentions and motives that produce them or with which they are brought into connection—more often than not retrospectively. As a result, works and products are neutralized and devalued, while the importance of the motives and intentions assumed to lie "behind" them increases. What develops then is the tendency, both in "public political" and in "private" life, to pay less attention to the actions and, instead, to speculate about the underlying "motivations." Finally, a state can be attained both in community and in politics where it is sufficient in order to gain social respect, votes, and political approval to successfully demonstrate a generally admired or comfortable point of view, meanwhile renouncing political action or rather declaring the demonstration of one's point of view to be political action (see Sennett, 1983). To use the biblical language of similes, a good tree now no longer needs to bear good fruit; it is enough for it to look pretty good in other respects.[29] And, conversely, a tree that bears good fruit must submit to an "analysis" of its reasons for bearing them.[30]

This shifting observation and the guidelines for observation to the control of motives and intentions leads, according to the direction the observation takes, to the rediscovery of an old enemy of mankind, an enemy residing within the individual, occasionally ruling him and thereby appearing to be both within him and without him—affect and impulse, that something which forces him to be "like a beast" (Psalms 73: 22). It is that something that Satan is riding and that one later will simply call "id," that, however, urgently wants to become "ego." Regardless of who or what this enemy is, he must be conquered, or at least disciplined.

Not only the symbolic figure of the "inner enemy," but also that of the battle with this opponent has a long tradition, in which two very different battle techniques and victory plans emerge. While the one—and in this the monastic discipline of the active orders and the Calvinistic discipline of industriousness resemble one another in a central aspect—regulates and controls action and "external" lifestyle in every smallest detail, the other aims at controlling the "inner world," the thoughts, opinions, intentions, desires, imagination, fantasies, and dreams. While the one tries to discipline the inner world by way of controlling the "external world" and by way of "inner-worldly asceticism," thereby hardly leaving room nor time for the individual to observe himself, the other aims at controlling action by way of controlling the motives, that is, it lays its stakes on the hope that the "external world" might change if only one could successfully create order in the inner worlds (and should this hope prove to be misguided, then it suffices to "live in peace with oneself"). While the one sees the justification of man revealed in his *actions,* the other sees him justified through self-revelation in his *words.*

Luther returns to this second tradition via his re-awakened and radicalized forms of presentation and self-presentation of "biblical man." Re-forming and newly forming, or rather changing in principle the nature of confession, as well as training and schooling his followers in the new "form," create not only new guidelines of observation and judgment; they also create a new *type of articulation,* which subsequently becomes more and more differentiated. Without it and the ensuing refinement of observation and expansion of topics, we would not have today's forms of self-revelation in therapy nor the role of self-thematization, reaching from talk-show to bar talk, and the resulting culture of gab under the auspices of the new sensitivity or "sensibility." It is an almost inevitable result of the rules of self-thematization and self-revelation, released from the sacred grounds and thus become self-referential, that conversations—not only in the media but also in everyday "middle-class" or "new class" contacts—acquire the quality of a "show," of a self-presentation and self-demonstration. Social contacts thus determined become markets of autobiography, stock markets of particularly "authentic" model identities. This parting with oneself, inherent in the public revelations of autobiographies, becomes a sell-out of oneself through which social recognition can be acquired.

This tendentially universal capacity for self-articulation was still alien to the reformer himself, however good he already was at observing his "doll's sins" (see above). He was fluent in it only within the regulated religious tradition in which he had grown up. Nonetheless, he created—as I hope to have demonstrated here—the structural preconditions for this new type of articulation and the capacity for articulation that later evolved. And more—under his influence, a new biographical configuration of meaning developed as a result of the shift of interest by those observing and articulating, from the "works" to the intentions, from the deeds to the motives. And by this new configuration, isolated occurrences acquire a causal background. Divine and human motives or intentions constitute the connection that renders meaningful the connection between individual events. A unique causality pattern emerges that appoints a "because" and an "in order to" to every event, thereby eliminating coincidence and making every autobiography an individual story of salvation and failure. Autobiography becomes tellable. It acquires legitimation via a supporting scheme of storytelling and reasoning that is organized according to "causal" and "final" principles. It guarantees a formal cloak within which every detail and every individual story can be wrapped. This cloak is offered to the individual, well-trained in isolation; it waits to be filled, waits for a tellable "individual" story.

The Two Kingdoms

"So that we may recognize thoroughly what a Christian is and what is the freedom that Christ won and gave him, of which St. Paul writes much, I would like to advance these two tenets: A Christian is a free man above all else and subordinate to none. A Christian is a subservient vassal to all things and subordinate to all" (Luther, 1983a: 125).

The following reflections are aimed at uncovering the unifying element, or structure and meaning, of this linking of contradictions, and so contribute to reconstructing a configuration of meaning which Luther reform(ulat)ed and passed down. A configuration of meaning that, as implicit but at the same time differentiated as both formal-structural and material-symbolic form of knowledge and presentation, has to this day retained its effectiveness. In fact, it has retained its effectiveness particularly in the type of articulation that belongs to self-referential subjectivity. Of course, collective acceptance of Luther's formulated and lived-by-him configuration of meaning influenced more than just the patterns of (auto)biographical symbolism and articulation discussed here—it encompassed everyday life in its entirety, from family life to political behavior, from "individual" faith to state concepts, from working life to educational institutions.

If, in connection with Luther's theology and his way of life, the symbol of the "two kingdoms" is mentioned, then it is usually in reference to his "political writings."[31] It is Luther's opposition to the eschatological medieval teachings of God's kingdom on earth that is emphasized, and rightly so. Unlike medieval theology, Luther strictly differentiates "between a spiritual and a temporal regiment of Christ.... Only in the spiritual kingdom does Christ reign directly through God's Word, he has laid down the worldly sword."[32] However serious the political consequences of this differentiation,[33] it still shows but *one* consequence and *one* form of Luther's more encompassing, symbolically formed image of the world and of man, an image that stands and perseveres to this day in the tradition of the "biblical man" concept (see above).

The foundations of Luther's beliefs and teachings rest in his conviction that "every Christian being...is of a twofold nature, spiritual and physical. According to the soul he is called a spiritual, new, inner man, according to the flesh and blood he is called a carnal, old, and external man" (Luther, 1983a: 105). Even in the case of the "liberated" human being who has joined the faithful—and it is this human being alone whom Luther means when he speaks of the "Christian being"—the freed soul remains in the unfree body of the "old Adam," all that liberation notwithstanding. For the liberation in Christ is "a spiritual dominance which reigns by suppression of the body" (Luther, 1983a: 135). Even though the "inner person" of the Christian can be "one with God, happy and joyful" (139), he finds—at times particularly in those moments—"in his flesh a recalcitrant will which seeks to serve the world and seeks its own pleasure" (139). This, of course, "cannot be suffered by the spirit of faith which gleefully attaches itself unto him so as to dampen and hold that will in check" (139).

Thus, the battlefield within each individual is the scene both of this basic, irreconcilable dispute and of a daily, nerve-wracking struggle between the liberated Christian and his old Adam, between the freed soul and the unfree body. From the strength of each of those disputes, then, "every one...can himself decide the sensible measure of castigation of the body; for he fasts, holds vigil, works as much as he sees the body requires to dampen his wantonness" (125). Luther's basic attitude is already fully developed here, five years prior to the writings on the "unfree faith" (1525) (see above), and typically the writings on the *freedom* of the Christian being. The doctrine of the "two kingdoms" suffuses his whole view of the world and of mankind. To be precise, the world as battle site between spiritual and worldly kingdoms reflects that fundamental dispute between "inner freedom" and "external servitude" taking place within the individual human being.

This individual, however, lives "not alone in his body, but also among his fellow mortals. Thus, he *can* not be without deeds toward them, he *must* always speak with them and have dealings with them, although none of those deeds are needed to lead him to piousness and bliss" (Luther, 1983a: 145) (emphasis added). From this connection of sociality on the one hand—which almost seems an "imposed" entity—and independence from "justification through deeds" on the other, Luther deduces the freedom to serve one's neighbor without an eye to the rewards—according to the model of Christ's services to mankind. "While every man has sufficient in his faith...he thus is "left all other deeds and life...to serve his neighbor with unfettered love" (146).

However convincing and conclusive this figure of thought is at first sight—particularly for members of a Christian culture and graduates of a Christian system of socialization—it appears stranger and more distant upon closer inspection. First of all, the individual has to be concerned with his own liberation and his own faith; once he is sure of this faith and freedom inside himself, then "he has sufficient in his own faith" (see above); now he has become free to love his neighbor—and he does this by serving his neighbor as Christ served all mankind.

This argument irrefutably places each individual in a position of supreme self-interest. Love for one's neighbor on the other hand becomes abstract and general, oriented toward an unattainable role model. It is a generalized love, a generalized service to all humans. Love of one's closest neighbor and of those furthest away conflate, become indistinguishable, find their expression in "service" and stem from the "freedom" of a self-supporting (in this case still by virtue of its faith) ego. The personal note, the personal service to a "close" human being, that tone which we hear in Luther's letters to his wife (signed "Martinus Luther—your heart's desire") or in reports on how he treated his own children, succeeds here just as little as does the *direct* connection of self-love and love of one's neighbor in the Sermon on the Mount. If one follows Luther's texts *as such* and informs one's life with their abstractness, the way many subsequently did in a "Protestant lifestyle," one lives in a new form of egocentrism and contributes structurally to a basically asocial attitude toward his fellow human beings.

As for the doctrine and conviction of the "two kingdoms," it becomes clear at this point that the demarcations between the two are much more far-reaching, that the schism between the two is far deeper, and the consequences for a human coexistence based on it far more serious than may at first appear. The boundaries run not only between spiritual and worldly kingdom, they also run within each individual—Dr. Jekyll and Mr. Hyde—and screen off the individual—inside his freedom, inside his space—separating him from his neighbor. But another decisive factor in the doctrine of the "two kingdoms" is the perspective from which the demarcation is seen: It is the perspective of the *individual* Christian. He is not only the paradigm for the division of humans and the world into an "inner" and an "outer," into a "being-soul" and "having-body," into "freedom" and "unfreedom," he is also the one who experiences this division most intensively within himself. He is the beast of burden for which both riders, God and Satan, battle in order "to hold onto him and take him into their possession" (Luther, 1983b: 47). And he accordingly centers his attention on the battlesite where the decisive battle is fought: himself.

It is not in the least surprising that someone who concentrates in this manner on the events within himself gains a certain "external" freedom. It is, in fact, the freedom borne of the lack of interest in other objects besides the security of one's own faith. It is an expression of the strength of a person who has no significant enemies to fear other than himself, because he barely perceives any other enemies. As a consequence, he emphasizes the battle within himself, in his own way of life, in his own, self-oriented, risk. We find examples for this not only in the performance of the individual, the "little monk" at the Diet at Worms, but also in Luther's daring to marry an escaped nun, that is, confirming all his opponents' preconceived notions and thereby exposing himself to ridicule. Luther's "own" path stands out particularly when compared to that of Thomas Müntzer, another exemplary figure of the time. Not to put a fine point on it: Müntzer fights and Luther gets married. Both consider their "deeds" to demonstrate a consistent attitude.

It is typical for Luther that he uses his "private" life as public demonstration and public argument: He isn't battling an old institution as representative of a new one in the public arena, he is battling as representative of a certain kind of faith and life against an "adulterated" faith and an "un-Christian" life. For him, the "authentic" church of God on earth is ultimately not a public, visible institution. That could not in any case be so: God works in concealment on earth. His church is a spiritual authority and thus equally concealed—*nota bene concealed (abscondita)*—not invisible (*invisibilis*), its saints unknown but not unrecognized: "abscondita est Ecclesia, latent sancti" (Luther, 1983b: 221). The Scripture on the other hand is utterly clear: "satis sit...praemisisse, Scripturas esse clarissimas" (227). The result of all this for the faithful is that they must visibly follow the clarity of the Scripture in their private lives.

Luther himself followed this path with great personal courage. For him, fear of his God and gratitude for His mercy were far more decisive than any pressure by "worldly" powers. Cravenness was not part of his make-up. Nonetheless, *structurally* he created, with his doctrine of the "two kingdoms," thereby splitting up world, sociality and individual, the mental precondition for the submissiveness to authority found in Protestantism, particularly in the German Protestantism so influenced by him. It was as a result not of political pressure alone, but also of a lack of interest in the Church as a public institution stemming from this mental attitude, that in the Protestant principalities, the worldly prince simultaneously became the head of the established Church. This was not simply due to necessity, but also due to the basic tenets of the belief that however important the Church might be politically as an "external," visible institution, its meaning was practically nil as compared to the "authentic," concealed Church or to the personal experience of penitence and mercy, rebirth and spiritual liberation or sanctification. In general terms: However important the "external," political, economic world may appear, a person's peace with God and himself is of greater importance.

The Augustinian hermit thus in a sense remains true to himself even as *pater familias*—although he riddles the spatial hermitage with holes while still living in the monastery, he reinforces the individual's mental and spiritual separation from the social world via the new, that is, radicalized old doctrine. He and his formulations are strangers to that Christianity of intuition and emotion (*Gemütschristentum*) which is to follow later, primarily in the nineteenth century (see Müller-Salget, 1984: 20). But his teachings help lay the foundation for it: that the individual, preoccupied with himself and his spiritual salvation, loses his societal and political horizons, that the individual explains all "turmoil," unrest, poverty and violence, by the fact that mankind has lost its "peace in God" and its "obedience to God."[34] Ultimately, this individual sees himself, his own story, his own experiences large and small, as so meaningful that it becomes inconceivable to him that there might be anyone who isn't interested in such a significant biography: The autobiographical monologue, camouflaged as discourse, commences.

From the Subject of Revelation to the Revelation of the Subject

The doctrine of the "two kingdoms," of the tear in the curtain of appearances, of the schism between body and soul, between the old and the new human being, between the individual and the distant neighbor, his partner, between the Church as public institution and the concealed Church, rests on a theological doctrine central, in my opinion, to Luther, a doctrine that is planted in and created by this breach, and one that can be applied both to the world and the whole of human life. God Himself can be experienced by human beings—of this Luther is convinced—only as a contradictory entity, as a revealed God (*Deus praedicatus*) and as a God who is concealed and works in concealed ways (*Deus absconditus*).[35]

This ambivalent concept of God seems to me to be the "structuring" element of Luther's creed and theology. From it emerges not only the bipartition of the world, of social life and of the individual, but also the core and center of Luther's theology: his doctrine. For every belief and faith that mankind considers a justification to replace works and deeds, a justification which is sought as "conviction of faith" and can be attained by "the grace of God," is severely tested by the "concealed God" in particular. And more: The quality of the faith itself is based on the conviction that God is experienced as a contradictory entity. For faith, according to Luther, is defined by being "oriented toward facts that one cannot see. But in order for faith to have room, everything that is believed must be concealed." But it cannot be hidden any deeper "than under the opposition to the material, to perception, to experience" (quoted according to Luther, 1983a: 44; 1983b: 206).

The basis for faith is the insecurity and fallibility of experience. Nothing is what it appears to be. Frequently, the "real" truth is hidden beneath a contrary appearance. Thus, God "conceals his eternal beneficence and mercy beneath eternal wrath, his justice beneath injustice. It is the highest level of faith to believe that He is merciful who blesses so few, who damns so many; to believe He is just who by His will makes us so, that it cannot be otherwise, damnable" (Luther, 1983a: 44; 1983b: 206). This "God, concealed in His majesty, neither laments nor recants death, but rather works life, death and all in all. For here He has not locked Himself within confines through *His word* (emphasis added), but rather has kept the freedom of Himself above all" (Luther 1983a: 108; 1983b: 253).

This "concealed God in His majesty," working in all and everything, standing behind all and everything, makes high demands on the righteousness of faith and also demands unquestioning subjugation to His will—regardless of what happens. For "God does much which He does not reveal through His word that He demands it.... But now we must look at the word and let that impenetrable will stand, for we must follow the word and not that impenetrable will. For who could follow a wholly and utterly impenetrable and unrecognizable will" (Luther 1983b: 253ff.) What remains is "to fear and worship."[36]

In the face of the omnipotence, freedom and impenetrability of the concealed God in whose plans self-denial enters as part of His basically untransparent will, it becomes evident that, in all God's works revelation, as voluntary self-revelation by God, is the exception (see Luther 1983a: 293). The ways in which the *Deus praedicatus* appears are embedded in the "concealed" workings of the *Deus absconditus*.

Obviously, this is not the proper context for entering into a theological debate on Luther's viewpoint. What I am aiming at is a brief, albeit—so I believe—accurate interpretation of the structure of Luther's God; and also of his image of the world of man, an exposé of the consequences of this configuration of symbols for the Lutheran Protestant interpretation of the world and the self.

The concept of the combined efforts of the "concealed" and the "revealed" God would not, in itself, have been of great consequence to the interpretation of world and self on the part of the Lutheran-Protestant believer. It became of consequence, however, by virtue of the fact that the division of the world into a visible but illusory one that is subject to deceit on the one hand, and a concealed but true, liberated and "real" one on the other hand reached deep into the individual believer. The latter re-experiences the bipartition within himself, the battle between the old, corporal Adam and the new, liberated Christian—even *after* the conversion. Worse yet, the liberated Christian experiences the unity and majesty of his God in His contradictoriness. The believer is asked to stick to the God revealed in His clarity in the Scripture—knowing all the while that the impenetrable free will of God continues to exist, too—the will of a concealed, majestic God who works through His equally impenetrable mercy, does not let Himself be committed by any Godly pressure, and conceals His plans from all humans: a God who demands that man believe in the concealed, and "measures" the strength of his belief according to the ability of man not only to believe in *what* is concealed, but also to believe in something *because* it is concealed.

Thus, God's being hidden and concealed not only pertains to the world and the Church, it also pertains to the workings of God within the human being liberated by Him. The "liberated Christian" not only finds within himself and at the same time across from himself the old Adam, he also believes in the concealed workings of God in himself. Thus, every one of Luther's "Christian beings" not only belongs to the world as though he didn't belong to it (see above, I Corinthians 7:30ff.), *he also belongs to himself as though he didn't belong to himself.* He knows of something within himself that is not him, that is concealed, in which he must believe and by which, ultimately, he is justified.

If the believer in his isolation—or, as he sees it, in his immediacy to God—wishes to speak with Him, then he first encounters the God revealed in Scripture, who has spoken and continues to speak to each individual through the Scripture. Here, he experiences not only God's mercy, but also God's demands. These give him the criteria, standards, and observation guidelines with which to discover his own sinfulness and keep pedantic account of those sins. God's unfulfilled and ultimately never quite fulfillable demands and commands for their part refer to His mercy—without mercy and the belief in it there is neither salvation nor liberation.

Self-observation is in the end always observation of sins, identification of one's own sinfulness, one's own failures. Trained self-observation makes evident the need for God's mercy. In the words of a paradox: By recognizing his own sinfulness, the believer experiences God in a *negative revelation*. His own sinfulness, insofar as it is perceived, comes about in reference to the workings of the concealed God in whose plans the God revealed in the Scripture with the "chartered" offer of mercy is included.

This negative revelation of God—the believer's perception of his sins—which in its turn refers to Scripture's positive revelation of God, and to a concealed plan of salvation, is in essence a feat of *observation* and *interpretation*. As long as the believer is convinced that it holds true—not only for the Scripture, but also for himself insofar as God works in him—that God Himself is the actual interpreter—both as subject and as object of the interpretation (see above)—as long as that conviction holds, he will find comfort in his belief in the visible and the concealed workings of God in his life. However, the construction of this figure of thought requires a nearly impossible feat on the part of every individual believer, once he has to fill it with life and translate it into life. The structure of the figure of thought is parallel escalation of the knowledge of one's own sinfulness on the one hand and—in connection with that—an increasingly urgent longing for grace. This grace should and has to be believed in particularly because although it is promised in the Scripture, it is not necessarily visible in one's own life. Kierkegaard's "leap of faith" (see above), based on a "*credo quia absurdum*" is, from this point of view, something other than what emerges in Luther's theology, that is the despair of the believer in his sinfulness, his despair growing proportionately to ever more detailed self-observation and the ever more desperate belief in God's mercy, based on no "facts of experience" whatsoever (see above). Paracelsus, a contemporary of Luther, knew what this meant in terms of demands on the individual, what it meant to leave the ritual protection of the "Mother" Church with Luther and to no longer have a protective representative positioned between the individual and his God: "Whosoever places his faith in the papacy rests on velvet; whosoever believes in Luther is sitting on a volcano" (quoted according to Friedenthal, 1983: 555).

This volcano erupts if the person's faith looks for some kind of foothold within his own life, if the despair can no longer be comforted by the vague promise of mercy revealed in the Scripture, and if the individual tries to find in his own life clues to the workings of the "concealed God" which will lead him to "salvation." For it is precisely the absolute majesty and sovereignty of the "concealed God"—in this, Lutherism and Calvinism reveal the same structure—that force man in his interest to "at least in the particular case look into [the concealed God's] cards and specifically to know his own transcendent fate, [is] an elementary need of the individual" (Weber, 1972a: 317).

However—and Lutherism and Calvinism differ here—Lutherism is focused on a different card game than Calvinism. While the Calivinist looks, in the sense of "practical interest" (Weber, 1972a: 317), to publicly visible success as a symptom of "being selected," the Lutheran turns his eyes inward. For him, there is no reliable answer to be found "outside," in the visible world. If there is any certainty to be found at all, it is only in his faith as an individual who must feel and experience the workings of God within himself. Only by directing his observational powers "inward" can he find an answer. Even the question whether the individual believer—qua individual reader—has understood and truly seen the Scripture in its "clarity" is something that the individual needs to decide for himself. It is especially the individual's direct prayer to his God which refers to that only authority which can receive an answer: that authority is the individual—isolated—believer himself. Forced to search within himself for signs of the "concealed God's" works, the Lutheran-Protestant believer becomes a virtuoso of self-observation and self-interpretation.

The observation of one's own life, the story of one's failures, or of one's sudden "illuminations," everything that is or can be remembered, every single experience is woven into a chain of symptoms in the search for clues of where the "concealed God" is effecting His works. Each individual experience, every detail, is given a reference structure. What we can observe here is a hermeneutic paradox that is active in nearly any interpretational work, a paradox which, unless it is controlled, leads to false assumptions albeit of an elegant and accomplished appearance, a paradox which in this form particularly brings about a uniform rounding-off of meaning in biographies. What I am referring to is the discovery, exact observation, extraction, and extensive interpretation of every single detail—be it an element of perception, experience, or of the text— with the goal of destroying it as a detail in order to comprehend it as symptom or circumstantial evidence for a larger, unified context.

This has two notable advantages for the biographical self-observation and self-interpretation, both in the individual's intercourse with himself and in his intercourse with others. On the one hand, all individual experiences and events are put into a context which, although constantly changing in the course of time and life, still is orderly in structure. In other words, coincidences disappear, everything has its motivation, everything rests within a motivational or causal relationship. On the other hand, a communicable repertoire of relatively cohesive stories is created—an indirect medium of self-presentation. *What emerges are concisely cross-referenced modi of a self-reflected, autobiographical subject: a subject observing itself, interpreting itself, a narrated and narrating subject.*

The Protestant-Lutheran believer at first is borrowing this subject and, via the borrowed subject, his security. For the subject of action, the subject and object of interpretation is the only one whom the quality of an individual subject, the quality of freedom, autonomy, and self-sufficiency befit: God. But what happens when the individual can find no answer in his observing, his self-interpreting, his praying, his inward-harkening? What if the revelation of God, which after all is the exception both in its message of salvation and in the life of an individual (see above), doesn't materialize, what if the questions the individual asks are answered only by their echo?[37] What remains if the individual searches for this subject within himself and does not find it? Where is he to search if he cannot find in himself the certainty of salvation even though the desire for salvation remains?

Experiencing the "loss of God" leads, in the Protestant-Lutheran tradition and history of consciousness, to various attempts at solving this innerworldly drama—either into insoluble despair, the "sickness unto death" (see Kierkegaard, 1959a), or into a final, desperate attempt at finding a path of return: to the "leap of faith." And there remains a further, more everyday reaction, rooted less in the Protestant systems of faith and knowledge, but all the more rooted in its subject-centered structure of observation, interpretation, and relevance. The search for an answer and the answer itself, the search for *the* subject, the desire for redemption and the hope for redemption are, in this solution, transferred into this world, into the individual. Not transcendence any more, but rather the individual himself is expected to deliver answer and redemption.

It is particularly the latter attempt at a solution that has become effective collectively because of the institutionalization of life in the community and the concomitant religious acts. Its effectiveness can be traced to the present day[38] with a certain continuity. According to their structure, the above-described attempts at solutions are the same; however, the latter is different from the former two by virtue of the fact that it breaks with the traditional religious concepts, leaving only—or so it might appear at first sight—the formal pattern of the now innerworldly, subject-referential symbolic figure of the "two kingdoms," of the subject's self-reflexiveness, his self-perception, self-interpretation, self-justification, and self-coverage. Regardless of the respective religious contents or varying attempts at a solution, within the symbolic configuration of the Lutheran-Protestant interpretation of world and self, historically, a virtuosity in self-observation and self-coverage develops historically ever more and ever more observably, combined with a shift to an everyday and taken-for-granted mastery of those abilities—especially among the bourgeoisie.

The "loss of God"—be it a personal or a communal experience—may bring with it profound distress in people who were both trained in this tradition and trained themselves in it. That doesn't, initially, change anything in the structure of the Lutheran-Protestant formation of individuality based on self-observation, self-interpretation, and self-coverage. However, it does redefine the thematic emphasis: the system of relevance acquires a new centerpoint. And now, after the traditional religious contents are abandoned, it becomes obvious where that centerpoint always had been as far as the structure is concerned. The human individual meets himself directly in observation and interpretation—without the detour via a God concealed, met, or imagined within himself. Now the individual is himself identifiable as subject and object of the interpretation. Again, very little has changed structurally in the isolation of the individual. But without the belief in a personally experienced God the isolation now becomes tangible—and threatening. In logical consequence, the desire for redemption also grows, but this desire must seek its goal in a different direction.

To summarize the thus-far identifiable "steps"[39] in the development of a new personality type, seen in the context of the history of consciousness: The Middle Ages seek—and find—that all-inclusive and all-founding subject who, as the only true subject, can by rights say of himself "I am who I am," in an ordered cosmos, in a universe in which everything has its secure place—just as every individual has in an ordered society. This concept of order, along with the firm, functional, and hierarchically

regulated, public-*positional* personality resting on this concept, safeguards
the individual human being. Individuality can hardly become a problem
here, because there is no occasion to make it into one (see Soeffner,
1989: 34). Luther seeks the encompassing subject that legitimizes everything, and thereby the individual as well, no longer in the tangible world,
nor in nature or society. He looks for the most general, the universe, there
where it seems to face him directly: in the *individual's* encounter with
God—an encounter that takes place *within* the individual. The Lutheran-
Protestant type of personality, co-existing with the loss of God and faith,
in a way turns himself into the universe: he not only observes and interprets primarily himself, he also has to legitimize his thoughts, motives,
and actions himself.

At this point it becomes evident that although the expression "loss of
God" has attained a certain explanatory function in the symbolic context
of the Christian religious tradition, it no longer is—particularly from a
sociological point of view (see Durkheim, 1912)—applicable in the description of a more general context. The reason: God and mankind's
Gods do not die. Nor are they lost. They simply go through numerous
metamorphoses and appear in ever new forms (see Luckmann, 1980:
161–72). What *is* sometimes given up are certain religious concepts that
are replaced by others. Thus, it becomes necessary at this point to un-
cover "God's new form" or the new disguise or concept of a traditional
symbolic figure.

A look at the shape of the Lutheran-Protestant personality type—which
had become focused on the inner world—of the kind that the German
Enlightenment displays and that is recognizable to this day, helps sim-
plify the matter. Here, the goals of the subject-orientation are already
formulated: freedom, autonomy, creative will (or, in modern parlance,
"self-fulfillment," "authenticity," "creativity"). One can easily identify
all these qualities as those which, in Christian medieval credo (and in
Luther's), befitted only one, the only subject: God. The in general unconscious transfer of the divine subject's attributes to an innerworldly concept of self, the concomitant omnipotence fantasies, justifications,
illusions—and disappointments—mark the "God" of one of the contemporary images of world and human being[40]: the self-reflexive, self-sufficient, autonomous, "emancipated" subject. And the Lutheran variant of
this type, its emancipation or "liberation" according to the degree of
"inner freedom," belongs to the new "Gods" and heroes who inhabit, in

the mental configuration of the Enlightenment, the new inner Mount Olympus up to the "generation of '68."

How, in structural terms, did the shaping of this personality type come about, and what are the consequences of this new symbolic figure—decked out with old props—for the everyday life of those who grew into this type and feel committed to it?

The Destruction of Practical Reason by Self-Reflexive Reason

"But to be subordinate to the speculative reason, and thus to reverse the order, one cannot expect of the pure practical reason, because ultimately, all interest is practical and even that of speculative reason is only qualified and is complete in the practical use alone" (Kant, 1785, vol. 6, II: 252). What Kant is clarifying here about the primacy for practical life of the "purely practical" over the "purely speculative" reason, about the inherent quality and autonomy of practical interest as opposed to the pure, theoretical, and thus "impractical" interest (see Soeffner, 1989: 10–50), is anything but clear for the concept of autonomy in the Lutheran-Protestant personality type, a concept oriented toward the "inner freedom" and committed to the self-reflexive self. The relationship of self-observation, self-recognition, self-control on the one hand and the daily need for action, the daily practice of action, and the everyday, practical interest in action on the other hand is here rather scholastically regulated before the fact: everyday life "in the world," the actions required there, the decisions to act and the interest in action do not have an "intrinsic" value. Just as formerly, the invisible realm of God devalued the "outer world" and its manifestations, now, under the dictate of the "autonomous" self-reflexive subject, the "outer" everyday life as the "unintrinsic" one stands under the primacy of the "inner world" and its independent causalities.

Prior to the devaluation of everyday action and practical interest one can identify a new, paradoxical, concept of action: that of "inner action," to which "external action" is subordinate. There is a fundamental difference here between Lutherism and Calvinism, their respective historical successors, their configurations of thought and formations of knowledge.

For Calvinism, the world, including the social world, never loses its inherent worth as God's creation. The world is the only material where the believer can and must prove him or herself through rational and ethi-

cal action. Thus what is required from the believer is "innerworldly asceticism." Proving himself in the world becomes his profession. But "profession" means here "the rational ethically ordered economy, run in strict
legality, economy whose success, as working for one's living, makes visible that God blesses the work of the devout and so, too, the piousness of
his economic way of life" (Weber, 1972a: 329).

Lutherism and Lutherans remain, as their founder ultimately did too,
committed to hermitage in the world, be it as a believer or as an "autonomous subject." For both—the believer battling within himself with the
"concealed God," as well as for the modern, self-reflexive subject who is
permanently occupied with self-therapy and self-analysis—"the sole concentration of acting on the active feats of redemption" holds true (see
Weber, 1972a: 329). Potentially always connected to this concentration
is a "departure from the "world," from the social and psychological bonds
of family, possession, and political, economic, artistic, erotic, and in general all creature interests" (Weber, 1972a: 329), in short, denial of the
world and world-denying asceticism.

In contrast to the Calivinist work in and on the world, the rationally
controlled, external activity as control and discipline of himself by the
individual, we have the controlled self-observation of the Lutheran, the
rational control over the inner world, the disciplining of motives and
intentions. The Calvinist tradition develops a publicness by having the
individual work in the public. The Lutheran moves in public as in a
foreign land. His home is the inner world. His actual work is—except for
external forms of presentation of an "inner" attitude—invisible; it takes
place in the "interior" as "inner action." The professional ethics of Calvinism require the taking-on of responsibility for the "public world". In
the Lutheran ethics of belief (*Gesinnungsethik*), the individual takes on
the responsibility for his inner world, for his intentions and his "experiences" with himself. Through the requirement to turn "outward" in everyday life, the Calvinist configuration of thought controls the individual's
public actions, while Lutherism tends to control the intentions and beliefs, insofar as they become publicly visible. However, they needn't or
shouldn't even become visible, for "the more inner, and true merits one is
conscious of...the less art (he will apply) to accentuate his favourable
sides."[41] The danger of thereby being misunderstood "from outside" is a
necessary consequence: virtue itself punishes the virtuous, thereby giving him the opportunity to further expand his "inner" growth.

A decisive factor in forming the Lutheran-Protestant type of biography—in contrast to Calvinism's configurations of thought and meaning, which prescribe for their clientele the direct public exchange in nearly all forms of social relationships—is that it results from the memories and reflections of an ego that communicates primarily with itself. The social opposite, the others, are but suppliers of self-experiential material, servicepeople of a sovereign preoccupied primarily with himself. And so it is not surprising either that the increasing refinement and art of self-observation and self-perception bring forth that proverbial sensitivity or "sensibility" of the subject, a sensibility that the subject finds and admires so incomparably within himself that it inevitably cannot be supplied to him by anyone else to such a degree, while the subject, equally inevitably, complains of the lack of sensitivity in his vis-à-vis and demands greater "sensitization" to that other-ego, meaning himself. Should two individuals of this same type meet, then we have the stuff of social comedy in the structural differences of the respective "self"-sensibility" and "other-sensibility," although the protagonists experience the situation as a tragedy caused by the lack of communication.

The art of self-observation and its increasing refinement, the interpretation of images of inner experience and inner texts shape and promote a specific memory pattern: the individual's history of experience as his history of communication with himself. Succinct memory and extensive interpretation complement one another. Both lead to a capacity to recount what is remembered and interpreted: experience and its retrospectively discovered deeper meaning, as a history of the insight into external occurrences which in turn represent references to an inner development. The history of memory and interpretation becomes a combining of symptomatic details into a meaningful whole, indebted to an inner causality: the basic pattern of psychoanalytic communication and of the type of knowledge, self-perception and report exigent for the pattern.

In addition, in the "alienation experience" of the individual who is confronted with his "concealed" half (see above), there is already a structural allusion to the invention and methodical exploitation of an artificially externalized, quasi-objectified "ego" as mirror, listener, and substitute interpreter analogous to what Freud's psychoanalysis would later develop. The ideal of this self-reflexive communication pattern would then be the self-sufficient trinity of experiencing, narrating, and interpreting ego. This much seems certain to me: The paradigm of psychoanalysis, emerging specifically from the Jewish tradition, is hardly explicable without the prohibition of images in that tradition, and the teachings and art of exegesis which thus were shifted to text-interpretation, now lacking the Jewish tradition of the extensive interpretation of detail, its experience in dealing with symbols, its parabolism and its talmudic-dialectic method of interpretation of meaning via the perpetuation of meaning. It is equally certain that psychoanalysis—as far as the art of remembering, narrating, and establishing the meaning of its imagination are concerned—could hardly have become so successful without the Christian tradition of confession and especially its refinement and focus, or rather ego-focus, through Lutherism. The reviewal and appraisal of memory, the genres of narration and forms of presentation of a textualized ego, in other words psychoanalysis' interpretational material would not exist in such elaborate editions without that tradition. And also the motives for entering into analysis: the suffering of guilt toward the concealed God within the self, or rather, an ego's suffering of supposed guilt toward itself, is indebted to the Judeo-Christian pattern of thought and self-experience.

It is the Judeo-Christian heritage that transports into the present, passing through various historical metamorphoses, the concept of the authority within the human being that works in concealment and is initially impenetrable; the hope of successfully giving meaning to existence, thereby rendering "clear and light" that which was formerly not understood; the centering on the self in psychoanalysis; the "denial of the world" that is structurally connected to that centering on the self; the hope in "innerworldly redemption" or meaning that can be experienced within the self; the teachings of the "two kingdoms, of the meaning behind the appearances, of the bipartitioning of the world into symptoms and worlds of meaning.

Even the trinity of "id," "ego," and "super ego" reproduces—recognizably enough—the Christian trinity of Father, Son, and Holy Ghost[42] as it is also interpreted in Luther's theology. There is the absolute, concealed God who acts "freely" and spontaneously in the dark, the Father who was before all else and who was the beginning itself, whose actions are recognizable only in the hard-to-discover references and symptoms. Then the Son, the "God incarnate," who implements the plans of the concealed God according to the latter's will, who Himself suffers and thus knows that He, as *Deus praedicatus,* is a manifestation of the *Deus absconditus*. And finally, the Holy Ghost that reveals Itself in the clarity of the Scripture, in the text interpretation and self-interpretation, as the proclaimed law and workings of the "concealed Father." Symbolically, the Trinity forms the structural pattern of a specific concept of self that was originally attributed to God and now is attributed to the human being. This structural pattern shapes, in an innerworldly oriented and thus changed symbolic form, the at present operative "European" theories of the individual subject as well as the self-understanding and the forms of self-presentation of individuals in their lifestyles. In this sense it is only to be expected when Freud, in his programmatic—not only in his estimation of religion—work, "The Future of an Illusion" (*"Die Zukunft der Illusion,"* 1974: 139 ff.), quotes Heine at the conclusion of the second-to-last chapter: "Let us leave heaven to the angels and the sparrows" (Freud, 1974: 183).

Freud thereby consciously enters into the heroic-Promethean variant of the Renaissance and the Enlightenment. *"Quae supra nos nihil ad nos"* was the former rallying cry in the same vein. God is no longer even mentioned as "resident of the heavens." But He has only seemingly disappeared. For to assume that a lack of interest in "heaven" and its God or angels implies God's "death" would be only too naive and also would in no way be in keeping with Freud's teachings. God has merely been brought down to earth from heaven. Initially still as Christian God—as for Luther—into the individual, then—after having destroyed this concept of God as well, after the "enlightened" patricide of "our God logos" (Freud, 1974: 187)—into the enlightened human subject.

Just as formerly, it was believed that nothing and no one could in the long run resist God, now the belief is "in the long run nothing can resist reason and experience" (Freud, 1974: 187). There is no end to the search for certainties and the belief of having found them. And, presumably, it is less fear of potential punishment that keeps the individual believer from giving up or testing his faith than fear of cracks in the worldly system, the repressed knowledge that there is no fundamental certainty, that nothing remains as it is, that even the "naturalness of the natural outlook" (see Schütz/Luckmann, 1984: 174) can end up in a state of crisis and be rescinded. The cause for faith in the Judeo-Christian tradition was and is the suffering of the "evil finiteness," of the imperfection, weakness, fallibility, failure, and necessary denial of one's wishes or wish fulfillment. From Psalm 90, verse 9: "We finish our years like a sigh. The days of our lives are seventy years. And if by reason of strength they are eighty years, Yet their boast is only labor and sorrow. For it is soon cut off, and we fly away," to the late Luther: "We are all laughter, fable, and carneval before God" (quoted according to Friedenthal, 1983: 633), all the way to Freud: "As for humanity as a whole, thus it is hard for the individual to endure life" (Freud, 1974: 160), the Judeo-Christian world and life pessimism are present in them all as well as the wish for redemption that stems from it.

The variously imagined concepts of redemption, but above all the concomitant paths toward redemption, have always had an effect on the believers' conduct in life. All visible and invisible religions tend to influence the everyday conduct of life with all its ramifications. In this respect, the "battle" of speculative-theoretical (including religious) thought against practical reason is presumably as old as the world.[43] But while many forms, particularly of elementary religious life and its practical maxims of faith pertaining to everyday acting, encourage rather than hinder the everyday conduct of life—especially in the area of practical interests, the universal pretension of cognition by the God "Logos" and his rational-speculative, "impractical" reason (i.e. reason that is under no obligation to the logic of action)—is directed against the practical interests of everyday action. "Social scientification of identity-formation and the denial of practical life" as described by Oevermann, are manifestations of a personality type and the, for it, binding subject model whose historical differentiation I have aimed to show in this essay via one line of development, that is, the Lutheran-Protestant line.

In the beginning of this particular development, the individual was confronted with an absolute subject in which it was, contrary to all reason and experience, supposed to believe. At the temporary conclusion of the development, we have a theory of the individual subject which has taken over the structural model of the Christian God concept = concept of subject, but now has made the individual the respective egocentricized subject. This concept of the individual subject, however, is supposed to be theoretically arguable, deducible from experience and reason, and scientifically not only identifiable, but also provable. According to this concept, the individual can consequently be guided in his actions according to the standards of speculative reason—with a "critical" eye, of course.

Today, the theories of the individual subject have turned into such an extensive self-theorization on the part of the subjects that even the details of how one conducts one's life, the details of everyday action, are affected by it; speculative self-theoretization catches up with and punctures the "practical interest" of practical reason. The apparent rationalization of practical interest by speculative, self-reflexive reason not only endangers the practical autonomy of action, it also tends to destroy the everyday potential for action and decision, the practical rationality: *the practical interest in action is subjected to the primacy of "impractical" interest in cognizance* and thus becomes "incomplete."[44]

This is particularly evident in the paradox of the premature legitimation of action: in the speculative, self-reflexive attitude of the ego that is in communication with itself, the legitimation of the action precedes the action in principle. The inner orientation from which alone action can ultimately be justified must be concealed before one *may* act. But since, for the personality type described here, it is not the "external" action, but rather the inner orientation as "inner action" that is significant, one may forego the "external" action. The individual persists in the pose of self-observation and other-observation. What crosses to the "outside" is no more than a publicly visible signaling of one's subjective attitude by which the individual marks his participation in the social events. He announces to the "outside world" how he is reacting within, whether in a happy or painful way, to his own observations—out of a legitimate attitude. This visible "being moved," the self-sensibility that is transported to the outside, becomes the social make-up of the soul. Attitude hygiene and make-up of the inner self's external appearance merge into a consistent social type of presentation: a comparatively trivial end of a personality type which contains only in traces the elements of the major conflicts and doubts from which it sprang.

Notes

1. See in this connection as a kind of "case study." H. Wenzel (1985): *Exemplarisches Rittertum und Individualitätsgeschichte. Zur Doppelstruktur der "Geschichten und Taten Wilwoldts von Schaumburg"* (1446–1519): 162 ff., in C. Gerhard, et al. (eds.), *Geschichtsbewußtsein in der deutschen Literatur des Mittelalters,* Tübinger Colloquium 1983, Tübingen, H. Wenzel (ed.) (1983): *Typus und Individualität im Mittelalter,* Munich; also therein: 11 ff.: H.-G. Soeffner: *"Typus und Individualität" oder "Typen der Individualität"?*
2. Thanks to my skiing companions, above all Dieter Gutzen and Horst Wenzel, for suggestions, discussions, and tenacious and helpful arguments against my theses in the following chapters.

3. All Bible quotations in the English version of this essay are taken from The New King James version, published by Thomas Nelson Inc., Nashville (1982).

4. See the report by Justus Jonas, a fellow student of Luthers in Erfurt, quoted from Richard Friedenthal (1983: 37): *Luther, sein Leben und seine Zeit,* Frankfurt; W. v. Loewenich (1983: 52); v. Loewenich refers to Melanchton and Mathesius, who connect Luther's entry into the monastery with the death of a close friend of his.

5. W. v. Loewenich (1983: 57). *Nota bene*: As patron saint of printers, it almost inevitably comes to mind, Saint Augustine certainly rendered outstanding services to his fellow monk in propagating the latter's Bible translation and pamphlets.

6. The fact that "Luther," that prototype of "reformer" emerged from history and stories, himself became model and passer on of the pattern he assumed and varied, shows yet again the power inherent to the structures of the history of mentality: The most prominent representatives of this pattern, Martin Luther King and Bishop Tutu, the "Luther of South Africa," carry on the heritage.

7. The mythical pattern that Luther follows here is also the foundation of the medieval "theory of music": The musical sounds and dissonances of "Satan," the spirit of melancholy, gloom, and bad humors stand in diametrical opposition to the heavenly harmonies and divine euphony. In other words, music is seen as the symbol of harmony and divine order: David the Psalmist's harp acquires a special meaning in this context, perpetuated in the "cult symbolism" of Protestantism. For instance, in the old Lutheran chapel of the castle in Dresden, the paintings on the organ depict the Elector of Dresden as a latter-day David, standing with his harp in front of the altar. See F. Herrmann (ed., 1967): *Symbolik der Religionen,* Vol. XV, *Kultsymbolik des Protestantismus,* Book of Illustrations by K. Goldamer to Vol. VII of the text, Stuttgart: 74 and 75.

8. One could continue the—mythical/legendary—parallels by referring to Saul's attempt, driven by the evil spirit, to "pin his enemy to the wall with his spear." The spear was merely driven "into the wall" (I. Samuel 19:10), and in Luther's legendary throwing of the inkwell at the evil spirit; it landed on the wall of his study. From spear to inkwell, from commander to interpreter, the images change but the structure remains the same. And in any case: In the "oldest version of the legend (1591) Luther did not throw the inkwell at the devil, but rather it was the devil who threw the inkwell at Luther" [W. v. Loewenich (1983: 191)], which represents the pattern of Saul/David much better.

9. According to this understanding, Luther defends suicidees as Satan's victims who meet their death not voluntarily, but rather, as a result of being violated by the "spirit of melancholy" (i.e., by the power of the devil). Here, too, we see the allusion to mankind's basic lack of freedom (see the following): Without God, man is unfree, prey to the powers of darkness. See R. Friedenthal (1983: 358).

10. M. Luther, *dass der freie Wille nichts sei* ("that free will is nothing"). *Martin Luther's response to Erasmus von Rotterdam,* translated into German by Bruno Cordahn, Munich 1983: 46 and 47; see also M. Luther: *De servo arbitrio,* in: Martin Luther: *Studienausgabe,* ed. by Hans-Ulrich Delius, Vol. 3, East Berlin, 1983: 20.

11. Pseudo-Augustin (1632): *Hypomnesticon contra Pelagianos et Caelestianos 3, II, 20.* MPL 45. Typically, the heretic quotes from a polemical treatise against heretics in his polemical treatise against a representative of the theological tradition.

12. The martyr's career is of no consequence for the ancient models, although it is of central importance for many examples and almost all of the "historically early"

saints. The fact that Socrates' "voluntary" death is frequently referred to in terms of a martyr's death, its wholly other motives and constellations notwithstanding, is a result of the collective effect of the martyr's pattern for *curriculae vitae* and the conduct of life in general: in the reduction of the typical martyr's *curriculum vitae* to a description of the end of his or her life.

13. See R. Friedenthal (1983), but also E. H. Erikson (1958), where Luther's problem with God translates into his problem with his father—and vice versa. In this connection, see W. v. Loewenich (1983: 37f); v. Loewenich quotes Luther's so-called table talk [M. Luther; *Kritische Gesamtausgabe (Weimarana)*, Weimar 1883 ff., 2. *Abteilung Tischreden*]; *Tischrede 2, Nr. 1559:* "My father once flogged me so hard that I fled from him and he was worried until he accustomed me to him again"; *Tischreden 3, Nr. 3566 A:* "My mother flogged me for the sake of one nut until the blood flowed. And with this harsh discipline they finally drove me into the monastery."

14. See in this context, for example, the great work of F. v. Sales Doyé (1929): *Heilige und Selige der römisch-katholischen Kirche. Deren Erkennungszeichen, Patronate und lebensgeschichtliche Bemerkungen,* two volumes with appendix "*Deutsche Heilige*" and "*Die alten Trachten der männlichen und weiblichen Orden sowie der geistlichen Mitglieder der ritterlichen Orden,* Leipzig." Characteristically, the motto of this work is "*Nihil obstat.*"

15. Michael Schmaus, et al. (eds.): *Handbuch der Dogmengeschichte, Band IV Sakramente—Eschatologie, Faszikel I a: Die Lehre von den Sakramenten im allgemeinen von der Schrift bis zur Scholastik,* by Josef Finkenzeller, Freiburg/Basel/Vienna, esp. 119 ff. The "sacred" or "mythical" number seven itself refers to the repetition of the timelessly valid order *also* in the sacraments.

16. Concerning Luther's attitude toward the sacrament of marriage see E. Bornkamm (1979: 104 ff): *Martin Luther in der Mitte seines Lebens,* aus dem Nachlaß herausgegeben von Karin Bornkamm, Göttingen, 1979.

17. Here, Paul is anticipating "Weber's thesis on Protestantism" in his concise use of "the language of the fall"; see also R. Bultmann (1956: 116).

18. Pietistic (auto-) biographies fulfill this pattern in an exemplary fashion. The structure is also indisputably in evidence in K. Ph., Moritz's *Anton Reiser;* see E. Jung-Stilling: *Heinrich Stillings Jugend.*

19. On the subject of Luther's entry into the "Black Monastery," see also W. v. Loewenich (1983: 53 ff.).

20. See Th. Kolde: *Die deutsche Augustiner-Kongregation und J. von Staupitz,* 1978. The Augustinian-Observants for their part follow in the tradition of the Franciscan-Observants, those most radical adherents to Saint Francis's rules of the order.

21. See A. Hahn (1982). Hahn points up convincingly the "protestantization" of the confession in the Counter-Reformation, that is, the shifting of emphasis from "the works" to the institutions.

22. Hahn (1982: 410) refers to historically preceding validation attempts which appeared in similar contexts. See also C. v. Schätzler (1860): *Die Lehre von der Wirksamkeit der Sakramente—Ex opere operato—in ihrer Entwicklung innerhalb der Scholastik und ihrer Bedeutung für die christliche Heilslehre,* Munich; and W. Knoch (1983).

23. It seems doubtful to me whether the philosophy of Abelard, which was material in the development of confession and "analysis of sins" (Hahn, 1982: 408) was also decisive at the IV. Lateran Council. Without doubt a purely "external con-

cept of sin" was as insufficient for the Council as for Abelard. But to bring the more "inner" concept of sin as one not connected solely to concrete works into general connection to the very modern connotations of "motive" and "intention" seems a bit over hasty. Thus, too, the "acquiescence in sin" (408) on the part of the sinner is, in the eyes of the Church, less an indication of intentionality than expression of a sinful basic stance, of a misconception. Equally, the "remorse" is seen far more as expression of repentance in the sense of a now corrected, correct insight than as "individual" repentance: The catalog of sins as well as the standardized course of questions, penance, and punishment are, and for the time being remain, collectively institutionalized to such an extent that it is hard to believe that, already in the early thirteenth century, there was such a thing as the "subjectivization of sin" (Hahn, 1982: 408) or repentance (*contritio* and *attritio*).

24. See in this context also L. Boff (1972): *Die Kirche als Sakrament im Horizont der Welterfahrung. Versuch einer Legitimation und einer struktur-funktional-istischen Grundlegung der Kirche im Anschluß an das II. Vatikanische Konzil,* Paderborn. The fundamental difference between Protestantism and Catholicism as regards the term and function of the "Church" is visible in particular in the way the traditional concept of "church as sacrament" is viewed exclusively in relation to Catholicism.

25. This tendency is particularly marked in pietistic groups and also, generally, in Protestant sects. See also M. Weber (1972b): *Gesammelte Aufsätze zur Religionssoziologie I, Tübingen, esp. 207–38 (Die protestantischen Sekten und der Geist des Kapitalismus).*

26. Ibid.; in addition Luther, unlike Zwingli, made no attempts to impose a firm organizational form on community life or on the community as an entity. He was primarily interested in questions of faith. See also H. Bornkamm (1979): 125 ff., 425 ff., as well as Luther's role in advising the German Order of Knights (*Deutscher Ritterorden*): 282 ff.

27. Kierkegaard not only thought this image, he also—in keeping with his "inheritance" from Luther—lived it as "biblical man": He lived, in self-reflection and self-description, a—sufficiently documented—exemplary Protestant life. See S. Kierkegaard, et al. (1960): *Werke I. Der Begriff Angst,* transl. by Liselotte Richter, Hamburg; (1959): *Die Krankheit zum Tode,* transl. by G. Jungbluth, Hamburg (1959a): *Gesammelte Werke. Die Tagebücher,* ausgewählt, neugeordnet und übersetzt von H. Gerdes, Düsseldorf/Cologne.

28. The *Deutsch-Katechismus* (German Catechism), later called *Der große Katechismus,* appeared in 1529, as did the *Kleiner Katechismus,* which appeared on tablets in the form of a placard. Both were furthered by the *"Traubüchlein für die einfältigen Pfarrer,"* included in the *Kleiner Katechismus.*

29. This figure of thought is already to be found in Luther's writings: "This is the Christian freedom, the pure faith which effects not that we can go idle or do evil but that we do not require deeds in order to attain piety and everlasting salvation" (Luther, 1983a: 131): *Von der Freiheit eines Christenmenschen,* ed. by E. Kähler, Stuttgart, see also 142f. Deeds do show up "externally, who is pious and who is evil...Matt. 7:20: 'Therefore by their fruits you will know them.' But that is all mere appearance and external" (143).

30. On a philosophically higher but nevertheless comparable level, the discussion between Kant and Schiller takes place, too—"Duty or Inclination?"—as motive for action. Whatever the answer is: what is decisive for the evaluation of the action is not the observable action itself but rather what lies behind the

action; not the dangers, risks, or success and benefit, but rather the motives for acting.

31. See above all M. Luther: *Von weltlicher Obrigkeit, wie weit man ihr Gehorsam schuldig sei* (1523), Martin Luther (1983a, vol. 3: 27 ff.). Also Martin Luther (1983a, vol. 3: 85 ff.): *Ein Brief an die Fürsten zu Sachsen von dem aufrührerischen Geist* (1524), as well as the writings on the peasant rebellion, published in 1525: Martin Luther (1983a, vol. 3: 105): *Ermahnung zum Frieden auf die zwölf Artikel der Bauernschaft in Schwaben. Luthers Vorrede und Vermahnung zum Vertrag zwischen dem biblischen Bund zu Schwaben und den zwei Haufen und Versammlung der Bauern vom Bodenseee und Allgäu.* Martin Luther (1983a, vol. 3: 134): *Auch wider die räuberischen und mörderischen Rotten der anderen Bauern*; Martin Luther (1983a, vol. 3: 140f.): *Ein Sendbrief von dem harten Büchlein wider die Bauern*; Martin Luther (1983a, vol. 3: 148 ff.).

32. Commentary on Luther's work "*Von weltlicher Obrigkeit*" (1983a, vol. 3: 27 ff.)

33. Typical for such an exclusively political, "one-track" interpretation of the "Doctrine of Two Kingdoms," see Loewenich's summary of the discussion on the subject (1983: 218 ff. and 224 ff.). See also H. Bornkamm (1979: 106 ff.).

34. See R. Müller-Salget (1984: 29). This interpretational pattern also has to serve, for instance, in explaining the "survey" of 1848. But it has also continued to "stand the test of time."

35. In this context, see particularly: M. Luther, *De servo arbitrio,* op. cit., 251 ff. See also the differentiation between the "*deus intrinsece*" and the "*deus extrinsece*" in Luther's commentary on Romans.

36. Ibid., 254, "*Timere (et) adorare.*" For a continuation of this "Lutheran" position in Protestant theology see H. Bornkamm (1979: 393 ff.); esp. 334, and also W. v. Loewenich (1983: 264).

37. This motif is taken up by German Romanticism in particular. Typically in the *Nachtwachen von Bonaventura* (1804), Stuttgart 1964, 134: "'What, is there then no God' he cried out wildly, and the echo returned to him the word 'God' loud and clear... 'It was the devil who invented the echo!' he finally said—'Since one cannot tell whether he is merely aping one or whether the words are really being spoken!'"

38. More detailed and exact proof for this thesis is to be brought in a later study. For now, I shall limit myself to a few references.

39. When I speak of "steps," I am not implying by this metaphor that there are types of individuality that take over one from the other or even replace one another. If a traditional context, as well as certain societal groups with their specific way of life, all indebted to one of these types, "survive," then the survival of that type is secure, that is in the reserve of the monasteries.

40. See Soeffner, Hans-Georg, 1 (1992): "Style and Stylization. Punk, or the Superevelation of Everyday Life" (*Stil und Stilisierung. Punk oder die Überhöhung des Alltags*), this volume.

41. Adolph Freiherr von Knigge (1977: 20): *Über den Umgang mit Menschen,* ed. by G. Üeding, Frankfurt. Knigge's book of advice is insofar a piece of practical enlightenment—become necessary for life in society—as it battles against the Lutheran-Protestant "inward orientation" already firmly entrenched by the educational system of the late eighteenth century. This inward-oriented conduct practically makes a guide for public conduct indispensable to those who "are misunderstood, overlooked by everyone" and thus "do not achieve anything at all" (introduction, 230). Accordingly, the first programmatic sentence of this

guide is: "In this world, every person counts only for that which he makes of himself: (37), and for Knigge, this unarguably means how he presents himself *publicly* and visibly.

42. Mead's conception of identity of "I," "me," and "self" is also indebted to this structural model. See G. H. Mead (1934), *Mind, Self and Society,* ed. by Ch. W. Morris, Chicago.

43. The Lutheran-Protestant type of individuality discussed here represents, in its present-day, scientifically enlightened form, an extreme position within this relationship. It is hard to overlook the polar opposites going in the direction of "scientification" at one end, and in that of self-reflectiveness and self-sensibility at the other (e.g. in "punks" and the "smooth operator" type of manager. See H.-G. Soeffner, "Style and Stylization. Punk, or the Superevelation of Everyday Life," this volume.

The far more encompassing thesis of the "colonization of the life-world," in which the Marxist metaphor of the "colonization on the inner world" is taken up in a characteristic fashion [see J. Habermas (1981), *Theorie des kommunikativen Handelns,* 2 vols., Frankfurt], apparently overlooks the structural difference between practical and speculative reason and thus not only subverts the quoted Kantian insight, it actually also proves that, as far as the domestication of practical life by theory or ideology is concerned, it does not differ *structurally* from what it is criticizing: everyday action is being spoon fed either way. In addition, it is not, on the whole, hard to recognize from the metaphors and figures of thought used in which tradition of thought the figure itself is embedded. Here, too, good and less good, "light, clear" and dark worlds stand in opposition to each other: *civitas rationis* and *civitas simplicitatis.* The speculative god "Logos" has taken the place of his Judeo-Christian predecessor without having given up the latter's structural concept of the "two kingdoms."

44. See the Kant quotation at the beginning of the chapter.

2

Style and Stylization:
Punk, or the Superelevation of Everyday Life

Max Weber considered the "religious stereotype [as] a creation of the products of the formative arts" to be the "oldest form of the creation of style."[1] He was referring to the close connection between the creation of types or stereotypes, formative arts or aesthetics, and religious expression independently of the more traditional use of the word "style" in his formulation. I shall use this remark as my starting point for the following chapter. I consider it more than a remark about the historical beginnings of the formation of style: I use it as a stimulus to investigate techniques and actions of aesthetic "superelevation" of the everyday in general, and to look at how much they already appear in concrete everyday interaction and possibly in that context already contain elements of the expression of religious experiences or religious views.

There are two primary reasons why I shall first turn my attention to the punk movement, a most striking group—on the one hand, stylization, creation of type, aestheticizing citation of everyday objects (e.g., safety pins or crown corks) are hard to overlook here, on the other hand there seems to be no indication, at least not at first sight—that these means of stylization serve to express religious experiences. So observing the phenomenon "punk" can also serve to test my initial assumption. I shall divide the undertaking, which admittedly is rather bold within this limited framework, into three steps: (1) First of all, I shall try to develop a concept for the terms "style" and "stylization" which can be used as a tool for empirical observation and at the same time as a concept for analysis; (2) I shall describe some striking, even if not demonstrably central, means of style and practices of stylization used by German punks, and I shall supplement these descriptions by tracing, in the manner of no more than a sketch, several connections between stylistic means or symbols used today and their historical predecessors; and (3) I shall formulate several hypotheses deriving from the analysis of our observations, but whose solidity must be tested by observing other groups and other phenomena of stylization.

The following observations and reflections are closely related to other case studies that my research group is working on. Our goal is to garner, by means of empirical case studies, information that will throw light on the forms of expression and contents in collective designs of self, others, and reality, designs which determine our contemporary societal life.[2] In other words, the focus of all these studies is on the symbolic and emblematic structures and structurings of social order(s) and the description and interpretation of observable manifestations of social forms of presentation pertaining to the reciprocal orientation of social groups.[3]

Style and Acts of Stylization

From the point of view of interaction theory, what I consider a specific historical style is first of all an observable (self-) presentation of persons, groups, or societies. Style as specific presentation marks and manifests the individual's belonging not only to a group or community, but also to a specific demeanor and form of life which these groups or communities feel compelled to maintain. A style is part of an extensive system of signs, symbols, and references for social orientation: it is expression, instrument, and result of social orientation. Accordingly, an individual's style not only indicates who is "who" or "what," but also who is "who" for whom in what situation. And the style of texts, buildings, clothing, art works indicates not only what something is, or where it can be classified, but also what something is for whom and when and what it "wants to be."

Thus, "style"—not only as applied *to* social interaction, but also *in* social interaction—is mainly a piece of and category of observation. Within human society, which has always been a society of observers, style is produced in order that one may be observed. Style represents and presents in social interaction the unity of presentation and observation. In this respect, "stylization" and "styling" can be understood as a bundling of observable actions that are paraded in order to achieve a uniform and coordinated presentation. Thus, the elements of a developed style are the frozen actions of stylization or actions that indicate style.[4]

But, since human beings always produce signs in their actions next to and in all activities or plans, thereby indicating what they do, think, or want, and who they are, it would be a senseless generalization to call only the significatory and typificatory presentation of actions or attitudes "style." Everyday life is ordered and orders itself through *typified* actions, perceptions, things, and persons, and equally through *typifying* perceptions and actions.[5] We live—ourselves types in the eyes of others—in a typified world. It does not mark an outstanding lifestyle just to move typically within this everyday world, to conduct oneself or act in it. On the contrary, in contradistinction to everyday typification, every style has, in addition, an aesthetic component—an aestheticizing superelevation of the everyday.

"To have style" is, in other words, the result of goal-oriented actions directed toward a "cultural superelevation" of the everyday. It is a visible, unifying presentation, in which every individual action and every detail is included with the goal of forming a homogeneous configuration (*Gestalt*) or "style," and of presenting it. In this sense, "having style" means being capable of consciously offering and staging a homogeneous interpretation both for others and for one's own self-image. This means that the member of a "significant" group must be able to represent the interpretation and presentation of his or her own group in an exemplary fashion in each individual case (which one has to stage oneself).

In this context, I would like to specifically point out that the "bearer" of a style needn't have an *explicit,* discursively communicable concept or an explicit prescription and reason for the style presented. What the bearer of a style—as the designer of himself—needs is to know those significant selections—and to introduce them in acting—by which a specific style is produced and staged. *Nota bene*: an individual can indicate his belonging to a specific group on the one hand in a stylized way by arranging a significant staging of group-conforming actions, attitudes, beliefs, manners, clothes, and the like. In this case, the individual generally knows that he is behaving in a "conforming" way. On the other hand, individuals can—and at present this is being demonstrated in our society—very strenuously try to be and appear "unique" or, in the vocabulary of current usage, "authentic." Then they are, in the eyes of the outside observer—in the circle of the many who feel committed to uniqueness—the conformist members of a group of nonconformists.

A person's style, or that of a group, an artifact, an object of everyday use, or that of a text, combines all perceptible details of its respective bearer into a representable configuration of meaning. And "style"—in the sense in which I use it here—must simultaneously be understood as a recipe for interpretation, acted out in front of an audience: as the presentation and expression of something that lends an aestheticizing, non-everyday accent even to everyday actions or objects. An interpretational clue for the concrete or potential observer (also for the designer of style as observer of himself) as to the configuration of meaning as a whole is worked into every detail of the style and the stylized actions. Thus, each individual stylized action and each element of style embodies on the one hand actual-concrete purposes, and on the other hand contains clues to a more encompassing and legitimizing "higher" unity of meaning: the style.

Accordingly, elements of style contain not only clues and points of contact to the style itself, but also to other elements, signs, scenes with which they are connected. In social interaction, a specific style is continually produced and reproduced via stylization of individual actions and details that refer to preceding, stylized details and scenes, and are picked up by succeeding ones.

This process, which is continually being defined in individual actions, cannot, in the system of reciprocal social actions and reactions, have recourse exclusively to familiar things, nor repeat or quote them alone. Rather, it must be—as far as the to-be-presented meaning is concerned—*structurally (relatively) closed* and at the same time *materially open (almost without limit)*. The latter mainly in regard to novel situations and materials, which can be worked into the styles's structure of meaning via stylizing activities, and adapted to the style.

I already mentioned that "style," within a society of observers and those who are observed, of interpreters and interpretees, is a category of observation *and* interpretation. In keeping with that, "style" does not mean the *quality* of a person, of an art object or an everyday object, of a text, and so on. What it is is a *product* of social interaction, observation, and interpretation. A style is created not alone by an actor who stylizes himself or certain products, it is created just as much by confirmatory complementary interpretations on the part of observers and interpreters.[6]

Here, the effect and the goal of "style" and "stylization" become apparent: A person who produces a style indicates in so doing that he or she distances himself both from himself and from his social environment, that is, the person in question also confronts himself or herself in the act of observing or interpreting. Thus, "style" becomes a means of expression and a form of presenting social *demarcation*. It illustrates "membership in" and "demarcation from" through conscious presentation and stylization of a self for interpreting others (observers).

The familiar thesis—this much is now apparent—that only the historical appearance of a so-called personal or private style constituted or brought forth an "individual" subject is not tenable. The consciously stylized contrasting of an "autonomous" self against others is rather a collective and widely shared answer to a situation in which the individuals have lost their social position in a securely ordered society, a position known and recognized by other individuals and thus familiar and visible.[7] In such historical situations, individuals try to secure what they have already lost: To wit, all those often desperate attempts and ideologies that try to constitute an autonomous "authentic" subject and to legitimize the striving for subjectivity, above all try to demonstrate how profoundly painful the loss of positionally secured subjectivity is felt. Not to put a fine point on it: the modern dream of the self-sufficient subject builds on the ruins of historically preceding orders and the integration and security of individuality within those orders—the illusory construction of an autonomous subject. This illusion of self-sufficiency demands from man as *animal social* something that he neither is nor can accomplish. Moreover, the perfect fulfillment of the norm of "self-sufficiency" and "autonomy" would mean nothing other than an objectively practiced form of antisocial behavior, however euphemistically paraphrased.

Independently of this thesis, which we shall return to later on, may this brief sketch of the concept of style as I use it suffice for the present. It is a concept in keeping with empirical observation and it contains both the colloquial expression "to have style" and criteria according to which it can be used as an observation category. Also, I hope to have clarified that the interpretation of a specific style is not, based on these preliminary remarks, intended to answer the question "*Why* has a certain style developed historically?" Instead, I think it makes sense to ask the following question and to seek answers for it: "What does a specific, observable style represent and mean?"

Possibly I shall succeed in making concrete the direction of question and answer in the following short description and characterization of "punk style."

Style and Demeanor

"Oh, yes, one sometimes does want to be a
good person—if only the good people weren't
quite so insufferable."[8]

In the same way as other groups we can now observe who consider themselves "outsiders" or are thus defined by others— such as, "the Alternative Group" (*die Alternativen*), "the Green Party" (*die Grünen*), "the Autonomous Groups" (*die autonomen Gruppen*), "the Sannyasin," and the like—the punks, too, have developed a form of presentation that is marked by the conspicuous preeminence of "symbolic actions," by a well-developed emblematism, and by highly ritualized acting in public. According to my thesis, the specific form and practice of staging "punk" as style and of "punks" as group members and designers of this style are the result of conscious stylization and of an implicit, collectively shared knowledge by the punks from which details and elements of a system of symbols must be selected and practiced in order to stage the right "performance" of "punk."

The data which I will use in the following consists of open interviews, videos, field observation, photos, punk magazines, punk-music album covers, and letters written to one of the members of my team, Thomas Lau, who does all the fieldwork in the punk project—gathering, cultivating, hunting.[9] Within the very limited framework here, this data cannot be described in nearly as great detail as a field study should do. I will limit myself to summarizing and typifying some central elements of the punk style, with the goal of elaborating on the raw form of the "ideal type"[10] (in Max Weber's sense) and of what I call the "configuration of meaning"[11] of the punk phenomenon. My point of departure (see above): I shall attempt to perform those interpretations that punks provoke me and others to do by staging their specific style.

Anyone who has ever seen punks will remember the strange and characteristic composition of the "Iroquois look" on the one hand—an allusion to a specific "primitive people"—and, on the other hand, at least in the initial stages of punk, the primarily black, rivet-covered and painted clothing. *Nota bene*: the predominance of black clothing for a while switched over more and more into garishly colored clothing, and now is returning once again to the color "black." Whatever official fashion picks up from punk design is immediately abandoned by the punks by way of a counter movement, and reformulated as antifashion. But, independently of this tendency, the outward appearance of punks is and was structurally determined by the contrast between eye-catching hair-styles and colors on the one hand and predominantly dark clothing on the other.

The inattentive observer might see a sharp contrast between the laboriously produced hair-styles (and often make-up as well) and clothing that seems—in a special way—neglected, dirty, worn, and often darned or patched. But, if one looks closer, one will realize that this first impression is deceptive: the seemingly tattered and shabby garb is carefully put together and arranged. A lot of it is handmade, not exactly according to fashion magazine dictates: rivet patterns, patches, glued-on buttons, emblematic painted patterns (e.g., the anarchists' emblem) and letters, provocative slogans, or names of bands.

Instead of belts, some punks use(d) ropes, and many of them "decorate" their jackets and trousers with patches. Facial make-up either aims for striking pallor or consists of ornamental painted patterns—a conspicuous allusion to war and hunting paint used by the American Indians. Scars are seen as ornaments of pain or of aesthetic stigma: the famous safety pins in the earlobes or cheeks point in the same direction. Characteristically, the stylized self-injury, which evokes associations of pain and uneasiness in the observer, is demonstrated by, of all things, the diversion of a "safety" implement from its proper use.

In short, it costs much effort, time, and, at best, discomfort to maintain the high standards of punk make-up, bodily presentation, and dress culture (probably more than a *dame de Vogue* or a "Cosmopolitan-woman"). And even if the effort were comparable, the goal remains another: "Punk" is the elaboration of a specific aesthetic of the ugly—and, by implication, of poverty and shabbiness. The aims of this aesthetic are exactly the opposite of the usual efforts at make-up—they mean to demonstrate strict animosity to luxury, mass consumption and serial, reproducible beautification.

Considering all these efforts—Iroquois look and all—that a central European adolescent invests in order to produce the image of a "child of nature" (we are not referring to the fashionable nature-man or jungle dressman as evidenced by Camel cigarette ads), then one has a fitting example and concrete historical expression of the stylization and expressive superelevation of an "artificial naturalness."[12] Considered thus, punk style is the consciously arranged and, regarding the aesthetic pleasure involved, playful reversal of that *conditio humana* that Plessner called "natural artificiality."

Any attentive observer will notice that punks know what they are doing and toward what symbolic expression they are investing their antithetical style. The Iroquois look does not represent the Indian as a "child of nature." On the contrary, by calling themselves "urban Indians," punks deliver a further proof for the formal principle of their style—for its *antithetical structure* as well as for the principle of construction and expression of contradictions, which are valid *within* the style, too. Contrary to the "Green Party," the "Alternatives," and/or "ecological" movements, punks don't hold with a late resurrection of Rousseauism nor with a return to nature. They merely quote the myth of the "original, natural order" of things, pointing out that it has been irrevocably destroyed. *The antithetical structure of the punk style is directed inward and outward.* It refers to the internal principle of the connection of emblems, symbols and referential signs as much as to the "outward"-directed, provocative and caustic reversal of the "current" fashion.

The way symbolic traditions are cited—itself a symbolic procedure—and connecting, antithetically, symbolic quotations and fashion that is in constant counter motion to the current fashion, even where the latter adopts punk style as in the use of the color "black" in punk clothing and cosmetics. Black, emblem-covered clothing was one of the supporting elements of punk style in the beginning of the "movement."[13] When general fashion began to invoke this style, punk turned to color; when this, too, began to be consumed in mainstream fashion, punk returned to "black".

Black as a dominant color in clothing has a long tradition in Central Europe, nurtured by very different and contradictory movements. It is this Central European tradition alone that I want to turn my attention to here briefly. In its turn, it is the foundation of our implicit knowledge about the ambivalent symbolic content of clothing of this hue. "Black" is not so much "beautiful," but it does affect our perception in a very specific way: It puts the body, clothed or painted in black, in a most conspicuous contrast to colored or light-colored surroundings. It was and remains the color of meditation and concentration—visible sign of the denial of sensual pleasure and sensory openness to the world. Thus, it was not only the color of specific, transitory, ritually transformed experiences, occasions, or "passages of life" (i.e., mourning, widow's garb, or old people's clothing). The traditions of the formal, the worldview, and the social contrasts all complement one another.

When Philip the Good of Burgundy (1419–1467) was the only one to appear in monochromatic black amidst his colorfully clad court, it was a representative expression of his socially elevated position. When, on the other hand, the Renaissance generally recommended black clothing, purportedly because the human face stands out most effectively against black, this recommendation laid new emphasis on the presentation and observation of human expressive behavior. The "little black dress" is a leftover from this tradition. And the Spanish court-dress in the sixteenth and seventeenth centuries stylizes the expressiveness of the—pale yet "glowing"—human face into the masklike immobility of pure courtly representation: court painters serve the masklike white face up on a large white collar so that it hovers above the black-clad body as though it were on a platter.

The official Lutheran vestments as well as those of other Protestant churches were, or rather are, black—just like the "worldly" garb of Protestant laypersons—visible sign of a withdrawal from the world and of a self-referential attitude, that is, self-exploration. Black as the color signalling a withdrawal from the world and at the same time as the color of protest thus complement each other. Similarly, the German romantic of the early nineteenth century, with his secure worldview and secure style, wore a black instead of a white cravat in order to symbolically give the "night-side of life"—at least in this minute way—its right. Black as the color of anarchism has its place in exactly this tradition (who could forget Juliette Gréco's long black sweater?), signalling the connection between anarchism and existentialism.

Yet another symbolic context—another line of tradition—should be mentioned in the discussion of black clothing: black as the color of "élite" military troops.[14] The black chain of often dubious élite forces winds its way back through the centuries, from the "Black Cavalry" of Count Günther of Schwarzburg [*Schwarzburg* meaning "black castle" (fourteenth century)], over the "Black Army" of Matthias Corvinus, the "Saxon Black Guard," Florian Geyer's "Black Troop" (in which the members' faces were also dyed black), the "Black Band" of Emperor Maximilian, the "Death's Head Hussars" of Frederick the Great and the Duke of Braunschweig (Brunswick), all the way up to Mussolini's "Blackshirts" and Hitler's "Waffen-SS."

Many more symbolic uses of the color black could be listed. But for the present investigation, let it suffice to have made visible some of the main strands of those traditions in which the self-presentation of individuals, groups and collectives, and the presentation of emotions, passages of status, and worldviews are expressed by the use of the color black—in an "external" sign as reference to an "inner" attitude, opinion, or membership.

It is perfectly evident that when they use the color black, punks do not have explicit knowledge of all the traditions, meanings, and symbolic contexts listed above. However, they do know some of those contexts from books, comics, mass media, and the visual arts. In any case, this kind of symbolic context is not passed on or kept alive by perusing the *Emblematum liber*[15] or an encyclopedia of symbols. They remain alive through social action chains[16] whose elements and forming principles they are. They are learned through usage and one uses them without knowing explicitly that one has learned them. They help form our implicit knowledge; they make up part of our implicit knowledge.

Let me name yet again the basic characteristics—the symbolic presentation of social attitudes—of the extremely ambivalent symbolic configuration expressed in the various types of black clothing. At the same time, I would like to point out that in punk style (see above), nearly all symbolic and emblematic stances are connected in a special way. These are: social distance, contrast and opposition; piousness, religiousness, world-denial, meditation, renunciation; protest and battle. In terms of *structure*, all these stances bear the characteristics of isolation and separation. In terms of *contents*, this feature is almost invariably marked by the consciousness of belonging to an élite—or, to put it pointedly, an élite of renunciation.

This structure becomes discernible under all the feathers and finery, and a direction emerges where one can search for the antecedents of the punk "movement." The emphasis is on "antecedents"; they are not "models"—representatives of historically lived and symbolically presented attitudes—not ahistorical casting-moulds. Punk—as attitude, not style—shows conspicuous parallels to lay mendicant orders in the Middle Ages, in particular to the lifestyle of the Franciscans *before* their legalization by the Church and their subordination to the basic tenets and the universally binding symbolic system of convent orders.[17]

The structures characteristic for lay orders that consciously parade stylized poverty and demonstrative opposition to luxury, combined with the emphasis on the "simple life," the attention to an "endangered nature," the conscious return to simple virtues, a vagrant life, a life marked by derision and indignation from the rest of society—all these closely approximate the implicit norms of "punk" lifestyle.

In the interviews we made, it becomes clear that emblematic allusions to convent habits in punk clothing are deliberate. Using a rope instead of a belt was, according to an interviewed punk, borrowed from those "monastery dudes." One need only compare the stylized, patched garb of punks to the patch-covered habits of mendicant monks in old engravings—in particular, depictions of Saint Francis of Assisi. But all these allusions could be seen as a purely aesthetic game with historical costumes, as a parody of traditional clothing of the Church and others, if there wasn't also further evidence to support the theory of a specifically "religious" pattern. We found such evidence both in our interviews and by observing the norms of everyday life among punks.

A casual observer of the urban punk scene, of punk groups' frequently rude behavior and their provocative patches or T-shirt messages ("I fuck like an animal") will find it hard to believe the norms expressed in interviews and observed in the field, as they seem to be so antithetical to all appearances and stagings of provocation. A brief synopsis of those norms follows:

1. A more or less *impersonal friendship,* not linked to individuals, potentially with all members of the group—whoever they may be and wherever they may come from. It can further be observed that punk is the only so-called youth subculture that not only includes all social groups—from the child of blue-collar workers to middle and upper-class high school students—but also contains—the "Iroquois do" is a symbolic allusion to this[18]—approximately equal numbers of male and female members.

2. *Hospitality* toward members of the group. Punk is a traveling or vagrant movement. Punks "travel" throughout *all* of Europe and increasingly also through North and South America. Whoever—visibly—belongs to the group can find lodging with other punks for free, without having to refer to anything except their lifestyle.

3. *Enmity toward luxury* and—by the standards of the rest of society—blatantly paraded *lack of possessions.* All one needs is the right music—concerts and hot albums—and the presence of like-minded and like-styled co-punks.

4. The intact community of "authentic" group members. ("Where there's punk, the world's O.K. You can count on every one of them. Just

as long as you watch out for those weekend punks.") This community is a unity of "shared minds" and a shared lifestyle.

5. *Internationalism:* Punk has no regional or national, nor racial borders—an accomplishment unmet by any other youth "subculture."

6. A specific *innocence* and *purity*, expressed by not letting oneself be seduced by a "shallow," "phony" way of life, by "keeping clean."

The genuine lifestyle of punk moves within these simple norms and values whose religious provenance is irrefutable and whose continuing existence in the present has been guaranteed by certain groups—the successors of those orders created in the Middle Ages, groups that, in the words of Halbwachs, "continue, in part, to live among the ruins of the past."[19] The manner of returning to these simple norms and values also follows a traditional pattern of behavior: that of radical conversion, which includes leaving behind "normal" life. Those who convert to the "punk" lifestyle not only are given a new "wardrobe," he/she is also given a new name[20] and schooled in a new language—a new system of social typification. Once the conversion is completed, life has, in accordance with the conversion pattern, no further developments—at least not as long as belonging to the group and its lifestyle determines one's everyday life.

Those who have reached this point in their observations will hardly be surprised that for their performances, punks have not only a *provocational milieu* (railway stations, public parks, shopping malls, etc.), a *narrower group milieu* (concerts or pogo meetings in different "locales"), but also a further-reaching, more *"ceremonial milieu"*: peace marches, peace demonstrations, and Church congresses, both Protestant and Catholic. They are to be found here on a regular basis, the "provocateurs" of the "silent majority," not as opponents, but rather as participants or—above all in the Protestant Church in the then-GDR—as participants *and* refuge-seekers from state powers and state morality.

And here, too, the punks' distancing, antithetical style keeps them from making the transition from being distant participants of the new mass ceremonies to being members in a community of convictions and emotions. They reject the collective ceremonial, religious, or worldly chorals, stagings of inner orientation and demonstrations of faith, or else parody them. They consider that lullaby of hope "We shall Overcome," sung by Belafonte, barely worth one "pogo."[21] "Punk" as style and stance doesn't live on periodically staged, more or less isolated,

collective emotions or ritualized creeds, but rather on the "permanence" of the everyday conduct of life. A contrast to collective movements based on conviction or persuasion, punks present themselves as virtuosos in attitude and style.

The unmistakable religious elements in "punk" lifestyle, however, have one conspicuous characteristic: The European habit of always seeing and defining religiosity in connection with a conception of God is absent here. That should, in theory, lead to a sharp rift between punks and other religious groups. For the term "God" is not mentioned, not as name, "person," or idea. Punk represents religiousness without God and, thus, a form of that "invisible religion," invisible to most members of our culture. This religion, then, is not only "non-ecclesiastical,"[22] it has also merely *replaced* God, not killed Him off. For ultimately, "God" never dies, He simply changes the image that society endows Him with. This "natural" religiousness is nurtured by the transcendency experiences— based in the life-world—that precede every "developed" religion.[23] It is obvious: God has been replaced by the group itself—for them, intact nature is destroyed, a hereafter is not imaginable, past paradises are lost and future worlds of salvation are not to be hoped for. Transcendency happens *in the* and the hope for salvation refers *to the* here and now: Punk is one of the currently concrete forms of the "world-piousness" analyzed by Plessner, and of the innerworldly desire for redemption expressed in this "religiousness."[24] In the punk system of style and symbol—but also, albeit in a different way, in the public presentations by peace movements and ecological movements—a now in-all-truth post-Lutheran and post-liberal-Catholic, innerworldly religiosity lends expression to its worldview.

God has, as we mentioned, disappeared from there, not, however, the concomitant imagery, the saints and sinners, the heroes and villains, the images of the golden old times, the bad here-and-now, and the either darkly apocalyptical or utopian end of the world. Album covers, buttons, clothing, pseudonyms ("Pope Pest") are full of primarily apocalyptic motives and allusions. Innocent, suffering saints and heroes have their good—and hopeless—place in them.[25] What happens here is that on the one hand, the formal, aesthetic-antithetical style of the punks turns into a life stance; on the other hand, it is hard to discover clearly articulated "messages" that are connected to this attitude or have clear proselytic or missionary goals.

The Superelevation of Everyday Life and of the Individual

A style must be represented—an attitude lived, at least ideally. In other words, representatives of an attitude that expresses itself in stylization must stage the style in such a way that the style refers to more than itself, that it refers to a background which legitimizes the style itself. The style in question thus becomes a system of allusions, and the respective staging an intimation. The actors accordingly see themselves as "animators" for observer and interpreter.

For example, in the "provocational milieu" of public places, railway stations, and parks, punks regularly stage a piece that could bear the title "Juvenile Alcoholism" or "Orgy Non-stop." Beer bottles are rolled in front of the feet of passers-by. Loud burps are heard. Now and again one splashes oneself or the pedestrians with beer.[26] Our (public) interviews had to be "paid" in beer, according to the express wishes of the punks. But in spite of the theater of intoxication permanently on stage, we have to date rarely seen a completely drunken punk. Public demonstrations of that particular state are left entirely to "normal," petit bourgeois weekend drunkards, army reservist groups and the like. As a rule, punks exit from the stage without much fuss and still on their feet after their "performance." Their means of provocation is a familiar pattern: that of "winos" or other "transients" who are to be found in similar public milieux and are recipients of alms and public revulsion all at the same time. By using this pattern, punks can hardly be said to be staging a drama of social criticism called "Public Poverty"; their allusion is not to a group of the "humiliated and insulted" members of this society, but to the society itself: the target of this publicly staged alcoholism is a society of (I quote) "closet alcoholics" who are less afraid of the drinking itself than of their lapses becoming public knowledge. They call to mind Henscheid's provocative motto: "I'd rather be known city-wide as a boozer than be an anonymous alcoholic!"

Deliberate provocation through "obscene" messages on patches (see above) exploits the same device. Whoever imagines, in these patches and signs, promiscuity, wild excess, "damaging tendencies," and "signs of decay"[27] in a marginal group of young people suffers from remarkably poor eyesight and powers of observation. In contrast to the serial animalistic Playmates, the Playboy bunnies, the copulating rabbits on bumperstickers, the very clear and personally formulated punk messages ("Willi

Wucher fucked me"; "I fuck like an animal") are pure provocation—and not an expression of collective desires tacked onto those illustrated fable creatures that are precisely the targets of these punk attacks.

The provocation of public violence also follows the same pattern. The punks stand out with their rudeness and "bad behavior"—offences for which educators/parents are in theory responsible. But the latter—from family via school to the Church—do not react, or rather react with diffuse and hence meaningless understanding. In other words, the desired and necessary partner removes himself from further discussion. There is nary a material-normative opponent in sight. Drunkards call drunkards drunkards, libertines complain about libertinage, political opportunists and lobbyists warn of moral decline and demand "change" in ringing tones. The punks have, in a certain sense, brought about this change according to an old pattern of conversion—and not only in their own opinion. Now it remains for them to show which "pillars" of society still remain, on what the social order is actually resting.

These "pillars" of society, as well as the order they guarantee, can be identified—according to the punks in interviews—as hollow shells: the social system of order presents itself as a formal regulatory system, not as a system of values. Accordingly, the trustees of this regulatory system are seen not only as depersonalized, but also as "devalued" functionaries of a now but formal order, behind whose superficial functioning a battle for power and sinecure rages. The consequence of this hypothesis is that one now seeks the opponent needed for a normal development and who, at home, in school, and at church, is refusing confrontation and fleeing instead into a nebulous but formally well-trained "communication" mechanism, in a place where one can be sure to obtain the desired reaction: among the police, the social trustee of formal order.

If one observes the direction that the necessary normative dispute between parents and children has taken in many families—not least of all under the influence of handbooks dispensing do-it-yourself recipes for family therapy—transforming the by nature intimate family life into a communicational and social-technological "family *conference*,"[28] then one will not be particularly surprised at the provocational patterns developed by punks, nor by their choice of substitute opponent. It is *one* of the possible reaction patterns to a diffusion of norms that has permeated the "classical" authorities that socialize and establish norms—from the family via school, which is now wholly oriented toward the technology of instruction, to the Church. This trend is particularly evident in the churches: The fact that first the Protestant and now the Catholic Church, too, have opened psychotherapeutic counseling centers and incorporated them into their respective parishes gives rise to the question "What religious and theological contents are the churches representing when they substitute therapy for pastoral care and, without further reflection, new institutions of innerworldly-oriented religiousness for the traditional form and content of faith?"

This briefly described tendency of traditional socialization institutions toward an empty or padded, but formally often well-developed technology of "communicative" behavior—leaves punks searching for and finding an opponent that cannot be a socializing authority, but by which the presumed, purely formal and thus deficient character of one's own societal order can be illustrated. Discussing the norms is not possible, according to the above hypothesis, so the point is to break the rules, specifically those that on the one hand are relatively insignificant, but on the other hand are of "public" interest. So what is to be done? The answer given by the avantgarde and also by the punks is: collective "bad behavior" in public.

And so the punks sit, foul-mouthed and guzzling beer, in the cities, public parks, railway stations, and pedestrian zones. They don't attack any of the large symbols of society (e.g., government buildings, flags, monuments, churches etc.); they are merely sullying the lace doilies of the nation. The provoked—formal—organization for the maintenance of public order appears on the scene as expected and skirmishes ensue, also just as expected. The subsequent fistfights are—at least on the part of the punks—a far cry from the brutality of common bar or amusement park brawls on the one hand, or "politically" motivated mass brawls (e.g. with skinheads) on the other. In the beginning they let themselves be beat up more than they beat anyone up. Their goal in a firmly and "ritually" regulated pattern for skirmishes and one of the goals in the quasi-game of "cops-and-robbers" in the provoked chase is to verify their own hypothesis about society for all to see, to show what formerly was but allusion. The hypothesis: This society's sole interest is to maintain a beautiful illusion.

And it is particularly in respect to the destruction of this "beautiful illusion" that the antithetical character of punk style becomes visible and its effect so profound. What we have here is a "youth movement" playing with contemporary ideology and advertising design, with the images of "youth," "attractiveness," "dynamics," "beauty," "authenticity" and a future filled with a "let's-do-it mentality." These young punks place ugliness, shabbiness, and cynicism squarely across from the image of youth that advertising helps support and style: theirs is a different form of youth, caricaturing the media-made image. Nowhere else is the punks' toying with ambiguousness and the semantic range of the term "punk" as clear as here: In good provocational style, punk is: (1) "tinder" for the public whom one is provoking precisely by (2) "messing about" and presenting oneself as (3) the "trash" and "scum" of society; as (4) the "nouveaux misérables." The whole thing takes on the guise of a "youth movement," which at the same time parodies its own romantic or romanticizing antecedents (e.g., the *Wandervögel* (a German youth movement founded in 1895, mainly associated with outdoor activities, especially hiking and singing folksongs around the campfire).

As impressive as the antithetical style, the aestheticizing shabbiness, the distancing/parodistic, moral protest, and the citing of religious traditions may be in the sense of innerworldly piousness—almost all interpreters of punk judge the punks to be lacking in expressiveness, aesthetic games, and provocational skills. The reason: one is accustomed to "messages," at least in this day and age, in connection with social movements. And there are none to be found here. Except for what seems to be a provocation per se. The usual sermon, the appeal are absent. And there are generally no speakers, no spokespeople, no leaders. What remains is a group of disciples without master: an hierarchical order within the group is just as little in evidence as "official organs" or authorized proclamation. And yet the group and its style have survived for years now, gathering proselytes and continuity. So where, or what, is the message?

The answer is simple: Punk *has* no message. Punk as a way of life and a lived style *is* the message. The group doesn't "proselytize" through teachings, appeals, or messages, but rather by demonstrating a unified, moral—albeit costly and risky (because of the constant sanctions accompanying it)—lifestyle. The group has no charismatic leader; it lives on the self-charismatization of the group and its lifestyle. Its means of expression and proselytizing are style and attitude rather than doctrine. At issue is "succession," not dogma. The group is testing field, testing authority and goal all in one. The group transcends both everyday life per se and all individuals. Collective presentation and orientation are secured through the media of the style—emblematism, antithetical aesthetics, music—and through the deliberate public deployment of the style. In this manner, the public stage and the public reaction guarantee the cohesion of the group within the arrangement as a whole.

By consciously placing the group's everyday life on the public stage, it becomes the unaccustomed and non-everyday, and as long as the public in the audience reacts by imposing the expected sanctions, punk is safe from "becoming an ordinary, everyday thing."[29]

It is not only the desire for "innerworldly redemption" but also its potential fulfillment that this group demonstrates through its means of presentation and above all through its self-charismatization, a type of presentation that it shares *structurally* with the also "leaderless" peace movement which, unlike the punks, relies on the masses as ornament and carrier. "This evil world" is not overcome by hoping for a "better other world," it is overcome, as far as the group is concerned, by living a "better" here and now.

However, the superelevation of everyday life and of the individual by a charismatic group is more than simply a reaction to certain existing structures and lifestyles in contemporary society; it is also a reaction to the historically preceding canon of values like "emancipation," "self-fulfillment," "creativity," and "autonomy," in other words self-sufficient subjectivity as represented by the bourgeois sector of the preceding generation, the generation to which the punks' parents' generally belong. The subject-oriented antiritualism of the so-called generation of '68 that portrayed itself as in the tradition of the Enlightenment is confronted today with societal forms of a community-oriented ritualism as represented by the punks, and not only by them.

Both forms—individual-oriented antiritualism and community-oriented ritualism—follow a far-reaching European tradition of religious patterns of presentation. The goals of individual-orientation—creativity, self-fulfillment, autonomy (self-sufficiency)—are easily identifiable as those traits which, in the Middle Ages, were accorded only one Being, the only one who was, in His quality, "individual," and that one was God. The (usually unconscious) transfer of the divine subject's attributes to an innerworldly constituted human concept of the individual,[30] the concomitant fantasies of omnipotence and the illusions, disappointments and antiritualism based on the egocentrism of the subjective perspective, characterize the one strand of tradition that is generally considered the "enlightened" one. The other one—the self-charismatization of the group—originates in the "early Christian" community, in the expanded group of disciples who had lost "their" master and experienced their epiphany as a *group*—albeit in their role as representatives. So although it is a sort of borrowed charisma we are faced with here, the type of charismatized group is nonetheless easily recognizable as historical interim between the "real" leadership of Jesus, His later otherworldly leadership, and the still later representative leadership in the world. That legendary early Christian community also, incidentally, followed the tenet that the best sermon is the visibly lived principle and attitude, in a certain sense the continuous consecration of everyday life.

Yet both manifestations signal, in a sociologically remarkable way, what they lack and what they continue to threaten: The value system, consisting of the ideals of the "non-everyday society," "solidarity," and "supra-personal community-generated friendship," *exceeds*, and thereby endangers, the primary everyday life relationships: family, personal friendship, and neighborhood "close communities." Hegel's insight continues to hold true here, even more for the "universalistically" oriented mass movements of our time than for punk:

> Love of mankind which should encompass all humans, even those of whom one knows nothing, whom one doesn't know, with whom one stands in no relationship, this general humanitarianism is a shallow but characteristic emotion of those times that cannot avoid setting up idealistic demands and virtues against a merely thought object, in order to appear quite magnificent in such thought objects, since their reality is so lacking.[31]

The concurrent value system with its ideals "emancipation," "self-realization," "autonomy," "self-sufficient subjectivity" on the other hand *falls short* of the primary everyday life relationships, thereby endangering them as well.

Both developments are costly for the "close community"—in the one case in favor of the illusory abstract ideal of a subjective autonomy that cannot be realized in everyday life, in the other case in favor of the equally illusory abstract ideal of a "higher" community free from everyday life that is self-supporting, and charismatizing. In both, it is a case of the old Gods donning new clothes, but without having found their places in everyday life—yet.

Notes

1. Weber, Max (1972), *Wirtschaft und Gesellschaft. Grundriß der verstehenden Soziologie, 5*, revidierte Auflage, ed. by Johannes Winckelmann, Tübingen: 249.
2. See in this context Soeffner, H.-G. (1989), *Emblematische und symbolische Formen der Orientierung*, in Soeffner, H.-G. (1989), *Auslegung des Alltags, der Alltag der Auslegung: Zur wissenssoziologischen Konzeption einer sozialwissenschaftlichen Hermeneutik*, Frankfurt: 158–84.
3. It is quite possible that these studies also clarify how the current myth of the "New Obscurity" came about, and which patterns of orientation are expressed in this so-called new obscurity. See Jürgen Habermas, *Die neue Unübersichtlichkeit. Kleine politische Schriften V,* Frankfurt, 1985. And, incidentally, the idea of calling the observable present at any given time "unclear" or "obscure" is one of the few ideas of great—and hardly surprising—continuity.
4. See also Soeffner, H.-G. (1989), *Handlung, Szene, Inszenierung. Zur Problematik des "Rahmen"-Konzepts bei der Analyse von Interaktionsprozessen,* in Soeffner (1989): 140–57.
5. See Schütz, Alfred, and Luckmann, Thomas (1979/1984), *Strukturen der Lebenswelt,* Vol. I., esp. 227 ff., and Vol. 2, 178 ff.
6. See Strauss, Anselm (1968), *Spiegel und Masken.* Die Suche nach Identität, Frankfurt.
7. In this context, see Luckmann, Thomas (1980), *Lebenswelt und Gesellschaft. Grundstrukturen und geschichtliche Wandlungen,* Paderborn; Soeffner, H.-G. (1983), *"Typus und Individualität" oder "Typen der Individualität"?,* in Wenzel, Horst (ed.) (1983), *Typen und Individualität im Mittelalter,* Munich; Beck, Ulrich (1982), *Jenseits von Stand und Klasse?* in Kreckel, R. (ed.) (1982), *Soziale Ungleichheiten,* Göttingen, 35–75; Beck, Ulrich (1984), *Perspektiven einer kulturellen Evolution der Arbeit,* in MitAB, I (1984): 52–62.
8. Eilert, Sömmering, *Titanic 4* (1984): 86.
9. Field studies, interviews, and video tapes were made primarily in the Ruhr district. Th. Lau supplemented these data with field observations from England, extensive collections of "fanzines" from all over Europe and overseas. The correspondence—initiated by individual punks and continued over time—is from the entire area of the FRG, and also from England, the U.S., and Brazil. Nonetheless, we know that that part of the field best known to us—the Ruhr district—is only partially representative for an international phenomenon such as "punk" is. Especially the punks in the U.S. seem—judging by my own observations and those of Anselm Strauss—to differ from the ideal type developed in the following.
10. Weber, Max (1972), *Wirtschaft und Gesellschaft,* op. cit., chap. I: 1 ff.
11. Soeffner, H.-G. (1980), *Prämissen einer sozialwissenschaftlichen Hermeneutik,* in Soeffner (1989): 66–97.
12. Plessner, Helmuth (1929), *Die Stufen des Organischen und der Mensch,* Berlin/ New York (3, 1975): 309 ff.
13. The same is true of "rockers," "teds," and so on, where, however, no clear contrast between clothing and "make-up" can be determined, nor an "internal" antitheticism in the stylistic means of expression. What we see here is merely a fairly simple threatening gesture and a not-at-all ironic provocation of the "rest" of society.

14. See also Nixdorf, Heide, and Müller, Heidi (1983), *Weiße Westen—Rote Roben.* Catalog for the special exhibition at the Staatliche Museen Preußischer Kulturbesitz, Museum für Völkerkunde, Abt. Europa, and Museum für Deutsche Volkskunde, Berlin.

15. Alciatus, Andreas (1531), *Emblematum Liber.*

16. See especially Maurice Halbwachs's reflections on "collective memory." Halbwachs, Maurice (1925), *Das Gedächtnis und seine sozialen Bedingungen,* Frankfurt (1985): 249, and others.

17. In addition, see Foreville, Raymonde (1970), Lateran I–IV, *Geschichte der ökumenischen Konzilien,* ed. by G. Duneige and H. Bacht, Vol. IV, Mainz: 354 f.

18. As Irene Woll-Schumacher has noted, Iroquois society has, in contrast to other Native Indian Tribes of North America, a structure characterized by a kind of "equality of the sexes" in wide areas. Woll-Schumacher, Irene (1972), *Gesellschaftsstruktur und Rolle der Frau. Das Beispiel der Irokesen,* Berlin.

19. Halbwachs, Maurice (1925), op. cit.: 249.

20. For Thomas Lau, the interviewer, it was initially difficult to maintain contact with individul punks (e.g. via written correspondence or telephone) because the group members don't use last or Christian names among themselves, but only the names given and used by the group. The names themselves are given according to the typification pattern of individual traits, and not with the intention of coining "nicknames" ("Clod" refers to a person's physical build, "Saw" to one with a harelip, "Pony" to a horse lover, etc.)

21. Observed at the "Great Peace Demonstration" in Bonn, 1984.

22. See Luckmann, Thomas (1963), *Unterscheidung von Religiosität und Kirchlichkeit,* among others in Luckmann, Thomas (1963), *Das Problem der Religion in der modernen Gesellschaft,* Freiburg, particularly 14 ff. and 32 ff.

23. See Schütz, Alfred, and Luckmann, Thomas (1982), *Strukturen der Lebenswelt,* Vol. 2, op. cit. On the topic of transcendencies in everyday life see 139 ff.; Halbwachs, Maurice (1925), op. cit.: 256 ff.

24. Plessner, Helmuth (1959), *Die verspätete Nation. Über die politische Verführbarkeit bürgerlichen Geistes* (= Gesammelte Schriften VI), ed. by G. Dux et al., Frankfurt 1982.

25. See the extensive documentation compiled by Thomas Lau.

26. "Harder" liquor is rarely involved, nor are "hard" drugs—if one doesn't count "uppers" (Captagon, Preludin) as "hard."

27. Utterances by prosecutors and judges in youth court proceedings.

28. See the German bestseller by the same title, *Familienkonferenz* ("Family Conference").

29. See Weber, Max (1972), *Wirtschaft und Gesellschaft:* 142 ff.

30. See Soeffner, H.-G. (1983), *"Typus und Individualität"* oder *"Typen der Individualität"?,* op. cit.: 38f.

31. Hegel, Georg Wilhelm Friedrich, *Der Geist des Christentums, Werke I, Frühe Schriften,* Theorie Werkausgabe, Frankfurt, 1970: 362.

3

Rituals of Anti-Ritualism—
Materials for the Non-Everyday

I

The title Ernst Jandl gives the following poem is "According to Old Custom":

> in the end no-one wanted it.
> in the end everyone did it.
> that sounds like a lie and is one, too. (Jandl, 1980:34)

If one concurs with Malinowski that *custom* means "any traditionally regulated and standardized form of physical behavior" (Malinowski, 1944: 104), then in my contribution, the focus is on a specific class of customs, namely, rituals. With the help of two specific examples, I shall try to describe both the societal use of collectively "produced" or collectively meant and condoned rituals, and the effects and reality accents achieved by rituals. The question of truth or fiction is not one I shall pursue. I shall, however, pose the question of "subjective meaning" that people give their ritual behavior, as well as the question of objective meaning and effect that often occur as involuntary side effects of ritual behavior.

As a starting point, I shall take a thesis put forth by Mary Douglas. In her work, *Ritual, Taboo, and Body Symbolism* (Douglas, 1974), she describes the essential features of two collective forms of expression and self-presentation, both anchored in specific societal structures: (1) "ritualism"—a form of presentation oriented toward highly ordered and organized social behavior and toward a common worldview, which at the same time represents this worldview and order; and (2) a counter movement that battles the supposedly rigid and superficial or "purely exter-

71

nal" form of ritualism, and which is also anchored in specific societal structures (usually looser, less hierarchical social groups)—in other words, "anti-ritualism." In concluding her work, Mary Douglas voices the suspicion that we, the modern or even "post-modern" people and societies, move within various forms of anti-ritualism, a supposition that would appear to be supported by an at least superficially identifiable destabilization or reordering of obsolete social patterns of order and hierarchies.

My thesis, however, runs as follows: We do not live in a time of engaged anti-ritualism, even if some of our political and religious movements might make that claim. Rather, we move within an *unrecognized ritualism,* as illustrated by two extreme manifestations: (a) a ritualized anti-ritualism; and (b) a change in a traditional rite brought about by naive, inflationary ritualism.

The former manifestation can be demonstrated in rituals of contemporary "social movements" in Central Europe, particularly in Germany, the latter in the description of the Pope's trip to the United States in 1987.

Before I turn my attention to my cases, though, I would like to try and characterize, very briefly, the theoretical framework within which the descriptions that follow must be seen.[1]

II

In social interaction our body is, both to us and others, the visible actor, medium, material, and "form" (*Gestalt*). It functions as visible interpreter and as interpretee. Plessner described this phenomenon as "being (in) body" and "having body" (Plessner, 1970: 162 ff.). He characterized our approach to the world and to ourselves as "mediated immediateness" (Plessner, 1929: 321 ff.). In a fairly broad sense, we are at the same time communication's subject, object, material, and sign. In this respect there is little sense, within concrete, pragmatically directed communication, in differentiating between communication on the one hand and "communication's materials" on the other. But at the same time, the direct connection of action and interpretation in human interaction explains that ultimately, all human societies consist of highly specialized interpreters of their respective forms of presentation and their realities.[2]

Within the context—characteristic for humans—of ambiguous behavior and the resulting need to interpret, gestures and signs that we have learned to use "significantly" in the various phases of our socialization constitute the specific relationship of individuals amongst each other. Gestures, signs, and language help to overcome the boundaries between individuals. But, simultaneously, they function as markers and signposts for these boundaries. Each time I employ gestures, signs, and language, I step outside the area of *my* immediate "individual" experience: I already begin to generalize at a very early stage. On the other hand, I am also, by using signs and gestures in order to communicate and draw attention to myself, signalling to my opposite that as *my* gestures, they also represent something that is outside of *his* experience and scope both in time and space and in individual quality of experience (see Schütz and Luckmann, vol. 2, 1979: 178 ff.).

By means of a "natural artificiality" (Plessner, 1929: 309 ff.), constituted among others by the institutionalized use of signs, human society as a society of sign users makes its way toward a specific artificial naturalness. What the way one presents and secures oneself seeks is nothing other than "the restoration of the fundamental relationship of instinct and catalyst on the higher level of the forms of conduct which are arbitrary, learnable, but which have to be stabilized" (Gehlen, 1973: 26). Once these forms of conduct are firmly established in collective habits, then the habits can provide their own impulses (see Gehlen, 1973: 35), under the condition that their form is both known and socially accepted. If this be the case, then it is true that "forms are the food of faith" (see Gehlen, 1973: 24)—they secure the social construction of reality. They are the corset of human society whose figure they shape.

To speak of rituals[3] in this context means focusing on some of the plastic stays (the days of whalebone being long gone, of course) in society's corset.[4] As every self-respecting corset has its lace and frills, so, too, does the societal corset. Behind a playfully decorated facade, it conceals the stays whose pressure is not diminished by the ornamentation. And they leave us in no doubt as to whether it is worth our while to unlace the hooks and eyes or whether it wouldn't after all be better to content ourselves with the lacework and accept the beautiful illusion. The evolutionary transitions from social forms of organization that were manageable such as clans, tribes, and small communities, to urban cultures, nations, and macro-societies change not only the interaction, but also the meaning and the *knowledge* of the meaning of collectively enacted behavioral rituals. While smaller forms of society are generally characterized—based on a social control taking place directly in face-to-face communication—by an extraordinarily conscious, collective treatment of behavioral rituals, more complex societies seem, at first glance, rather to dismantle rituals and ritually determined behavior.

But as soon as one examines—as Goffman has done—everyday life in those so-called complex mass societies, one quickly discovers to how great an extent life in these societies is permeated by "interaction rituals." Nonetheless, one can hardly still speak of a consciously controlled and cultivated use of those rituals. They are now used in a more implicit way, and the knowledge of how to use them rarely reaches the light of consciousness. So, although ritualized habits of behavior permeate our everyday life, even if less conspicuously, it is almost de rigueur, in contemporary sociological studies, to point out that we live in a complex, diffuse, transient, comparatively unstructured world, "confusing" in big and small ways—compared, of course, to the so-called simple world of past and/or simpler societies.

In all that, one thing becomes evident: The transition from small, clearly structured societies to more complex ones is, simultaneously, a transition from social interaction and organization "at first hand" in long-term, immediate living together, to a second-hand social organization and interaction in which the interaction partners frequently change, are hardly known intimately outside their primary group, and in many cases no longer even meet "face-to-face" (because of the largely anonymized contact with bureaucracy, press, media, etc.). The organization of rituals must now—insofar as rituals continue to exist, and it is my contention that they do—be able to carry itself, while in the first case it is directly controlled and perpetuated by all participants.

In the first case, the community forms and passes on the rituals, thereby stabilizing itself. In the second case, using interaction rituals establishes the range of possibilities for creating temporary interactional communities where all participants maintain a pretty much implicit and anonymized context of order for social action.[5]

In complex societies, the more the share of knowledge acquired through the media grows and overlaps that part of knowledge acquired in one's personal or communal experience, the less it (the knowledge) acquires a "personal" admixture. It becomes impersonal—both in the good and the bad sense of the word. Within this evolutionary context, those ritualized gestures and forms of presentation that are not secured by permanently institutionalized contexts or conscious traditions increasingly develop their own, apparently free-standing, balanced existence. Separated from their tradition of context and far away from their original *raisons d'être,* they now carry structural meanings and effects that have little to do with the new applications in which they appear, and are practically unfamiliar to those who use them. At the same time, the empty space left behind by the history of the origins can be filled up with new, "current," symbolic contents without necessarily affecting the fundamental—and now forgotten—range of meaning.

This phenomenon not only lends support to Gehlen's observation that the reasons for the creation of institutions—here: of institutionalized behavioral habits—differ, as a rule, from the reasons for which one conserves them (Gehlen, 1973: 34). It must also be added that the findings show that there are obviously also institutionalized forms of ritual behavior during which *neither* the reasons for its existence *nor* the reasons for employing and/or preserving it become explicitly conscious.

The (necessary) search for a concrete inner meaning in individual rituals often obscures one's view of the rather formal orientation structure which is, however, fundamental to social forms of organization,[6] a structure that is established and secured not least of all by rituals. Ritual behavior is behavior that is fully formed, predictable, in a certain sense *calculable,* and it guarantees *orientational security.* It is—as far as its value in human society is concerned—a predecessor, a kind of elderly relative of the rational calculation with which it shares at least the above-mentioned structural traits, even though it doesn't share the same degree of consciousness and planning.

The inertia of such detached rituals that now supply their own motivation ultimately imposes on all those who submit to them a specific range of meaning—even though those concerned rarely have more than a vague idea of why they are submitting to a specific ritual or actually believe they are acting "spontaneously" and at a far remove from all forms of ritualized behavior. Regardless of what attitude they take, as soon as they actively perform rituals, thereby submitting to their (the rituals') scope of meaning, they are surrendering to the rituals' specific influence—they don't know what they have taken on or what they have surrendered. They believe that a will extraneous to theirs is their own (see Scheler, 1957: 271). Mass rituals constitute the best examples. Whoever has entered into them and then attempted to withdraw again, even for a moment, will have felt that extraneous will—and will hesitate to expose himself to it again.[7]

III

Before attempting to describe in my first case history—a collectively staged, ritualized gesture—a social form of self-presentation which I shall call "ritualized anti-ritualism," I would like to outline the contexts of action and staging within which this gesture is to be found. I am aware of the fact that this outline will have to remain more than a bit rudimentary.[8]

Since the second half of the 1960s, one can observe both in the United States and in Western and Central Europe political demonstrations that can be called, in the true sense of the word, "mass movements"—masses moving in favor of a "movement." One hundred or three hundred thousand people, occasionally as many as one and a half to two million people, come together for a relatively short period of time (usually just one day) in an apparently relaxed, more or less "self-organized" form, in order to demonstrate for or against something—in order to show themselves, together with a multitude of others—to be participating in a collective attitude. Unlike the large political mass rallies between the world wars or the mass rallies organized by the trade unions, the more recent mass demonstrations have neither a universally recognized leader—according to taste and creed, the charisma is split up into smaller portions—nor is there a durable, tight and centrally run parent organization. Instead, the movements consist, only seemingly by coincidence, of church groups (both Catholic and Protestant), wings of the "large" but also of the smaller and smallest, frequently antagonistic parties, feminists, trade unionists, homosexuals, "gray panthers" and the like, not to mention the numerous children and babies whom their families "invest" in the general enterprise.[9]

However colorful and coincidental the general arrangement may appear, it not only expresses a conception of world and self that is—in spite of differences in content—presumably the same structurally, but it also unfolds in always the same order: in carefully arranged, "relaxed" form, colorfulness and "spontaneity." In the face of collective forms of presentation identifiable as an arrangement, but not created by a centrally organized authority or a charismatic leader or *animateur,* the question necessarily arises as to what mortar connects, on the one hand, the various social bricks for a limited time, and which, on the other hand, is evidently easily dissolved and reused. The common answer to this question—given by the "members of the movement" and accepted unquestioningly by social scientists and journalists—is as follows: The mortar is made up of shared ideas and a common value system. These alone supposedly are the reasons for demonstrating for peace or disarmament, for the right to life (of endangered human, animal, and plant species), for the right to abortion, against pollution, and so on. All these answers make the claim that a specific idea is the only or certainly the leading motivation for the movements. But they touch on only one—vastly overestimated—aspect of the whole arrangement: Ideas that are not molded into stabilized forms of social knowledge and action, and thus secured, move nothing and no one permanently, they merely move temporary collective fantasies. Fantasies may be the perfume that attracts—but in the end, it is not the perfume that satisfies the desire it arouses. That satisfaction requires a concrete and material basis, namely relatively stable and secure expectations and, thus, forms in which the promises made can be realized and given shape as something definitely to be expected. But rituals, whether performed consciously or unconsciously, are building blocks, material for those forms in which human actors—individuals, groups, gatherings—lend expression to their expectations and thereby give them "shape" (*Gestalt*).

The total arrangement of the form consists of various elements of which I shall examine only one in detail. The others I shall content myself to merely outline. My first example shall be the "form" of the peace movement.[10]

First, the clothing. In the beginning one saw, more conspicuously than today (but some similarities remain to this day), peasant smocks from Southern Germany and Westphalia, striped Dutch and Friesian fishermen's shirts, work clothes such as overalls, coveralls, workers' caps, handknitted sweaters and watch caps, handmade clothes from the "Third World," such as hats from Peru, ponchos from Mexico, Palestinian scarves, and the like. This medley of clothing created the impression of a political group in regional folk costume. In the middle of a Western industrialized society, and presented by a predominantly urban middle class, there is a romanticism expressed here that likes to dress up by citing clothes from a lifestyle of distant, "simple," rural shepherd and peasant societies or of artisan trades and proletarian traditions that are on the way to extinction.

Just as conspicuous is the widespread use of emblematic means of expression: buttons, stickers, posters. Practically the whole surrounding area of the movement becomes a billboard: the participants' clothes, cars, windows and doors of apartments and offices[11] (principally in the "free space" of universities), street signs—almost everything is be-buttoned, be-stickered, and, in addition, festooned with banners and "original," portable signboards. Public space becomes advertising space for mottos and slogans. At the same time, a huge flock of white doves before variously colored backgrounds refers to the scope of various possible memberships within the movement. Blue background for the "regular" adherents of the movement; purple—with the addition of like-colored bandannas—for the "Christian" groups, and, last but not least, the white dove of the opposition, the so-called "*Geißler*-dove" on black-red-gold background—referring to that other national "peace movement" in the services of NATO. There have even been fliers showing a white dove wearing a boxing glove over its wings. Very pugnacious, but can it fly?

All this printed and sticky matter is sold, along with a wide array of healthy snacks, by a swarm of eager small merchants and dealers in convictions, the eco-retinue accompanying the movement and supplying it with exactly that prestamped emblematic articulation that lets it turn the "inner" emotions and convictions, the group emotions, to the outside. Thus everyone is able to read the "inner" convictions of the demonstrators from their external appearance immediately and easily. In the emblematic expression—primarily in it—the "group soul" (Scheler) finds its articulation. Cloaked in the movement's emblematics, the actors form their respective specific "ornament of the masses" (see Kracauer, 1963), and they do this mostly without words, as far as their own speech is concerned, with the exception of some isolated slogan chanting. It is the emblems that do the talking.

The ornamentalism of the movement consists of a relatively broadly strewn repertoire of figures of expression that is nonetheless easily identifiable as typical for the movement. The names for those figures of expression themselves combine, in a characteristic manner, humanistic, peaceable sentiments with aggressive, military ones: "peace marches," "symbolic mass dying," "memorial vigils," "human chains,"[12] "sit-down strikes," "peaceful blockades." The ambivalence of this terminology is no coincidence. It represents, also linguistically, a part of the inner contradiction of a movement that seeks to reconcile the irreconcilable in the "non-violent resistance," the "fighting pacifism" and the "battle for freedom." All these various ornaments and forms of expression are the cement holding the actors together. But some of the elements of that recognizably "ritual" total arrangement seem to lead independent lives: *They reappear, in very different contexts, in the identical form.* They refer to a motive that establishes itself beyond the articulated contents and convictions and seems to be independent of them. My focus is on precisely these elements and on the social reality they constitute, on the *structural* motive beyond the *intended* one.

I have picked out what may seem an unimportant detail from the total arrangement, one of those significant ritualized gestures in which the arrangement of the spontaneous finds its expression. The people hold each other's hands, lift them skyward, and begin to move first their intertwined hands and arms, then their whole bodies, like the stalks of wheat in a field form waves in the wind. This human field of wheat sways to the rhythm of very diverse songs and hymns. When one asks the individual participants of this collective undulation about the meaning of the gesture, there are two different basic answers: (1) I'm doing this because I feel good here, together with the others; we are expressing our common experience here. (2) We are demonstrating that we all belong together without exception or difference.

The remarkable thing about these answers is that one gets exactly the same ones at very different "events," from very different groups, and before the background of very different feelings on the part of the members of the groups. The only thing these events, groups, situations, and emotions seem to have in common is the gesture itself and the answers to the question concerning its meaning. One can find both at Protestant Church congresses and Catholic Church congresses (where especially young people, but not they alone, initiate that typical "movement"), at peace and environmental rallies—but also at pop concerts, ice hockey games, at the final ceremonies at the Olympics in Los Angeles (1984), at the German Gymnastics Festival, among soccer fans (not only in the ill-reputed "western curves"), and finally, at Carnival meetings. The repertoire of songs and hymns that accompany the ritual is just as varied: It unites in a sort of patchwork medley "I Pray to the Power of Love," "Where the Hell Are We Here and Where's our Beer?," "Sultans of Swing," "Brothers, Join your Hands in Union," "But It Will Last, It Will Last Forever: The FC (Schalke, etc.) Will Never Go

Under," "Such a Day, as Beautiful as Today," "*Freude schöner Götter-funken*" (Beethoven's Ninth), and finally, "We Shall Overcome."

Obviously, the same ritualized gesture can appear in all these various contexts (1) because the form has become, to a fairly high degree, independent of the specific total arrangement and, what is more decisive (2) because the form itself has taken on its own, inner context. The form gives itself its meaning and independent motive. It imposes purposes on the participants in the ritual applications which can be far removed from the motives for action intended in the contents. (3) As various as all these situations within which the ritualized gesture makes an appearance are, they all have one thing in common: They are situations in which a large number of people, who as a rule do not know each other, meet in a public setting. The setting itself has the nature of a demand: As a member of a community of faith, as a fan, club member, happy participant, and so on, one is to make oneself identifiable as such. In short, one must, within a specific framework of time, present oneself as a member of a transitory community that has, so to speak, a limited lifespan.

In this context, it is especially the independent and impersonal character as well as the mobility of the ritual which allow anyone to "use" it and thereby in communal action to become united with all those present.

Individuals who are united only temporarily for common action and/or experience thus lend to their transitory commonality the appearance of a relatively stable community. Not only does the effortlessly comprehensible form and the organization of common behavior increase the willingness on the part of the participants to become engaged, to declare their faith or conviction, and to demonstrate their feelings, but they also represent a relatively standardized and thus easily "legible" repertoire of expression and presentation. And, with the help of this repertoire, each individual's *subjectively experienced "inner world"* can be *collectively* turned toward and expressed to the *outside*. The uniqueness of such communities that their participants experience and aim for over and over again lives on the illusion of the cast that they are in a community of individuals and *not* what the ritual, after all, visibly turns them into—a "mass" that is anonymous, however thoroughly organized its details are. The existence, form of expression, and intensity of the temporary experience of commonality owe their "half-life" to the ritual's pattern of order and form.

But at the same time, the varying quality of the different communities points up the fact that the *general* meaning and message of the ritual do not consist in believing in a God or in the Dire Straits, the FC Schalke 04, peace, freedom, and so on. The central point is not the belief in something external to the community in question, it is above all the experiencing of "community" itself within the largest and most single-minded, collective form of expression.[13]

By becoming "ocean, field and waves" in the rhythm and song, the mass of arms and bodies of the individuals mimetically represent the appropriation of the communal soul by the communal body—and they are enamored of each other. The crowd loves watching itself in the arenas, the crowd itself is the "game," the spectacle it has come to watch.[14] It enjoys reacting to itself, translating "inner" into "outer" motion, increasing it and repeating the form (the ritual). Through the ritual, the community lends expression to itself and survives as long as the form is maintained. At the same time, the process in which subjective feelings and experiences are transformed and elevated into a common experience through the collective form of presentation becomes a process of "self-charismatization" by the community as such.

The interplay of rhythm, strophic form of the songs, invariance and repetition of the rituals lends an appearance not only of permanence, but also of the possibility of repetition to the fleeting and temporary character of the community. In this manner the—structurally determined—transitoriness of the charisma the community lends itself is elevated to a charisma of the enduringly unique and extraordinary which, it is paradoxically enough implied, can be planned and staged cyclically like the Olympics or county fairs, or on the basis of expected recurrent events. Its ritual organization is the guarantor not only of the appearance of durability, but also of the actual repeatability of the total arrangement.

In the ritual's symbolic form and rhythmic order, time seems to turn back upon itself. In this cyclically organized time—combined with the experience of the extraordinary—the point is more than just the appearance of permanence, it is a permanently offered "presentness" of the community which, however transitory it may be, can still be recreated over and over again. The *temporal* dimension of meaning in the total arrangement becomes visible in the cyclical structure of ritual action that is geared toward repeatability. In the first place, the process of self-charismatization by the community is substantially supported and propelled by rituals (albeit not by them alone). The *social* dimension of the charisma thus results from the collectively secured combination of the non-everyday, the unique, the authentic. The temporal dimension of this specific combination is the present or, to be precise, the permanently possible presentness of the extraordinary.

However, the rituals of collective mass arrangements not only produce a special temporal structure, they also constitute the collectively produced dimension of meaning of the communal *space*: Mass assemblies and mass arrangements do not actually "use" the space—they occupy and cover it, they appropriate it, turning it into a visible component of the communal form. All those mass aggregations whose individual elements move in space in a formally ritualized manner shape the initially unformed and spontaneously occurring event into a *monument*. In this characteristic trend toward monumentalism, just as in the temporal structure of the total arrangement, it becomes evident that the transitoriness of the aggregation must be overcome. In the one case through the illusion of the moment set toward permanence, in the other case through the illusion of *stability* of the monumental—presented through and in a collective *movement*. Nonetheless, in spite of all those identifiable ritualizations in them, collective total arrangements remain unstable and threatened by the danger of becoming unrepeatable, as long as they do not become institutionalized and integrated into lasting forms of organization, as for example Church congresses, Olympics, Carnival parades. Collective mass arrangements are threatened by their own transitory nature, as are all their participants; they are practically forced to give themselves and their form of community the appearance of durable cohesion and stability in the rituals. But the outside observer sees the monument *against* transitoriness precisely as a monument *to* it.

The structural meaning of the individual ritual described here refers to the structural meaning of collective mass-arrangements in general. It consists of the tendency and attempt to transcend the everyday character of life in society, and this attempt occurs in three ways: (1) In transcending individual experience through the illusory evidence of a collectively represented intersubjectivity. This, although on its own quite credible, purports to follow concrete contents and ideas, but ultimately expresses no more than the desire—fulfillable in a transitory way only—for a higher community which has primarily itself as idea and content. (2) In transcending individual space and individual range through the individual's active collaboration, the latter presents himself as part of the communal body and soul and becomes absorbed into the monument to the community. (3) In transcending time and transitoriness with the help of the illusion that time is arrested in the ritual, that the permanent "presentness" of a "higher" community is secured, and the transitory communal experience permanently provided.

But since communal soul and communal body, as representatives of a "higher" community, primarily refer to ritualized and, as a consequence, symbolic materials of action and presentation, the desired "higher" community can also easily be fobbed off with symbols and symbolic actions. For "if...God expresses himself only in symbols, then He can also be satisfied with symbols rather than realities" (Weber, 1972a: 248).

This explains why the field of practical, political action *in* the social institutions and organizations is so neglected, and why the monumental presentation by the movement is preferred. Founding organizations or even ongoing work in them is "felt" to be stereotypical, ritually empty, and unsatisfactory. And in fact, the charisma of the movements would evaporate in the practical constraints and routines of everyday existence. Even though the present political "culture" and its carriers successfully endeavor to convey stereotypes and emptiness, it still cannot be overlooked that the new social movements often exhaust themselves, even without that kind of help and support, in "symbolic actions." The political program is replaced by collective mentality, political action is replaced by the presentation of collective emotion. The movements do not *have* a program, they *are* the program.

The existence of such programmatically higher communities has political consequences not only for public life, but also for the everyday life of people who feel indebted to such societies. Between the universalism of the "higher" community and the—devalued—everyday life as usual in society, the individual perceives a deep gulf that he finds harder to bridge the more the non-everyday in his life claims to be the actual, "important," "fulfilled," and "authentic" life.

The observer of this societal phenomenon can hardly avoid concluding that the efforts for an authentic presentation of emotions, convictions, and beliefs as they are expressed in the new "mass movements" on the one hand, and the striving by the individual on the other hand to also "privately" lead an "authentic," fulfilled, "real" life, demonstrates two sides of the same coin: two forms of expression of a subjectivity that is oriented toward self-actualization and self-fulfillment. Herein, the present type of argument that can be traced throughout all intellectual history becomes evident: cloaked in the vocabulary of the Enlightenment it suggests, paradoxically, that the human being can be liberated from religion by making him the sole and self-sufficient object of religiosity, but so that he doesn't recognize this act of "self-liberation" as a religious act (see Luckmann, 1980: 173–89, and Soeffner, chapter 1, this volume). And, presumably, the everyday, "primary" life communities pay the cost for this development.

The claim to authenticity and uniqueness by this subjectivity cannot allow a conscious ritualism, must perforce see in it the enemy of "authentic," "singular" and unmistakable emotions. In fact, though, the structure of social interactions admits—whether or not we consider it paradox and lamentable—"uniqueness" and "spontaneity" of collective actions only within the framework of ordered co-orientation and action. So collectively desired and planned "unique" events have to rely on elements of order such as rituals. In them, one can only too easily surrender oneself and one's ideas to an as such unconscious ritualism. The alternative would be to try and make room for the ideas in everyday life, by which they might acquire a certain accent of reality.

IV

When Pope John Paul II goes traveling—one of his trademark activities—the photographers in the countries he visits wait for every move, every gesture, a description of which I leave to one of his chroniclers:

> The airplane "Ciudad de Mexico" has landed. At the door near the cockpit a figure all in white appears. The *representatively composed group of people* (emphasis added) that has been waiting for hours on the airport grandstands cheers: Viva el Papa. The pope greets them smilingly, descends the stairs, kneels on the red carpet, kisses the ground, sways as he gets up again because his mazetta has been blown forward into his face, obscuring his vision and orientation for a moment. Then he is standing again. (Lüning, 26)

Wasn't the pope perhaps already robbed of "vision and orientation" in his choice of the ritualistic ground-kissing as a form of greeting, long before that particular visit to Mexico? By making this ritual his individual trademark ["Near Eastern people kissed the hands, feet, and clothing of sacred images. Pope John Paul II kisses the ground of the countries he visits" (Eliade, 1987: 463)] he probably had the best of intentions, but not the insight into its potential range and structure of meaning. I have no

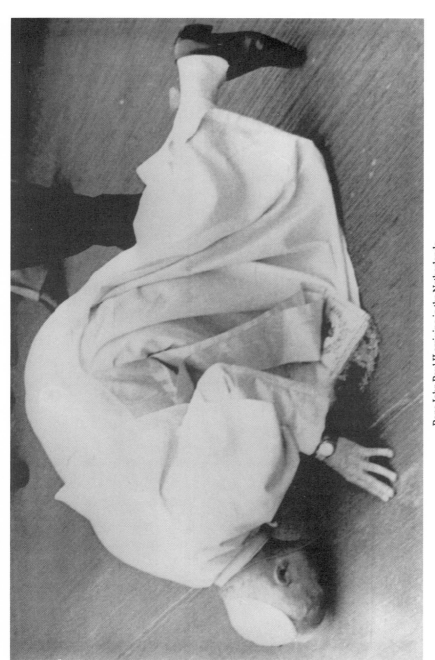

Pope John Paul II arriving in the Netherlands

idea whether he believed himself to be treading the firm ground of Roman Catholic ritual[15] in his choice. But the context into which he placed this ritual and which it seems to answer to is well-known: the voyage.

Papal voyages are certainly nothing new. However, frequent and voluntary trips abroad by popes are, at least in recent centuries, unusual. And around-the-world trips by the pope can be seen as a new trademark altogether. Whether it is an individual trademark or whether it will be continued by John Paul II's successors remains to be seen. It is not very clear—not even within his Church—how one is to interpret this wayfaring pope and what exactly the purpose of these trips is. Is he apostle and missionary,[16] "conqueror" and bringer of peace at the same time,[17] "Virgin Mary Pilgrim,"[18] or representative of a "global Church"?[19] All of the above? A conqueror whose Church already administrates the territories to be conquered? An apostle, founder of communities, and emissary whose communities are already founded and whose legations are already flourishing? A pilgrim in a jet, in other words precisely how Ambrose Bierce defines "pilgrim" in "The Devil's Dictionary," namely, a "tourist who is taken seriously" (Bierce, 1986: 82)? A frequently traveling Pope, especially one who celebrates masses in extravagant locations—for instance, on top of a mountain in the Alps—poses several problems for his followers and the followers of the Catholic Church's traditional ritualism.

The saint as prophet, pilgrim, and founder of religions wanders and travels in his proselytic way until he comes to rest at the end of his path, a path paved with trials. In the institutionalization of his religion, in the organization of the community and clerics, faith, too, comes to rest: in the fixed form and canonization. The stations of the wanderings turn into holy places which are visited by subsequent pilgrims. But the holy object that has come to rest, or rather its memorials and representatives, and its places of birth, death, and works, as well as its highest representative, remain immobile. The holy object does not travel, one travels to the holy object.

Pilgrimages as such were and are more than the mere means of reaching one's goal as quickly as possible. They are part of the rite, mental preparation for the goal, a sign of faith, the willingness to sacrifice, and one's membership in the religious community. On this trip, the individual pilgrims grow into the community which in turn offers them stability. For the religious community then, the pilgrimage itself is just as important as arrival at one's goal. After all, the holy goal cannot be reached without effort. And if, as in the uncounted legends, it literally came to meet the believer or even the nonbeliever, then it would be as a surprise—that is, neither according to a schedule nor in form of an epiphany with the times of broadcast listed in the T.V. guides. The holy object removes itself from fleeting and temporary approaches arranged in a familiar pattern of plane schedules and world tours.

And the traveling around of His representative is difficult for God's parish and Church, too, not only for His "representatives," as a kind of inflationary epiphany, just as the traveling pursuit of his prodigal sons and daughters by their "holy father" is. It was the return of the prodigal son, not his pursuit by his father, which made the reconciliation between them possible.

But once the holy object/the holy being has decided to travel about and visit believers and nonbelievers, it should be carefully avoided, from the point of view of a conscious ritualism and with insight into structure and meaning of symbolic and ritual action, that the holy one as traveler should begin competing with other prominent travelers, that is, that he should become the white-clad V.I.P. in the colorfully clad traveling V.I.P. show.

It becomes inevitable, at least as long as no further thought is wasted on it, that the pope, as head of the Vatican, is accorded the same arrangements as presidents traveling on state visits, since there aren't yet any tried and true ceremonial settings for official traveling saints: presidential jet, private train, state limousine, red carpet, honor guard, hymn, flags, children bearing bouquets, childrens' choirs bedecked with flags, and so on. The obvious has come to pass. The rituals of state visits also decorate the papal visits, albeit in light camouflage. Jet, private train, red carpet, flags, and children remain relatively unchanged. Honor guards and hymns are supplied by the Church and its personnel in its own special manner. The black state limousine becomes the white "popemobile."

Unlike presidential visits, a decisive part of the framework of the pope's "performances" is one that cannot be precisely calculated: the "people" that attend the visits. While a president can count on a larger or smaller number of people, depending on his prominence, and always on that typical blend of casual spectators, interested spectators, followers, and curiosity seekers, the pope could so far be sure that the greater part of participants in the Easter mass in the Holy City, for instance, considered themselves members of the Church and the religious community. Presidential visits are not in principle dependent upon the audience, but rather, on the political demonstration for which the audience serves as means to an end. Not so with the pope and his entourage. Here, all present form a community that submits to the same belief, the same ritual, and a lasting mutual commitment. If this community would dissolve into the same mixed crowd that comes to watch presidential visits and celebrity shows, then the religious community itself would necessarily be damaged.

The traveling pope who is subjected to the state visit arrangement will have seen or suspected this danger. But how was one to meet this danger once he made up his mind to do the traveling? Something clearly had to be found that transcended the official charisma and insignia which are all too fleeting, especially on such trips and under the constant pressure of the media presence, something that bursts the confines of the "secular" arrangement of the state visit. And this something became, for John Paul II, the kissing of the ground: a signal of significance with which the trip and the country being visited is supposed to receive the stamp of the extraordinary, the holy, the venerable.

It would be impossible to describe exhaustively the scope of meaning of that symbolic action by the pope which repetition and predictability have shaped into a ritual. In the brief sketch that follows we can at best try to extract its central supporting structure of meaning. That which is touched by the holy being or object has a special meaning in all religions; and cultures can be attributed not least of all to the fact that in the act of touching or being touched, that is, action and emotion, that which touches and that which is being touched, are connected directly and reflexively. Something touches me by my touching it. There is truth in "touch is the mother of the senses" (Crooke, 1961: 739). This association is expressed in a very interesting way in the kiss as a symbolic form of appropriation derived from the acts of feeding, eating, and tasting (also see Hastings, 1961, vol. 4: 189). Affect, love, veneration, and possessiveness enter a close conspiracy here, in varying mixtures depending on context and circumstances: Lovers kiss one another (in our cultures) on the mouth—among other places. Equals (in Greek and Judeo-Christian cultures) kiss each other on the "cheek"—nothing expresses better the presumptuousness of Judas Iscariot's kiss. Subordinates and people of lower social standing kiss hands, feet, clothing of those of higher standing, and so forth. Repertoire, vocabulary, and shades of meaning in kissing represent the possible proportions of the listed emotions from love to hate, from veneration to disdain, from elevation to lowering of status, from taking possession to giving away, from direct affect to abstract stylized gesture, from orgy to ceremony.

The range of meaning inherent in the kissing of the ground, the earth, the dust, the land, moves within narrower boundaries, but adds new meanings to the existing repertoire. Kissing the ground of holy sites (temples, graves, stones, etc.) is customary in many cultures, just as kissing the threshold of the house before entering it or touching holy objects to one's mouth: Just as specific sites are consecrated by the kiss of the divine or saintly being himself, the faithful for their part win participation in the sacred object by kissing the holy consecrated sites and objects. "God, heaven, spirits kiss...blessing the earth, making it their own" (Grimm, 1956: 2874). In the same way, Eichendorff's sky kisses the earth—silently—and people kiss the consecrated ground in reverence, in order themselves to become consecrated. The kiss of blessing or consecration on the one hand and the kiss of veneration on the other are interrelated.

But "kissing the ground," "the earth," "the dust" are also synonyms for "dying,"[20] be it as metaphor for a lost duel or as an image of the death wish. Both the expression of veneration and gratitude and the admixture of the meaning of—conquered—"death" and "dying" merge in the shipwrecked sailor's kissing the ground when he has finally reached dry land or, in a somewhat milder form, the kissing of the ground by one who has returned home after long wanderings. Finally, let me make mention of yet another admixture that is expressed in the oldest and most ubiquitous customs: the magical kissing of the earth (gardens, fields, vineyards, sites suspected of holding gold and treasure, paths, bridges, etc.) or of specific objects (talismans, charms, tools, cards, dice, roulette balls, boxing gloves, etc.).[21] What is at play here is the luck-bestowing effect of the kiss. Veneration and fear, hope and apprehension blend and mingle in the magical action.

However, it is not as easy as it would at first seem to file away the pope's kiss of the earth within the outlined spectrum of meanings. It is true that the "shipwrecked sailor"—even as metaphor—can quickly be eliminated. But to exclude the "home-comer" from the range of meanings is more difficult: God's creation is—particularly for His representative—not limited to a specific country, it is everywhere. The representative is returning home wherever he goes and the Holy Father's children have prepared for his homecoming.

But if God's creation can and must be worshipped everywhere, why then—time and again—on an airport runway on which a red carpet has been rolled out? Because the pope is setting foot on the ground of this country for the *first time*? If it is the individual country as such that is meant, then the anonymity of international airport architecture is least appropriate for doing justice to this uniqueness. If it were the people of the visited country who are meant, then one could approach them directly. Equally, a gesture of humbleness should be directed, as the Bible states in no uncertain terms, not to red carpets but directly to the apostles or the religious community itself. John Paul II's method is a different one: He kneels on the carpet, but stands, sits, or towers, enthroned, over his parish—either at the monumental altars built especially for him, or in the "popemobile" that has so very little similarity to that donkey in the New Testament, or to the traditional litter. To assume that the kissing of the ground can be seen as a kiss of blessing—which (see above) would be possible, too—is also out of the question. It would be blasphemous—God's creation can hardly be reconsecrated by His representative. And in any case, consecrating runways would seem to make little sense. If one would finally limit oneself to saying that John Paul II's kissing of the ground represents no more than just that mixture of "affect, love, veneration and possessiveness" (see above), then one would not be doing full justice to the specificity of this new ritual.

No, what is specific about this kissing of the ground is its diffuseness and mixture, that ambivalent symbolic reference network that contains elements of humility and gratitude as much as the "appropriation" of the kissed earth, adoration as much as the aftertaste of blasphemy, elements of the traditional rite as much as of the magical action. This diffuseness is the result of a decision that an *individual* has made for himself, an individual who is not seen as such by the majority of his believers or interpreters, but rather as a "conservative" pope, as, in other words, a representative of the Church whose actions preserve and perpetuate the traditions in full knowledge of them. But the "kiss of the ground" does not preserve the tradition, it endangers it. It (the kiss) is the result of an individual decision, not bound to tradition, made in favor of a diffuse ritual which is inserted into traditional ceremonial contexts. In the process, the ritual itself is first elevated and secured by the pope's official charisma.

This elevation by a tradition-bound, trans-individual representative of "the holy" turns out, upon closer inspection, to set the concrete individual John Paul II apart by means of the ritual that is typical for and characteristic of him. The expression of the collectively religious is diluted into a declaration of the individual, the peculiar. The rigidity of the teachings—as accredited to this pope—and the change in the ritual complement each other. *Both* are an expression for the no longer conscious and thus no longer sovereign employment of tradition. The direction of this development points to a basic reshaping of the handed-down ritual by naive, inflationary ritualism: the search for security and stability in the—new—ritual leads to a destabilization of the traditional rite. Where John XXIII was still the representative man within traditional ritual which he was fluent in, John Paul II strikes a path via the ritualized man as representative toward ceremonial self-presentation of an individual within traditional rite.

At the same time, the symbolic crossing of the border implicit in this ritual acquires an ambiguous structure: In the trans-personal quality of a collectively secured and consciously practiced ritual, the individual as such fades into the general. But here, the individual actually stands out because of his individual, no longer traditionally consistent choice. In the collective, sacred ritual the individual, secured by the collectivity of the form, crosses the threshold to "the holy" in which it dissolves. In the individually chosen and founded ritual, the individual crosses outside his own everyday existence and elevates himself in the ritual emphasis of his own singularity. Thus, the individual John Paul II crosses the boundaries of precisely that rite the representative of which he should be. But a pope—"representative" of a God, of a collective belief—who crosses the borders of collective symbolism into individual singularity, moves into nothingness. And more: the representative central figure of a community of believers is proving himself—structurally—to be a "deviationist."

For the record: The central configuration of meaning for mankind's contemporary interpretation of self and world within "Western cultures"— that subjectivity that is directed toward self-actualization and self-presentation (see above, III)—leaves its traces even where one would least expect it to have any influence, in the preserve of religious traditionalism and symbolism.

The result of the naive, unexamined ritualism and dogmatism embodied by John Paul II can easily be read from the reactions to his second visit to the U.S. The mixture of inflationary use of the sacred on the one hand—both the eagerness to travel reminiscent of a Central European foreign minister whose name we won't mention and the "twenty-four-hour presence" of the pope on major television channels give evidence to that—and ritually dogmatic stereotypism on the other hand has an effect that is easily identifiable. The expected large masses of believers are increasingly absent—not only in the U.S. "Well, the man was here in this country once already in 1979, and I think the thrill is gone" (*San Francisco Chronicle*, 19 Sept. 1987: A 12). Instead of the faithful, the curiosity seekers came: Photoreporters were able to discover one praying believer amidst the zoom-lens-equipped amateur photographers (*San Francisco Chronicle*, 19 Sept. 1987: A 10). The "Holy Father's" visit becomes a tour, a cross between state visit and celebrity show.

The jet rushes from one city to the next, the popemobile from one church to the next, the pope from one mass to the next. In the stadiums, the popemobile circles the arena like a victorious football team or a pop star's Mercedes before open-air concerts. And in Carmel, the town in which Clint Eastwood ("Dirty Harry") is mayor, a button is printed with the picture of John Paul II and the interpretation of that papal visit perfectly expressed in the words: "Go ahead—bless my day!" Dirty Harry ("Go ahead—make my day!") and John Paul II (official button: photo of the pope with the subscription "bless you!") enter a significant connection. Also, we seem to enjoy both performers most in the media, if possible at home on the sofa: "I think Catholics are probably turning into couch potatoes like the rest of us" (*San Francisco Chronicle*, 19 Sept. 1987, A 12). In the media, John Paul II—now a kind of serial actor—meets with interesting competition: "KGO-TV (Channel 7) said the pope outpulled some daytime soap operas, but did not do well against others" (*San Francisco Chronicle*, A 12). The final evaluation of his visit from this point of view, a point of view for which John Paul II is co-responsible: "The visit was hyped as the *greatest show* (emphasis added) on earth and heaven and in the end that's bound to disappoint" (*San Francisco Chronicle*, A 12).

V

In the two manifestations of currently observable social action described above, both (1) the ritualized anti-ritualism and (2) the changes in a traditional ritual through naive, inflationary rituals, one of the most prominent collective symbols of current interpretations of self and world has become visible as background: the social orientation of individuals according to the dictates of a fulfilled, self-sufficient subjectivity.[22] Subjectivity, uniqueness, and specific form of meaning (*Sinngestalt*) thus paradoxically become both collective role and collective, innerworldly religious model. Gehlen suspected that such a "culture of subjectivity (can) not, by its very nature, be stabilized. It has to end in a massive, ephemeral, surplus production" (Gehlen, 1973: 23). Although the preceding case studies would initially point to just such a tendency, they then also show up a different aspect. Initially, that subjectivity which supposedly rests within itself and is content there is collectively secured. Peculiarities or deviations (within *this* framework) are no longer threatening but rather accompanied by mutual goodwill on the part of the unique individuals.

At the same time, resistance by the primarily self-oriented subjects to the functional world of work and administration grows, a world that is organized according to the principles of the division of labor and that is highly regulated; that is, the resistance against a public-social sphere that is experienced only as an "un-authentic" zone of sociality ruled by the pressure imposed by the system and thus hindering the self-fulfillment of the individual. The mass movements of interconnected subjects and groups of all sizes respond to this—among other things—just like the subjective exaggeration of a traditional ritualism. Both refuse a *pragmatic* social consensus and a mutual commitment to rationality and argumentation. Instead, they quote the universality of higher communities and goals which are so far removed from the individual's everyday life that neither arguments nor obligations to cooperate can catch up with them.

In a way similar to how the universalism of communities is applied as the bonding agent against both the partialization of individuals and against the anonymity of functional and public role acting, the mass rituals close the dangerous rift between subjective personal and collective meaning. In the ritual of the public arrangement, closeness and emotional equality are suggested. But in the "private sphere," in the expression of the subjective, it presents the collective meaning. The "surplus productions" of the subjective and/or the universal are captured, in this case in the ritual, are then domesticated and, as concerns their "public" effect, dissipated and rendered harmless.

Notes

1. This theoretical framework was not, incidentally, invented by me. It dates back to reflections by Plessner, Gehlen, and Luckmann, and has its place within the

tradition of ethnological, social-philosophical, and sociological theories of signs and symbols. According to scholastic ritualistic form, let me refer at this point to Darwin, Wundt, Mead, Bühler, Malinowski, Schütz, Lévi-Strauss, Bourdieu, and Geertz.

2. So when, on certain occasions and within specialized contexts of work and meaning, the abstract differentiation is made between communication on the one hand and its materials and sign system on the other, then this also shows that the privileges of scientific work and attitudes always lead one into the temptation to neglect and overlook the practical experience of the material world. In this disassociation from the material and the practice of life, that is, from the conceptual form of the concrete social phenomena, it becomes possible to speak of communication, the constitution of signs, and sign systems "as such": to speak of an immaterial world of abstract-ephemeral objects, in which social life and its phenomena are no more than shadowy forms.

3. In speaking of "rituals" or "ritual behavior" as specific forms of presentation for human co-orientation, co-operation, and communication, one often overlooks the fact that the *observational* category "ritualized behavior" hardly refers exclusively to a specifically human form of behavior, that in fact it can, with good reason, be used to describe both human *and* animal behavior.

4. Many, but certainly not all, presumably not even most ritualized gestures are linked to language (in the narrower sense of the word). In the repertoire of human signs, language plays a significant, but perhaps not the dominant role that we attribute to it. What is certain is that we tend to overestimate language and its influence on our behavior. For one, language puts at our disposal a highly developed—and above all, well-described—potential for dealing with other human beings, with our environment, with our memories, with the collection and passing-on of "knowledge," and so forth. But another reason is that our profession is defined both directly and indirectly by language: We are members of a reading, speaking, story-telling, and blustering profession.

5. At this point, the order shared by both *routines* and *rituals* is emphasized. However, there is a considerable difference between routines as such and rituals. While the former could quite generally be described as behavioral habits that have been seen to be successful and, hence, have been preserved, the latter—including interaction rituals!—belong to the *symbolic* actions: rituals are *symbolically molded* routines of border crossing (see below).

6. For a more detailed description of the ordering of ritual action see Soeffner, H.-G., *Emblematische und symbolische Formen der Orientierung*, in Soeffner, H.-G. (1989): 158–84.

7. See Halbwachs, M. (1967), *Das kollektive Gedächtnis*, Frankfurt/M. 1985: 19: "A social movement of thought is generally as invisible as the air we breathe. In normal life, one feels its existence only when one tries to resist it."

8. I offered a more detailed description of the overall context at the 22. Deutscher Soziologentag in Dortmund (9–12 October 1984).

9. See Neidhardt, F., *Einige Ideen zu einer allgemeinen Theorie sozialer Bewegungen*, in Hradil, S. (ed.) (1985), *Sozialstrukturen im Umbruch*. Karl Martin Bolte zum 60. Geburtstag, Opladen: 193 ff. Neidhardt coined the expression "mobilized networks of networks" [*"mobilisierte Netzwerke von Netzwerken"*] for this context.

10. Sociology is a science of reality: it describes and analyzes the real possibilities and the possible realities of social action and social organization. Perforce its attention is—particularly where it defines itself as a *material* sociology of knowl-

edge—on the structures, forms, *and* elements of the social construction of reality. To practice social sciences as a profession means to observe, describe, and interpret from a structurally imposed distance and a necessary multiplicity of perspectives, that is, to approach the objects of observation with engaged disinterest and to approach the manifestations and expressions of the social fabric— of which the sociologist too is a part—with interested disengagement. Sociology, as one of the humanities practiced by human beings is, almost inevitably, indebted to the people and societies which it tries to describe and understand with dispassionate or disillusioned sympathy.

11. Involuntary and deliberate (?) parodies enter a delightful alliance where, for instance, besides individual offices the men's toilet, too—why only the men's?— is declared a "nuclear-free zone." (Out of sympathy, I shall refrain from naming the university in question.)

12. In the expression "human chain" there comes about a truly exemplary combination of ornament (jewellery) and coercion. The individual links of the chain are imprisoned in an ornamentally formulated, symbolic community.

13. We can see that ritual actionism, too, follows the same law of formal certainty even when empty of "content," and has no other goal than that fleeting yet repeatedly invoked community. We see it in the following statement of a member of the "Autonomous Party": "What separates us from other people is the stone in our hand and the truncheon at our neck. We are most autonomous when we're in a fog of teargas. *What holds us together above and beyond that, we do not know"* (Emphasis by H.-G. S.). Quoted from the magazine *Der Spiegel*, Nr. 46, 41. year, 9.11.1987: 19. The contradictory unity of autonomy and fleeting, inevitably empty, determined community is already easily recognizable here.

14. The "human chain" represents a significant exception. One can no longer see it directly *"as a whole"*; that only happens on the television newscasts in the evening: Filmed from a helicopter, delivered into our livingrooms, the phenomenon only attains its intended shape through the medium. It is an exemplary case for what is true of all arrangements mentioned. They serve as media for the media.

15. Inquiries at theological faculties in the FRG and the U.S. as to the specific meaning of this kissing of the ground and the reason for choosing this gesture elicited only uncertainty and speculation. The encyclopedias, too, remain silent—at least on this point. They had plenty to say on other points (see below).

16. See *Ein Papst erobert die Welt. Johannes Paul II. reist für den Frieden,* ed. by R. A. Krewerth, Offenburg 11/80: 158 ff. "Gehet hinaus in alle Welt." Die sieben Reisen um den Erdball.

17. Op. cit., see title and subtitle.

18. M. Malinski, and H. Pauels, *"Maria wir preisen Dich."* Johannes Paul II. als Marienpilger um die Welt, June 1983: *Der Papst auf Besuch zu Hause,* Pattloch Verlag.

19. *Der Papst kommt, Johannes Paul II. besucht am 1. und 2. Mai 1987 Stadt und Bistum Münster,* Aschendorff Verlag, Münster 1987: 14.

20. See *Encyclopedia of Religion and Ethics,* III, op. cit., P. 741: 744; also Grimm, *Wörterbuch der Deutschen Sprache,* op. cit.: 2874.

21. *See Encyclopedia of Religion and Ethics,* VII, op. cit.: 743, ditto Grimm, op. cit.: 2869.

22. Those days seem to be over for the time being in which someone (Marlene Dietrich in a television interview) could respond to the question of how she feels and interprets herself by saying "I'm none of my business."

4

Flying Moles
(Pigeon-Breeding Miners in the Ruhr District):
The Totemistic Enchantment of Reality and
the Technological Disenchantment of Longing

I

When I was ten years old, my family moved from a small town in Southern Germany to a city in the Ruhr district. Only a few streets from ours there was a housing estate for miners. Most of my schoolmates lived there, and so naturally, I became a member of their "street corner society." After school, I hung around with them, profited from the postwar blessings of the miners' status (coal, wood, and food rations), and watched in the evenings as many of the miners headed straight for those beings who seemed to hold the greatest attraction for them: their pigeons.

The pigeons—their breeding and health, their feed and price and, between spring and autumn, the pigeon races, flight performance, and wagers—were the topics that, as a matter of course, overrode other conversational and "life" topics such as soccer, politics, and work.

The view from my room was onto the then still smoking coal heaps, the pithead frames and factory walls. In the evenings, I watched the miners coming, freshly showered, out of the colliery gates: On their way from the dark, dusty, subterranean passages, seams and caves to the pigeon lofts, to their white or blue-gray birds. All this conflated into *one* image long after I no longer lived there, an image to which my fantasies, obsessed with meaning and symbol, gave the name "the flying mole."[1]

This formulation plays with contradictory concepts. It sets itself up as paradox: as something that contradicts, by its appearance, ordinary experiences (Mauthner, 1980: 231 f.), or at least in its linguistic form, contradicts ordinary use of language. In their appearance, paradoxes parade as specific rhetorical figures; but they are more than that. They illustrate one fundamental form (next to others) dealing with contradictoriness and oppositionality: They represent individual contradiction and the process of its harmonization *simultaneously*. They mark a considerable step within a process of overcoming problems that begin in the experiencing of insecurity, followed by reflexively ascertained contradictoriness and doubt, which we then, however, smooth over in strenuous work of the imagination to a playfully canceled balance of opposites, to an aesthetic equilibrium of contradictions. In short, paradoxes refer to those practically achieved processes of harmonization that are imposed upon us by our "eccentric positionality" (Plessner, 1929: 288 ff.). They point to the necessity of living with and in contradiction, and at the same time point to one of the means of dealing with these contradictions.

Formulating paradoxes is part of the symbolic work by which we draw a network of meaning over our visible and invisible construction of the world.[2] And it is not least of all the symbols that secure these constructions. This capacity is due to their ability to accentuate paradox and ambivalence while at the same time suffering them and transforming the dissonance of contradiction into aesthetic consonance. We use this unusual characteristic of symbols to combine various seemingly irreconcilable meanings, emotions, values, and tendencies into a graphically rounded contradictory unity.[3] On the other hand—and this is no contradiction to our preceding contentions—the "symbolism" [the original unit (coin, shell, ring, etc.) that is broken and then is supposed to come together again] serves friends, relatives, lovers as the identifying sign of recognition: as a sign of the inviolable community. The special accent attributed to symbolic action and expression, particularly in religious presentations and experiences, shows clearly how much our interpretations and life with others must be understood not only as life *with* symbols, but also as life *in* symbols. One of the most secure currencies in the social household, namely the social emotions, would have but a weak and fleeting existence without symbols (Durkheim, 1912: 316). Symbols, especially those we consider collective symbols, are the products and instruments of human effort at and with the conditions of living together in a group, community and society. And these products and instruments have to constantly be re-confirmed. In this respect, collective symbols constitute the feeling of community just as they help secure the community's (collective) consciousness and continuity.

Pigeons in the Ruhr District

Unlike the reflexive syntax and sequence of causality, symbols constitute immediacy. They contract the contradictory into a unit, the unsimultaneous into the simultaneous, the next-to-each-other into *one* form. Whenever the symbol postulates its own reality, it aims at divesting the argument of its existence. Overly determined and ambivalent as it is, it represents an aspect of the human construction of reality that doesn't shatter against its contradictoriness, but instead lives on it, expresses it, and suggests the unity of contradictions.

By exploiting this structure, central collective symbols represent a myth in which all details of life-world experience are bound together to an integrated higher meaningfulness, coincidence is eradicated, and each individual phenomenon is transformed into a cipher of power and effectiveness of precisely this myth. The significance of collective symbols as elementary parts of concrete social constructions of reality is due less to their referring to specific objects, events, persons, etc. *Rather, the decisive meaning of a collective symbol consists in the social reaction it evokes,* in its influence on the collective perception, orientation, and action. As Karl Jaspers said, it creates "community without communication" (1932, vol.II: 26).

The concrete historical phenomenon that around the middle of the nineteenth century a diffuse mass of peasants, artisans, and agricultural laborers from various countries, cultural and linguistic regions, driven and held together by a specific type of industrial labor, "chooses" as its collective symbol the pigeon makes any observer immediately suspect that this romantic image represents fissures and dissonance far more than any harmony, and that this romantic heraldic beast of the miners is the product of collective work on contradictions, unfulfilled wishes, disappointed hopes and illusions. The conspicuous contrast between the black, subterranean moles and their airy symbol shows that the intersubjective construction and the subjective experiencing of this collective ideal image is a symbolic expression of the concrete historical structure of a specific form of social existence and a way of life.

In the following, then, I shall attempt to answer these questions: What is it that makes the chtonic, earthy mole find his air-bound ideal image in the pigeon as heraldic beast? What makes him leave the ground? What particular flight techniques and goals does he choose? I shall approach these questions by describing—a first analytic step—the semantic associations that structure the lexical content of the symbol "carrier pigeon" and its relationship to the miner of the Ruhr district.

II

Unlike many of its symbolic relatives, the pigeon (which, in avian terminology, includes the dove) is both a heraldic and a domestic animal: practical and symbolic sides, pragmatic and ideal meaning, are closely related. The pigeon is at home on all continents. Its cultural history spans a period of 7000 years, and it is estimated that at present about 80 million pigeons ply the skies between St. Mark's Cathedral in Venice, the "Inner Palace" in Beijing, the Capitol in Washington, D.C., and the pithead towers in Wanne-Eickel. There are about 800 different varieties of domestic and wild pigeons and doves. They all derive from the rock pigeon: the mother of the traveller pigeon and the grandmother of the carrier pigeon.[4]

Whoever has read their way into the history and accounts of pigeons is tempted to spin stories forever, to tell of all the tricks that pigeons, wild or domestic, can do: stories about their mysterious and unexplained sense of orientation, about records in flight distance and speed, high, low, and long distance flights, loopings, aerial somersaults, and the like. Of course, this is all part of their cultural history, but I shall touch upon it only briefly, insofar as it concerns the questions I am seeking to answer here.

The oldest known witnesses of this cultural history are to be found about 5000 B.C. They are the first in a long row of pictures, inscriptions, statues, and stories. The sites of discovery, beginning in Mesopotamia, are strewn over all continents. One finds early traces in Egypt, Babylon, Greece, India, China, and Central America. The white doves of the Babylonian Goddess Istar/Astarte, the mysterious sounds emitted by the pigeons in Bali and Java, the carrier pigeons that flew as messengers of love from King Solomon to the Queen of Sheba, and those that Brutus sent out to his co-conspirators, the famous dove that marked the end of the Deluge, but also Hans Albers's "La Paloma," Picasso's dove of peace (painted in 1949, the year his fourth child was born, a daughter who was named "Paloma"), and finally the carrier pigeons of "Taumvater Jupp" and "Kumpel Karl" in the Ruhr district—they all are links in a long chain of mankind's practical and symbolic interaction with pigeons and doves.

Sometimes there are similar pearls within the long chain, pearls that make up their own pattern: In the year 444 B.C., the year of the eighty-fourth Olympic Games (there are no Olympic Games without doves, to this day), one of the winners, Taurosthenes, sent off carrier pigeons to his native island of Aegina, some 160 kilometers away, in order to let his friends and supporters know of his triumph (Hoffmann, 1982: 105). Following his lead, carrier pigeons were still being sent out, in the 1950s, by the fans of the *SpVg Erkenschwick,* the *STV Horst Escher,* the *Sportfreunde Katernberg,* and *Hamborn 07* (German soccer clubs). During the half-time breaks, fans and players were thus notified of the half-time results. In the history of culture too, 2000 years can often seem no longer than the beat of a wing.

There is a whole history waiting to be written of pigeons in the service of information and disinformation, a history to which the Rothschild Bank could contribute a characteristic episode. After Napoleon's defeat at Waterloo, the Bank informed its London branch, via carrier pigeons, three days before the mounted messenger got to the English court with the news. Enough time to "let (stocks and money) work" via the spreading of rumors and misinformation.

From the early days, training and breeding of the carrier pigeons were the precondition for their successes as messengers. But it was Akbar the Great of India (sixteenth century) who first methodized and instrumentalized pigeon breeding. His court is said to have enjoyed, or suffered perhaps, the presence of close to 20,000 pigeons. The mogul distinguished, with great scientific precision, seventeen different species amongst his pigeons, and he developed eight new breeds by trying to isolate and improve the "best" traits of existing species through crossbreeding. The new birds showed their appreciation by delighting the court with artistic performances—aerial somersaults, looping the loop—during concerts by the court orchestra.

In 1760, the Persian poet Sayzid Mohammed Musari wrote the first known history of the pigeon. Pigeon breeding and training have seen methodical development ever since—nowadays especially in Western Europe. In all this, the symbolic interpretation accorded the pigeons by the individual societies were in keeping with the respective social and political conditions and changes that characterize those societies. In Dutch society, carried by the bourgeoisie, pigeon breeding reached its zenith in the eighteenth century. At the end of that same century (in 1789), the dovecotes in France were destroyed as symbols of feudalism and the Church. Four decades later (1818) in the Belgian kingdom, which was in the process of developing its own coal and steel industry, the first pigeon races were held—and Belgium became the home both of industrial mining and of carrier pigeon and pigeon breeding on the European continent. To this day, the "Belgian hybrid pigeon" holds first rank in the hierarchy of noble pigeon species.

After the first longer race from Toulouse to Brussels (1818), others quickly followed. At first, these were flights from Paris or London to Brussels but then, after various way stations, the distances increased: In 1850, the stretch was from Rome to Brussels. Today, three-and-a-half million pigeons darken the Belgian weekend sky (see Hoffmann, 1982). The Germans were late starters by comparison. At the courts—and then at *the* court—the greatest popularity enjoyed by pigeons was in their role as hors-d'oeuvre. Still, in 1845 the first pigeon-breeding club was founded in Buchholz (Saxony); Frankfurt followed in 1869—and then, as befits German club mentality (*Vereinsmentalität*), the whole of the pigeon-breeding clubs were brought together under the umbrella of the "Association of German pigeon-breeding clubs" (Cologne, 1884). Today, the members of about 8000 clubs feed and train six million "German" carrier pigeons out of a total European air fleet of 15 million pigeons. And next to the artists of races and messenger flights,[5] one must not forget those white doves, the ones that magicians pull out of their hats. Twelve or even more doves have "space" in the commodious tails of the trick experts who exploit all that other magic of white doves.

The multifarious carrier pigeon's military career has its very own place in history. Already the Pharaoh Djozer (First Dynasty, 2600 B.C.) is said to have used carrier pigeons as his couriers. Julius Caesar, Chinese emperors, Christian crusaders, Turkish Sultans, and many others followed his lead. The Dutch let fly carrier pigeons against Alba, the British against the Boers, carrier pigeons flew and "fought" on all sides during the First World War, the French Résistance battled the German Wehrmacht with their help, British parachutists for a while wore jackets with a pigeon-pocket on the left side, pigeons with little cameras strapped to their backs like rucksacks were used as reconnaissance flyers, and the U.S. military forces swore in their avian air force to the sound of "Stars and Stripes" (Hoffmann, 1982: 133). Where there is a military, there are necessarily, according to its interpretation of itself, heroes. Thus, for example, the pigeon "G.I. Joe" was presented with the "Dickin Medal for Gallantry" by the Lord Mayor of London, because it had saved more than a thousand British soldiers with its messenger flight. "Cher Ami" (Hoffmann,

124 ff.), a participant in World War I, had the dubious honor of showing visible signs of its valor all over its body: It was the last of six carrier pigeons (five had already been shot down by German snipers) which was supposed to save an encircled American battalion from its own artillery that lay too close. "Cher Ami" took off in flight, was hit, fell to the ground, surprisingly rose again, and disappeared with its message from sight of the encircled men and the snipers. And the messenger arrived at his goal, having been shot through the chest and left wing and having lost his left leg. General Pershing himself took on the job of honoring the pigeon after its recovery, and ordered that "Cher Ami" be given an officer's cabin on the voyage across the Atlantic. The hero died in 1919, was stuffed, and can be admired (just like the tobacco box of "Old Fritz" with its gunshot scars can be admired in the Castle of Hohenzollern) in the Smithsonian Museum.

To this day, armies place some of their hopes in carrier pigeons. For instance, the Swiss army continues to train carrier pigeons. One reason is that they can pass through radar undetected, another is that that way, there will still be a "functioning" information system if, in case of nuclear war, all electronic information systems collapse through interference by the so-called NEMP (nuclear electronic impulse). But what would a military tool be, be it even a pigeon, without a matching description in a manual so that the well-informed soldier can look it up? What, in that case, is the "Swiss Military Pigeon"? Answer: It is "a self-reproducing small flying object on a biological basis with precisely programmed, automatic return from any direction or distance" (Hoffmann, 1982: 134).

III

The more or less profane, practical qualities of pigeons and doves and the resulting semantic content are—at times invisibly, but more often clearly identifiably—connected and saturated with those meanings nourished by myth, fairy tale, legend, religion, and literature. Once again, I can but briefly sketch this semantic network in a few of its basic patterns and colors.

Its central motives are closely connected to pigeon myths and pigeon cults around the already-mentioned Babylonian deity Istar, the Semitic Astarte, or the Syrian Atargatis. From here, there are traces one can follow to the myths surrounding Aphrodite/Venus, to the Pleiades (or *peleiaz,* meaning wild dove or pigeon[6])—the priestesses at Dodana, the site of Zeus' oracle—but equally, to the Indian Rig-Veda and the myth around the birth of Semiramis, who was fed and saved by doves after being abandoned as a child.

Istar dies in autumn with nature, when the leaves fall. In spring, life returns with her when she celebrates her "Holy Wedding" with her eternally young lover Tammuz, the later Adonis. Already in this early myth cycle, the accompanying symbol, the dove, combines very different and contradictory elements: Bird of life and death,[7] messenger of love and misery, the identifying mark of the holy Hetaerae ("temple prostitution"), of the priestesses of Astarte [compare their impoverished German great-granddaughters in the term "asphalt dove" (*Asphalttaube,* meaning prostitute)] and at the same time, soul bird.

Christian mythology takes over all these elements from its historical precursors, but each one of them, including death, misery, and suffering, is imbued with a new emphasis, one that implies redemption. From the doves Noah sends out that mark the end of the Deluge, all the way to the dove that "brings visibly to the eyes" of John at Jesus' christening, and later on to the disciples at Whitsun the presence of God (of the "Holy Ghost") and the promise of grace and redemption. In keeping with this, the council at Nikaea determines the semantic framework of the symbol "dove/pigeon" as follows: It is the symbol of peace, of the Holy Ghost, of the redeemed soul, of the burial of ghosts. To this day, the dove embodies, in the cultic vocabulary of symbols in the Catholic Church, "the Holy Ghost, the inspiration of the Holy Scripture, the soul that passes away in God's peace, as well as, multiplied by twelve, the twelve disciples" (Hermann, 1960: 84).

Fitting into the web of traditional myth, Jesus' sacrificial death also follows the mythological pattern of the Jewish tradition. In the symbolic equation both of the innocent, persecuted people of Israel and the innocently suffering Christ with the dove as well as the lamb—both are holy sacrificial animals—old myths come together naturally in new myths, and find their total form, which sounds as simple as it is cryptically worked out into the smallest detail. The most perfect expression of this can, I believe, be found in Bach's St. Matthew's Passion:

> At evening, hour of calm and rest,
> Was Adam's fall made manifest
> At evening too, the Lord's redeeming love,

At evening, homeward turned the dove;
An olive leaf the while she bore.
O beauteous time, o evening hour!
Our peace with God is evermore assured,
For Jesus hath His Cross endured.[8]

The Christian symbolism of the dove enters into new configurations in art, popular beliefs, and superstitions, or takes up old strands of the semantic cloth again: dove/pigeon meat, and especially their blood is considered, in some more magically informed circles, to cure or protect against stomachaches, strokes, eye ailments, warts, freckles, scorpion bites; the blood of doves or pigeons, pure or baked into patties, nowadays baked into pizzas, is considered an aphrodisiac (Wuttke, 1900: 119). Joan of Arc in legend and literature borrows, via the dove, the symbolic background of religion and fairy tale, just as did the Parcival legend, Wolfram's Parcival poem, and, of course, Wagner's Parcival opera that confronts every director of opera with the delicate task of getting a dove to float above the head of Anfortas at the right moment (act 3, the redeeming question).

Myth, religions, and popular belief praise—incidentally not without ethological justification—loyalty, love, and peaceable temperament of doves/pigeons. They are monogamous, enjoy a perpetually active reproductive instinct, as well as an equally remarkable capacity for love, and they are—even if only within the circle of their own kind—remarkably peaceable. Such obviously laudable traits lead one (e.g. the Physiologus) to countless stories, poems, and songs all the way from antiquity and Plautus, who is said to have introduced into literature the term of endearment *mea columba,* to Bert Brecht: "Mackie and I, we live like turtle-doves" [Jealousy-Duet, Lucy and Polly (Brecht, 1967: 451)].

Within precisely this frame of reference, the sentimental hit "La Paloma" fits right in, since it, too, the poor cousin of "higher songdom" cites almost all the significant elements of the dove/pigeon symbolism. Even the history of this song lets us enjoy that lofty teary melodrama on which it lives. It was written by Sebastian de Yradier, the voice teacher of Empress Eugénie, and had its première in 1864 in the Mexico City Theater. The famous Concha Mendezi sang the subsequently highly popular tango. Her most prominent listener was Emperor Maximilian—called "the Unhappy" in Germany—and he was moved to tears (Hoffmann, 1982: 100). The German text, sung in an unsurpassed performance by "the blond Hans" (Hans Albers), touches on all possible motives that connect seaman or seaside vacationer with the soul bird:

> If I should fall victim one day/ to the outraged sea/ a white
> dove will fly / to you here/ let it in by the window/ with the dove,
> my soul will come to you.

Of course, the world consists not exclusively of pigeon enthusiasts, of course the "rat of the sky" that colors our monuments and statues an acid grayish white[9] has aroused so much repugnance that there are never-ending discussions about sterilizing the love birds, and of course, given the emotional vehemence evoked by the birds, one might cheerfully and with good reason fall in with Georg Kreißler (the Austrian singer-songwriter) who wrote a song called "Let's go poison pigeons in the park!" (*"Gehma Tauben vergiften im Park!"*). The ordinary pigeons targeted here are, of course, not carrier pigeons.

IV

The long but necessary path through the pigeons' cultural history, necessary for our final argumentation, now leads back to one of their most loyal fanciers, the flying mole. But first we shall still offer some general data on pigeon breeding by the miners in the Ruhr district, for only then can a narrative interpretation be made out of the pre-interpretative narration.

Even today, there are about 30,000 breeders in the Ruhr district who, all told, keep about two million pigeons (the entire Federal Republic of Germany: 90,000 breeders, 6,000,000 pigeons). Pigeon breeding and "pigeon racing" became a hobby and a miners' sport in the Ruhr district at a time when the work day underground lasted twelve to fourteen hours, the average life expectancy of a miner was forty years, and his health and work capacity was constantly threatened by silicosis, unemployment, or both.

The first pigeon fanciers, who have meanwhile become legends in the Ruhr district, were *Taubenvatter Gustav* ["pigeon dad Gustav" (Pütt Baaker Basin)], *Taumvatter Jupp* ["pigeon dad Jupp" (Osterfeld colliery)], *Kumpel Karl* ["chum" or "miner Karl" (coking plant "Verlorener Sohn")]. These names alone, like the names of the collieries and the pigeon-breeding clubs ("Forever True the Old Ones," "Homesick at Schönefeld", "For the Fatherland") would be sufficient grounds for the sociology of knowledge to attempt an interpretation of the Ruhr district miners. But let us return to the carrier pigeons!

In the aforementioned "good" old days before industrialization, it was the pleasure of kings, moguls, the aristocracy, and wealthy citizens to breed and keep pigeons. Then the miner took over this art. For one of his means it is a costly pleasure; a good carrier pigeon costs between DM 300 and 500; top prices can be as high as DM 28,000. A pair of pigeons requires more than 100 kilograms of grain feed per year, and estimates quote agricultural profit margins of up to DM 50 million annually from pigeon breeding alone.

The pigeon lofts require special care. They have to be kept extraordinarily clean, otherwise the birds fall prey to disease and perish. In other words, the lofts have to be swept daily, washed out with baking soda, and treated weekly with disinfectant and insecticide. As one pigeon breeder put it, "All it takes is a grain of corn lying round, one pigeon shits on it, another pigeon eats it—and then you have the whole mess with diseases and so forth" (Hoffmann, 1982: 26).

Then there are the club expenses for the "cabin express," which ferries the carrier pigeons to their starting points in Vienna, Rome, or Copenhagen. These cross-country busses (which cost about DM 45,000) are exceedingly well equipped—dining and sleeping car in one: 9,40 meters long and 3,80 meters high. They carry 300 kilograms of grain feed with them and supply the birds with running water and special feed. And then, as if these expenses weren't already high enough, the breeder miners also seem particularly donation happy: The "Association of German Carrier-Pigeon Fans" (headquarters Essen) collected and donated, within ten years, DM 5 million alone for the "Aktion Sorgenkind" [a child welfare organization (Lau/Voß, 1988)], in a national charity bazaar: the so-called "little guy" making charitable donations for the even littler one.

Apart from the business of charity, that of betting is also alive and well. The highest stake is DM 30; some Ruhr district cities set the limit at DM 10,50; all stakes are played out. Still, betting itself is obviously more a social activity than a special passion. The metaphor that is always dragged in by the back hairs in this context, that of the pigeon as the "racehorse of the little man," may be humorous but is inaccurate (Hoffmann, 1982: 82). Unlike the racehorse, the pigeon runs (flies) its race exclusively on its own capacities and qualities, with no outside help.

There is neither an assisted take-off nor a demarcated racetrack, nor any kind of jockey substitute. Everything is up to the pigeon's instinct-guided navigation. Of course, success in the race depends on breeding, care, and physical shape of the pigeon. The traditional saying of breeders, "form is better than class" (Hoffmann, 1982) expresses something that is true both for the pigeon and for the breeder miner. Performance, not provenance, counts.

Generally, the racing career of a carrier pigeon begins at the age of six months and ends at six years. The "life expectancy" of the birds, however, is around thirty years, and these years are lived out under the tender loving care of the pigeon fanciers. Up to 30,000 carrier pigeons participate in the important races (e.g., Vienna—Ruhr district). The fastest among them take thirteen hours for that flight back home. If they are well-trained they fly, without interruption, at an altitude of about 100 meters. Around their leg they carry a narrow elastic band, which gives the exact starting time—day, hour, minute, and second, determined by a special stopwatch, the so-called *Konstatieruhr* ("establishing clock"). Upon their arrival back home, the breeder has to remove the time band from the pigeon's leg as quickly as possible and, with it as evidence, have the time of arrival (i.e. flight time) recorded at the local "establishing clock." The winner is not the pigeon that is the first to arrive on its own roof, and then stay there out of reach, thereby earning the name "roof-shitter," but the one who is the first to return to the breeder's hand.

In order to "motivate" the pigeons to achieve "maximum performance," the breeders, not exactly over sensitive, use a devious trick. According to the motto "We shall give wings to their longing," the "loyalty" and monogamousness of the pigeon couples are exploited. The euphemism "gentle method" is used for this system (Klein, 1981): The loving couple is separated. Shortly before the race, one lets the physically stronger male pigeon, which is to fly in the race, come together with his beloved. One allows the already feverishly longing pigeons a last foreplay of billing and cooing to intensify the heat, then separates the male "just in time" from his mate and sends him off. This deviously exacerbated longing lends extra wings to the lover on his return flight—to the point of complete exhaustion.

Apart from breeding, training, care, and the psychology of competition, the miners have yet another, more technical problem to solve: The distances between the individual pigeon lofts have to be measured with the greatest possible precision. And thus the miner discovers that the available city plans and street maps are not precise enough. He goes underground, into his professionally constructed and measured system of tunnels, using mining maps for the precise measuring of distances: The mole measures the surface of his world from the underground perspective.

V

There is no dearth of earthy self-interpretations, nor yet of lovingly empathizing outside interpretations of the pigeon-breeding miners. They all could be inscribed with the motto borrowed from Michael Drayton used in the preparatory symposium volume for a meeting in Dubrovnik (1989):

> I build my hopes a world above the sky,
> yet with the mole I creep into the earth.
> (The Paradox)[10]

And Hilmar Hoffmann can be named as exemplary among interpreters; it is to his "Pigeon Book" (*Taubenbuch*) that this essay is greatly indebted. To him, the miners' breeding of pigeons is an "act of liberation" (Hoffmann, 1982: 12) wherein the longing for spatial freedom is realized.

One has often asked why the pigeon has such numerous admirers among the miners—and the most tender, too. It is simple: Whoever descends into the night day after day, into the narrow crossways of a winding shaft, looks up into the regained sky often and with pleasure when he finally emerges again. That is where his pigeons fly; a ray of light over the gray monotony of coal heaps and pithead frames. With eight hours on the job and black coal before one's eyes, who wouldn't want to hold something light after coming off the shift, a white or dove-gray pigeon? If one spends one's life among rough, dead stone, one longs for contrast, for soft "material," for light creatures, a rabbit or pigeon. Heavy hands can be unspeakably tender. Pigeons sense that, too (Hoffmann, 1982: 14).

Like other interpretations that are borne by empathy, this one lives on contrasting two worlds: the bad, gray reality of industrial labor in the mine on the one hand, and the in part actively, to a greater extent however symbolically realized desire for freedom, warmth, and happiness on

the other. These interpretations are nurtured by the rhetorical development of the paradox, of the opposition of black and white, up and down,
heaven and (below) earth, constraints (imprisonment) and liberation,
narrowness and limitlessness (infinity), hard and soft, and not least of
all, life and death.[11] The lighter side of the oppositional pairs, the symbolically created and furnished world of fulfilled longing, defeats the
darker side of the world, the gray reality. The rhetoric of opposition acts
as paradox, but at the same time, the symbolic bridging of opposites
inherent in it elevates the contradictoriness to a harmonized unity, at
least in the symbolic action and the world of the imagination. In this
unity, the longing evoked by the evil of this world is seen as fulfilled.

Durkheim (1912: 325) recognizes in this form of idealization a general characteristic of collective self-presentation. Apparently, this ideal-
ism is a necessary part of our everyday life, an original utopianism that
proceeds according to the conviction that

> Heaven gives its glimpses only to those
> not in position to look too close.
> (*A Passing Glimpse,* Frost, 1958: 311)

However, this transfiguring fleeting glance includes but one side of the
social coin. The other side of the bourgeois marriage between the "principle of reality" and the "pleasure principle,"[12] which lives from the
smoothing-over of irreconcilable differences, shows the smoothing-over
process itself and at the same time, renders its background visible. In the
course of this process, a characteristic structural correspondence, namely,
the principle of affinity between the miner and his flying symbol comes
into view: An army of industrial workers, at first merely a mass that
moves into the new cities and is organized into troupes at work, chooses
as its heraldic beast a creature which, at least in the cities, appears in
masses and flies in flocks. The forever dirty work clothes face the el-
egance and beauty of the journeyman miner's uniform—and of the pigeons. The miner begins and ends his work like the pigeon begins and
ends its race—at the time clock.[13] The pigeon's flight time for the most
popular races (e.g., Vienna—Ruhr district), thirteen to fourteen hours, is
the same as a miner's workday used to be in the early days of industrial
mining—early days of his pigeon breeding, too. Training, discipline, and
work shifts—this is what is required of the miner and what he, in turn,

requires from his beloved pigeons. He disciplines his soul bird in the same way he has to discipline himself. What he experiences as his liberation in pigeon breeding and in the birds' flight has to do, among other things, with his carrying along as dowry into the pigeon relationship his own constraints: The kingdom of freedom he has created reflects all these constraints not only as their counterparts transformed into the realm of the good, it contains them physically.

However, the process of adaptation is not exclusively a one-way affair. To the same degree in which the breeder disciplines the pigeon, he himself is, in the true sense of the word, domesticated by the milieu he has created. The octogenarian pensioner Anton Schapler from Bottrop, for example, installed an alarm bell in his pigeon loft "so that he can get off the toilet fast enough when his pigeon comes back from a race. 'I've never traveled in all my life...never wanted to go traveling. Even Dortmund was too far for me. I've always stayed put, just 'cause of my pigeons.... I'm always up in my pigeon-loft'" (Hoffmann, 1982: 14).

Many of the other breeders are just as wedded to their pigeons as he is, to their pigeon lofts. Hardly a one changes his place of residence, even under the pressure of unemployment. Vacation trips don't take place. The pigeons and their breeders condition one another. Like the female pigeon, the breeder stays home, while the male pigeon takes the trip he has to take. The miners and their pigeons are lovers who impose upon themselves, too, a life-long mutual bond in precisely those gray and narrow places from which their longing and desire (purportedly) want to fly away.

The expression "identification," that hackneyed term in which the process of adaptation itself and its background are obscured or explained away in pseudo-psychological terms, does not fit the situation described here. The collier "identifies" just as little with the pigeon as the pigeon "identifies" with him. Both are made into victims of "identification" by their interpreters. Rather, the milieu of the miners and their carrier pigeons *as a whole* represents a symbolically fine-tuned and interpreted social form. Industrial labor, social origins, housing environment, traditions, habits of behavior, and interpretations—all these belong to the conditions under which the milieu, as a response to concrete historical problems, was formed, interpreted and made viable by those whose everyday life takes place in it. Attraction and repulsion, choice and rejection of possible actions, occur before a social-historically imposed background of problems and perceptions. This background influences action, interpretation and social organization in a decisive way. "Identifications" already belong to those ideologisms that originate in the specific perceptions of this historical situation.

Compared to earlier miners and pigeon fanciers, the miners have altered the original purpose of the messenger flight in an odd way. The carrier pigeons no longer carry messages, neither intimate love letters nor secret military information. Their new message is—if this be a message, indeed—the flight time, the "athletic" performance, the record. But the reader who recalls that up to 30,000 carrier pigeons participate in the races will doubt that this is a message. For the majority of breeders, the most important things are flight, arrival, and watching the pigeon, but above all the feeling of being a part of this total arrangement, this communally shaped social event.

If one compares the miner as pigeon keeper with his predecessors, the lovers, the commandants—in general, the letter writers, then one will find that the miners' pigeons are messengers without a message. Apart from their starting time, they are carrying "nothing" from somewhere to elsewhere. But, if there is something that *can* not exist within the human world, a world that is overburdened with meaning, significance and interpretations, then it is a symbolic action without that admixture of meaning that unites a social group, community, or society under its symbol.

What, then—from a sociological point of view—is the concrete message here?

VI

A collective symbol can, in general, be called the assembly, concentration, and organization of individual moods, feelings, and attitudes into a common reaction, a coloring of experience and feelings. The figurative form of such symbols enlivens the social worlds according to the image(s) of the respective societies that maintain them. Durkheim called the energies that nurture this invigoration of the world the "anthropomorphic instinct" (1912: 322).

In his attempt to reconstruct effect, appearance, and emotion of this energy, Durkheim comes across a social form of interpretation and organization that shows some fundamental parallels to the description of my "flying mole": totemism. Of course, this concept cannot be simply trans-

ferred to the phenomenon I described. The differences are too conspicuous between, on the one hand, the small, "archaic" groups that Durkheim,
Malinowski, and Firth described as totemistically organized and, on the
other hand, the mass of industrial miners in Europe in the nineteenth and
twentieth centuries. Nonetheless, the general principle of the collective,
symbolic self-illustration of a society that occurs in totemism can be
applied to the "flying mole" (by which I do not want to stylize the thus
described miner himself into a "totem creature" of the Ruhr district, even
though the coal and social politics of our country have occasionally acted
"totemistically" in this context).

The—to a great extent collective—decision by the miners to choose
pigeons as one of the symbols of their community proves the effectiveness of a network of conditions that produces something like a "totemistic
affinity." In it, along with the totemistic enlivenment, the enchantment of
the industrial world of the nineteenth and early twentieth centuries takes
place—all the way into "post-industrial" times. In this version of reality,
a (model) piece of the "old times" has an effect within the "modern" (or,
depending on one's taste, "post-modern") times, which in turn refer to
the old times by using the title "new age," obscuring their backward-
turning tendencies.

Neither the clan's God, its totem creature or its "flag of the clan" nor,
in general terms, the central collective symbol in which a community
portrays itself can be anything other than this community itself, "albeit
objectified and mentally imagined" (Durkheim, 1912: 284) under a symbolic form [plants, animal species, "more infrequently, useful inanimate
objects" (Malinowski, 1948: 6)]. Malinowski's descriptions of totemism
point in the same direction—in the belief in human power over a specific
species, we find expressed not only the belief in an affinity between the
nature of humans and animals or plants, but also a mixture of "utilitarian care of the necessary things in his environment" on the one hand, and
a preoccupation with things "that stimulate his imagination" like (for
instance) "pretty birds" on the other hand (Malinowski, 1948: 6).

Lévi-Strauss, in his short polemical treatise "Le Totémisme
aujourd'hui" (1962), discusses sense and nonsense in the use of the term
"totemism." He recommends, just as the German publisher who renamed
it "The End of Totemism" ("*Das Ende des Totemismus*") does, ending
the debate on totemism and forgetting the term "totemism" because of its
lack of clarity, or at least setting the debate to one side. But, while on the

one hand he gives the reader that advice, he is on the other hand quite obviously so fascinated both by the be-feuded word and the phenomena it is used for that he doesn't tire of circling round them reflectively and trying to include them in *his* method of thought.

In doing so, he comes to the same conclusion as I do in observing my "flying mole": "the animal kingdom and the plant kingdom are referred to not only because they are there, but because they offer human beings a method of thought" (1965: 22). Thus, in an expansion of my thesis, the chance arises to develop, with the help of a *symbolic* method of thought, a principle of social organization in which this method creates its own practical expression. Firth already described this principle in the abstract as the "core" of totemism (1930–1931). And in his interpretation of Firth, Lévi-Strauss, too, cannot help but concede the justification of this and thereby also of my thesis when he says that, although totemism is not a phenomenon *sui generis,* it is "a special case in the general framework of relationships between people" on the one hand and the elements of "his natural milieu" on the other (1965: 43).

Thus considered, totemism—I shall stick to the term—has two sides: One, it is to be seen as a form of organization of social groups and communities, a mode of organization in which the necessary activities and routines of everyday life are accounted for; two, it is a (religious) "system of beliefs and ceremonies" (Malinowski, 1948: 6).

Since the differences between a relatively anonymous mass of industrial workers on the one hand and a manageable number of blood-related clan members on the other are obvious, two questions then arise: (1) How is it that the miners in the second half of the nineteenth century revert to a very old principle of social organization—and to a quasi-totemistic, albeit (on the surface) religiously empty system of convictions? (2) Why do they choose carrier pigeons of all things as their symbol?

When the coal industry covered the Ruhr district with its collieries and steel factories in the 1880s, the population increased five-fold within a space of thirty years (from 605,000 to 3,000,000). People looking for work came primarily from the eastern parts or "Eastern Provinces" of the German Empire, many also from Poland, Italy, and Holland. They spoke different languages, came from different religious traditions, had different educational and work backgrounds. A large number of the workers were illiterate. Most of them knew or suspected that they would remain in the newly developing industrial areas for a long time, if not forever.

The mining companies began hastily erecting shabby mass housing. These housing developments were inhabited not only by the workers and their families, but also by chickens, pigs, sometimes even cows, but above all by goats and milking sheep—the "miners' cows." They were kept as vital food suppliers in the narrow backyards. At first, it was only the shared work, poverty, and the necessity of living at such close quarters that connected these workers and their families, not even the subsequently so strenuously evoked camaraderie and "solidarity." There was nothing that was precious to all alike, *although* or precisely *because it was not* part of their work life and the necessities of everyday survival, nothing that could thereby have bound them together: indestructibly and durably uniting dreams, wishes, and hopes.

According to everything we know about human communities and the principles of their organization, such a "something" could only be precious, indestructible, and durable if it did not threaten the specifically *necessary* structures of living together and of other vital activities—if, in fact, it promoted them. If such a "something" was to be acceptable to the miners as a whole, then no one within their own group must be hurt or excluded on the basis of religion or ethnicity, education or origin. In addition, this "something" had to fit into the shabby gray milieu of their habitation and work. On the other hand, it had to be capable of binding and uniting within itself all the various traditions, convictions, myths, legends, fairy tales, beliefs, and hopes of all the different groups. In short, it had to contain and visibly represent all tensions, contradictions, and differences of the concrete group, but at the same time cancel out the oppositions and overcome the tensions. It had to be a concrete collective symbol that fit exactly to this group, that the group had cut to order for itself.[14]

The interpreter as retrospective prophet[15] cannot but diagnose: If (but it could never happen in such a form) the miners would have consciously undertaken, say in a huge workers' meeting, to find that "something," they would have had no alternative but to select the carrier pigeon as the heraldic beast on the "flag of their clan." It unites all the different traditions, the dreams of freedom, the hope for happiness and peace, it embodies the longing for an unfettered existence and for physical space, it carries with it the aura of the sacred, of sacrifice as well as redemption.[16] And above all, the pigeon is adaptable practically without limit, just like its owner the miner, the human mole.

But there was more than the airy realm of dreams connected to the at first rather implicit choice of the pigeon as common symbol. In pigeon breeding and the organization of pigeon races, symbolic interpretation, symbolic action, and practical utilitarian purposes come together. In pigeon breeding, a principle of social organization had been found. From now on, one could interact in one's free time, particularly on weekends, yes, even "plan" that free time together, regardless of respective ethnic, religious, linguistic, social backgrounds. Pubs, houses (attics and rafters), and communal vehicles, Sundays and evenings, conversations, plans, communal kitties, all these were now organized under the symbol of the pigeon. This symbol imposed its mark on entire families with its lifestyle, its flight and food habits as well as its diseases. Pigeon breeding and air races established and guaranteed a "new" social order: The industrial miner, so distant from the semi-legendary collier of the Middle Ages in status, prestige, and historical timing, now no longer was merely worker—he became a "mate" (*Kumpel,* which subsequently came to mean both "miner" *and* "mate" or "pal" in German). In this term, the mass of miners identifies itself as a community. This foundation was in place long before the unions appeared on the scene; it was a decisive condition for the unions' successes in later times.

Everyday, practical orientation—a concrete social milieu and job constraints on the one hand, the utopian, upgrading re-evaluation of the constraints and one's own position in society on the other—illustrates not only the process of everyday life being superelevated, but also refers to *that which was in fact being consecrated: the new community and the task of maintaining that community.* In this way, the collective symbolism, in this case quasi-totemistic, creates the triumph of social meaning and tradition: the triumph of culture (Malinowski, 1948: 38) over the negative reaction of the human being to the constraints imposed upon him.

From an analytical point of view, the collective symbolism proves to be society's reaction to concrete historical problems for whose "solution" elements from the store of experience, the repertoires of symbols, and the knowledge of traditions' recipes (see Schütz and Luckmann, 1979: 37) usually seem inevitable or necessary. The solutions that are embedded in symbolic actions and interpretations contain problems and contradictions just as they contain their harmonization and the "superelevation" of the solutions: of the collective convictions which are in the process of establishing themselves. Symbolic actions are the responses to paradox, contradiction, and the experiencing of boundaries. They are remedies against "breakdowns." Moreover, one can read the respective social constructions of reality as well as the historical (and, in our case, the milieu-specific) conditions of the construction from the symbols, their usage, and their embeddedness in practical action. The life form of the flying mole is on the one hand determined by the historical-economic climate to which he must adapt—early capitalism, economic liberalism, industrialization. On the other hand, the resistance of everyday, practical action against an all-encompassing "colonization"[17] is apparent in the symbolic and living organization of one's specific life world.

However, in accordance with Hegel, one can observe that the development and recognition of paradoxes is almost always the result of a reflexive-analytic stance. It is the latter that divides harmony into its often contradictory elements, and traces the reasons for and process of harmonization. Thus, the sciences above all, but sometimes art as well, are the playground for paradoxes. In everyday life, the paradox ekes out a shadowy existence at best, but never flies freely over the roofs of the houses.

Notes

1. I have Didi Paus to thank for reviving these memories for me at the Soziologentag in Dortmund (1984) and thereby giving me the pleasure of tracking down my own fantasies as well as those of the miners and their (other) interpreters.
2. Talking about symbols also means using symbols: either consciously—by using their potential (e.g., the title of this article)—or unconsciously, by either not accounting for one's own symbolic expressions or by succumbing to the illusion that using a scientific language, "free" of images and metaphors and diluted into a "language of concepts," could suffice to shed the habit of thinking in symbols: language *and* thought are thereby diluted yet still they weave their own symbolic pattern.
3. Here and in the following, we are speaking exclusively of "real" or "transparency symbols." In this context see also: Soeffner, Hans-Georg (1989), *Emblematische und symbolische Formen der Orientierung*, in: Soeffner, H.-G., *Auslegung des Alltags und der Alltag als Auslegung*, Frankfurt: 158–84.
4. One of the loveliest and richest books on pigeons is by Hilmar Hoffmann. Although I consider Hoffmann's interpretation of the pigeon-breeding miners too empathetic and romanticizing, I am indebted to him for a wealth of information, inspiration, stories, and anecdotes. He saved me the trouble of doing a lot of my own research and at the same time offered me some highly pleasurable reading. Hoffmann, Hilmar (1982), *Das Taubenbuch*, Frankfurt.
5. Carrier pigeons as "information medium" of the press in the nineteenth century or in the year 1972 (Olympic sailing regatta in Kiel), in which a carrier pigeon conveyed press photographs from Kiel to Copenhagen faster than the Royal Danish Mail Service, made history just like those that were used by bootleggers during Prohibition in the U.S.
6. Originally "the gray-blue one."

7. In the depiction of a young girl holding a dove in her hand, the Greeks (in the fifth century B.C.) already linked the notions of bridal ceremony and death: That young girl was the allegorical "bride of Hades"—of the dead.

8. Bach, Johannes Sebastian, *The Passion of Our Lord according to St. Matthew's Passion*, transl. by the Rev. Dr. Troutbeck (1894), New York. Entombment, Nr. 74 recitative.

9. Already at an early date we come across the proverb, "He who wants to keep his house clean may not keep woman nor parson nor pigeons" (Hoffmann, 1982: 102).

10. See—as historical document—the reader for the colloquium *Paradoxes, Breakdowns, Cognitive Dissonance*, Dubrovnik, 29.3.—8.4.1989: 1.

11. In connection with the ever-present religious background to these motifs, see also Stefan Zweig "*Legende der Dritten Taube*" ("Legend of the Third Pigeon") "...she had flown out of the narrowness into the infinite vastness, from the dark into the light. But when she raised her wing now into the light, clear air, sweetly spiced by the rain, freedom suddenly surged around her and the grace of the unlimited" [Zweig, Stefan (1945, 1972), *Legenden*, Frankfurt: 224].

12. As a reminder of the origin of this terminology, see among others Freud, Sigmund (1920, 1975), *Studienausgabe*, Vol. III, *Psychologie des Unbewußten*, Frankfurt, "*Jenseits des Lustprinzips*": 213 (217)–72.

13. On the changes in the concept of time, the subjective understanding of time, and the organization of everyday life in the course of industrialization, see Thompson, E. P. (1967), *Time, Work-Discipline and Industrial Capitalism*, in *Past and Present 38*: 56–97.

14. The parallel to totemism becomes evident here, too: "Totemism standardizes man's practical and useful attitude of selective interest in his surroundings" [Malinowski, Bronislaw (1948), op. cit.: 37].

15. This characterization by Kierkegaard applies not only to philosophers, but also to sociologists. See Kierkegaard, Sören (1964), *Werke V, Philosophische Brocken*, Hamburg: 73.

16. And transfers that to the community that shares a common fate in the underground world—exemplarily invoked during mining accidents: In the worst case, the carrier-pigeon literally becomes the soul-bird of these "comrades-in-fate" (pointed out by Ulrike Krämer).

17. See in this context the discussion on Habermas's thesis of the "colonization of the life-world" by Richard Grathoff (1989), *Milieu und Lebenswelt*, Frankfurt, esp. 413 ff.

5

The Staging of Society—
Voting as Leisure-Time Activity

Introduction

When Alfred Schütz gave his lecture, in 1946, on the "well-informed citizen,[1]" he was seeking an answer to the following question: "What motives (move) adult human beings, who live their everyday life in our modern civilization, to recognize without question some parts of the traditional, relatively natural concept of the world and to question other parts?"[2] In the following, I shall deal only with the first part of the question and in doing so relate it to the concrete phenomena of electionlike procedures in German television shows.

Since, in addition, I fear I won't be able to penetrate to the heart of the "motives" that Schütz sought to discover, I will, while posing the same question, narrow it down yet again. I shall only examine the conditions that make adult people demonstrably accept without question, and in a wholly natural, everyday manner, a relatively precisely formed type of action—that of voting—which was originally related to the social framework of "politically responsible decision-making," within the new framework of entertainment programs on television. And not only do they accept and perform this type of action, they even seem to enjoy it.

I will consider only a few aspects of Schütz's lecture, but I must nonetheless present, in a very condensed form, some of the initial reflections which I share, in slightly different form, with Schütz. He described, in a fairly dispassionate way that distinguishes him from some of today's analysts,[3] above all without dramatizing bathos, as an "eminent basic feature of human life in the modern world...the conviction that the lifeworld as a whole" is never "completely understood" by anyone nor "completely understandable by any one human being."[4]

The structural causes for this conviction lie not only in the irrefutable and thus easily recited production of news and floods of information from mass media by which we are so threateningly surrounded that we can only find temporary shelter in islands of holiday quiet and contemplative, television-free Sunday hikes in the forest. The causes also lie, according to Schütz, in the social mobility which is to a large extent economically based and which encompasses nearly all areas of everyday life, in the concomitant transience and partial irrelevance of social relationships and the increasing uncommittedness and anonymity of many of the increasing social contacts "imposed"[5] upon us, contacts that we, according to our talent, perform in a routine, friendly, and "open" manner, or in a businesslike manner, but all in all in pretty much the same way. Just as our partners become for us, we become for them more and more "anonymous types who have no firm place in the social cosmos,"[6] with few exceptions. At the same time, though, we act and react, precisely because of our many social contacts, potentially within a framework of "hidden control by everyone."[7] Within this, admittedly very roughly depicted, situation characteristic of modern industrial societies, Schütz reconstructed, by creating three ideal types, the possibility of challenging, in public-political life, the unquestioning acceptance of imposed "matters-of-course." In these types, the differently structured approaches to everyday life are crystallized, in analytically pure form, according to action context, direction of attention, framework of relevance, and orientation of knowledge. Each one of us can, depending on the context we find ourselves in, realize *tendencies* of these three ideal type constructions. In his lecture, Schütz listed the ideal type of: (1) "expert"; (2) "the man in the street"; and (3) "the well-informed citizen."[8]

For the problem I am dealing with here, I shall confine myself to the ideal type of "the man in the street," which obviously includes "the woman in the street"—and ask why the studio audience that participates in certain entertainment programs doesn't abandon the "man in the street's" way of acting and knowing even when it is in a decision-making situation which—by all outward and formal appearances—is declared an election (1) with uncertain results and (2) between various alternatives. One would think that such a situation, again according to all formal appearances, would produce some uncertainty of action, that is, would dissolve the one-track "matter-of-course" into various "matters-of-course" and thereby tend to puncture the former.

Clues as to where one might find an answer to this question are already contained in Schütz's following characterization: The ideal type "man in the street" moves in his (also ideal typically constructed) social world helped by his knowledge of prescriptions for pretypified situations. "By following the prescriptions as though they were a ritual, he can achieve the desired results without asking why a certain procedural step has to be taken and why it has to be taken in precisely the prescribed order."[9] This rather vague knowledge is "*sufficiently* precise"[10] for all pretypified and familiar practical purposes. "In all affairs (however) that are not connected to such practical purposes of immediate importance, (the man in the street) allows himself to be guided by his emotions and passions. Under their influence, he constructs a complex of convictions and unclarified opinions on which he simply relies so long as they do not hinder him in his pursuit of happiness."[11]

However plausible this characterization is, it contains, as is proper for ideal types, on the one hand too many general regulations—in this case for practical action—and too few specific ones for the concrete situations such as we will be examining. On the other hand, it does point to a spectrum of potential development trends, without trying to anticipate concrete historical phenomena. In the following I shall examine one of these concrete phenomena.

Competitors without Competition

When in 1988 the Dortmunder Aktienbrauerei (DAB), a German brewery, called for a "nationwide DAB election" (*Bundes-DAB-Wahl*), the parody on the German Parliamentary elections (*Bundestagswahl*) was probably only accidental, albeit fitting. Such linguistic puns are, of course, obligatory for this type of advertisement. Advertising took up a pattern here that in turn cited political elections; on the one hand the pattern gave this ritualized decision-making scheme a different framework, and on the other it let the ballot run through more or less original metamorphoses.

Thus, in the show "*Wünsch Dir was!*" ("Make a Wish!"), hosted by Dietmar Schönherr and Vivi Bach, the television candidates were chosen by the viewers in their homes by flushing the toilet or turning electrical switches on and off. (The debate on wasting energy had not yet become "internalized.") In the stiff, yet carefully arranged opinion brawl in the television show "*Pro und Contra,*" the audience votes *in the* studio, by pressing buttons, in a competition between two "opinions" and their protagonists, although as viewers they are excluded from the discussion itself. The serial show "*Wie würden Sie entscheiden?*" ("How Would You Decide?") promotes the television viewer to the position of weekend judge in legal cases which are first (in realistic detail) reconstructed and shown in realistic detail. Some hit parades replace the lists of top sellers with a sort of absentee vote from their audience, or via the computer-controlled TED system which evaluates telephone calls. The Coca-Cola radio ads may accord even less intelligence to their listeners than our state accords its voters—it cuts in half the possible choices to a decision between only two alternatives (in this case: two songs). In addition, the absentee ballot method also was the godfather for the BRAVO (a German youth magazine concerned mainly with pop and rock stars and their music) Otto awards for most popular popstar, actor, and the like, as well as for other magazine and television elections. Here, the aim is to elect the "athlete," "computer," "car," "book," and so on, "of the year".

The Rudi-Carrell-Show (a German talk show) on the other hand, a show I shall be compelled to return to later on, has the audience decide, via the push of a button, not on opinions, but on the "best" performance of five imitation artists. In the show "*Wetten, daß?*" ("Do You Want to Bet?")—formerly hosted by Frank Elstner, now by Thomas Gottschalk—things appear to proceed in a perfectly natural way. Here, the best "audience bet" is voted on via the traditional "articulation repertoire" of audiences—clapping, whistling, howling, stamping of feet, and the like. This bawdiness however, well rehearsed and arranged in the studio, is precisely measured. The voting procedure is accomplished with the help of hit-parade-trained TED, the "votes" coming in from the generalized viewer "out there" (if that viewer owns a telephone).

One could go on listing the election possibilities[12] indefinitely. But our examples will have to suffice for the time being as reminder and illustration, even though it would be tempting to digress in order to consider the telephonic election of the "movie of the week." For that election shows in an exemplary fashion, like many other repeat broadcasts, the media's basic tendency toward self-reference. The collective memory of the audience, not only for entertainment programs, retrieves canned experience from the media's storage shelves in order to enjoy their own memories. Yet in both cases, the "meals" are chosen from a not exactly overly extensive nor, apparently, overly extendable menu, cooked and ultimately eaten in one and the same restaurant.

We will find, in the description and discussion of these phenomena, the general hypothesis that the audience—in other words, potentially all of us—enters an "illusory world" by "surrendering to the media." Where this hypothesis fails is where it cannot deliver what it would urgently require as proof: that "real world" whose "illusion" would be the other one. And then, it obscures the experience that is implicitly familiar to us all, that every one of the—many—social worlds is, as long as one's attention is on it, "real in its own way."[13] Thus it also obscures the possibility of describing what the conditions, actions, methods of attention, and attitudes[14] are by which we give—or remove—the accent of reality to how we experience our surroundings.

If one looks at the status that television—as an *activity* by the audience—has in the context of everyday activities,[15] how one is attentive to it, and what other activities, apart from the proverbial "getting up for a beer during half-time," accompany watching it, then one finds that watching television is not only overestimated as an activity for the reception of information or bad/good influences, but that the concentration with which the "normal" viewer performs this activity is also overrated. As soon as the medium has been introduced and given its place in the everyday life of a society, the activity "watching television" is accompanied by secondary activities, especially the genre "entertainment program" ("show," "quiz," etc.), which is made up of numerous subgenres.[16] Or it becomes a secondary activity itself. Particularly this type of program with its mixture of elements from musical, ballet, quiz, and contest, by its very structure encourages the combining of diverse activities. It permits the viewer—unfortunately only the viewer at home—to enter and leave the program at any given time.

Doubling the number of viewers with a "representative" group of viewers in the studio has, among many other functions, that of nailing to the show place—with the help of entrance tickets and contact-happy cameras—that small part of the public that is necessary in order to stage a live show. That part of the public is necessary; its applause is supposed to suggest suspense, atmosphere, and "acceptance" to those "out there," sitting in front of their screens. As all studies have shown, it is after all the camera facing into the audience that is more effective than canned applause and laughter.[17]

And applause makes recognizable that original voting situation that has always been tied to the dramatic arts, to shows—the audience judging an actor, a conductor, an author, a composer, an ensemble, a soloist, and so on. Consistent booing and whistling—although only when they in fact kept the audience away permanently—used to mean, in practical terms, performance and performers were deposed. The studio audience of today hardly has this option. On the contrary, it (the audience) is used, outwardly, as an indicator of the interest in the program itself. So that it cannot boo the performance *as a whole,* the audience has to become actor itself, be included in the ensemble, even if in a very limited way (e.g., in the full swing of booing).

An omnipresent actor is, apart from the largely anonymous audience, its so-called communicator: the show master (or "host"). The variables are, in our context of "request" programs, the stars and prominent guests. There, too, the mixture is decisive (apart from the general degree of familiarity, independent of personality): People from public life—today— are those who are present in the media (self-reference of the media). So each group, according to genre or type of media, must send its representative: the prominent athlete, the politician, the actor, the expert and, not to be forgotten, the showmaster of another show. Society portrays itself in the media the way the media portrays society. In other words: The media are a *reality* medium of society. They constitute forms of presentation through which society is attentive to itself and lends a specific accent of reality to this kind of attention *itself.*

So, since it is impossible to dis-elect the ensemble and almost impossible to dis-elect the showmaster as the audience's conversation partner, the self-reference and self-thematization of the members of the ensemble among themselves would lead to an inexorable demise of what is in fact the goal, the show, if it weren't for the "material" from the "outside," that is, those who are to be elected, the candidates. Where are they to be found? Or, to be exact, where does one find, *over and over again,* people who are familiar with the rules, the genres, the prominent personalities and their techniques of self-presentation, without themselves being from the first ranks of society? Among the viewers who have been trained in countless evenings in front of the television. Request programs like "Do You Want To Bet?" ("*Wetten daß?*") or the "Rudi-Carrell-Show" are performances in which a screen audience (those who determine television ratings) watches a partially participating studio audience. The studio audience elects members of the former screen audience as the best and most original, as kings and queens for the evening in a monarchy of one-day wonders.

Those who want to be elected have to be able to offer something in return for the honor. And if they have not yet taken a seat in the box of the theater of society, not yet attracted attention with the qualities for which boxes are generally bestowed, they have to choose the unusual as subject and performance material. The person in question thereby becomes "visible," but only temporarily and in the sense of the exotic and conspicuous. The consequence: In the show, he steps into the limelight: in society, he remains where he was, but now equipped with the devotional souvenir objects to remind him of the big moment: plaque, prize, video tape.

Facing the relatively small structural sector of possibilities of being temporarily elected is the sheer limitless repertoire of the unusual, by whose portrayal one hopes to be elected. The kings of wager share with the *Guinness Book of Records'* record holders the same social origins. If one would include the kings of wager in the *Guinness Book of Records,* then one would merely be expanding by yet another group this "Who"s Who" of those who have never had a share in media publicity and never could have, unless they stood out through exotic and unusual efforts or performances that border on the ridiculous. Here, the commonly not honored is for once honored, namely by virtue of somebody doing something that others consider not worth the effort —eating the largest sausage, smoking the most cigarettes simultaneously, crossing the United States on one's hands.

Still, this only describes one side of the social "dramaturgy of a chamber of absurdities."[18] The other side points up how much creating monsters serves us, the society as audience, how it secures and confirms our own social "normality." It secures our belief in the universality of the normal when we see the uniqueness of the extraordinary—but it also serves to "teach the newcomer clear differentiation between the various factors of reality as they are conceived in his culture."[19]

The candidates in our election programs then don't in fact compete with the opponent whom the society-as-audience has long before elected as the *"real"* personality, who in other words cannot possibly be beaten by those "little people" dressed up as exotic creatures. Nor do they compete—in the *classic* sense—with one another, since they line up in different disciplines. There are those who recognize—or not—crayons by their taste and those who can park a truck on beer glasses without shattering them: here, swimmers are competing with mountaineers. If anywhere, then it is here that that fundamental aspect of modern, highly labor-dividing society becomes visible, that for instance shows up as a background motive of increasing specialization in the *election* of a profession: avoiding competition[20] in what only appears to be a contest.

Nonetheless, the voters are supposed to compare the candidates in these election programs. Where, then, is the measure, if not in the comparison of the disciplines and performances? To look for the answer in a comparison of superlatives, that is, of the "most extraordinary," would merely show that the extraordinary becomes expected and ordinary in its perpetually newly staged frequency.

Container for "Perishables"—The Frame Makes the Message[21]

In the course of the seventeenth century, that genre we now call "news" gradually developed as international trade spread and organized. But its relatively stable form, astonishingly consistent to this day, only came about when a shift began, in the course of this development, from the pure exchange of market information to a mixture that generally contained everything that was, at first only for the "educated classes," interesting, new, and surprising, apart from the economic and political data.

Quite early, the rarely examined phenomenon occurred that hand-in-hand with the seemingly inexhaustible multitude and variety of news was a fixed form and a highly invariable framework, linked by the diversity and disparity of the new and classified and ordered according to sectors. It is but one of the visible consequences of this fixed form that early on, those social representatives who considered some newsreporter or themselves interesting or newsworthy, adapted to the new genre in their presentation and—in collaboration with the spreading pictorial media—submitted to a specific social iconography.[22]

A different, far more significant consequence of this framework constancy is that not the news itself, but rather the framework of the genre "news" establishes the credibility of the reported items for the audience.[23] Ultimately, it is not new and interesting facts that make a news program, it is the genre "news program" that makes a fact and a news item out of the "new" and "interesting" thing.

Thus the genre itself presents a strange picture: While the events seem to follow one another in rapid succession in the reports, the framework itself and its never-changing stage freeze into standing pictures.[24] If one looks today at the pictorial framing of television news from beginning to end—and there are only minor albeit typical genre deviations from one country to another—time seems to stand still. There they sit, the newscasters, world and state maps behind them, in front of them their microphones, and comment on the statesmen greeting each other and shaking each others' hands, the group photos from conferences, the low or high-flying goals in international soccer tournaments, the iconography of wars, earthquakes, catastrophes—always in the same order, the same time frame, at the fixed time, with the indestructible, time-resistant ensemble of newscasters.

The genre is both typical and style-shaping for the media. It not only represents the structure that is generally true for traditional genres: framing, forming, allocating, and evaluating social knowledge,[25] it also refers—as a specific form in which the same old familiar, daily special is concocted from the multitude of ingredients using the genre's principles of order and depiction—to a pattern that can be appropriated for other, similar purposes. It demonstrates prototypically how the constant "need-to-be-new" or "extraordinary," the seemingly disparate (competition, musical, ballet, wagering, video clip), and the participant ensembles can be linked by a specific *form* that doesn't allow any deviations and yet maintains the illusion of independence.

Everything seems to be in constant motion. The "never-before-seen-or-heard" is obligatory, only to be filed away immediately after it has been aired. The whole practice of performance suggests a change that in fact does take place *outside* of the television programs. But "while everything changes incessantly, [the] members [of society] have to be...convinced that society does not change—at least not within a certain period of time and in certain aspects."[26]

Copied Copies—Social Duplication without Original

The relatively high constancy of the frame corresponds with the constancy of the roles within the ensemble. This is particularly evident in that group that shows the greatest turnover of personnel and hence seems to change the most: the audience. The formula applied here is: Constancy through structural redoubling!

As for the—respectively different—situations of viewing, reception, and action of screen audience and studio audience, these I have mentioned above. This outline of the action and attitudinal background before which the studio and screen audiences move as voters for the king or queen of wagering, or other dignitaries, shall now be amplified a bit. Obviously, although the foot-stamping, clapping, whistling, booing viewer is a voter, he is not visible as an individual, but only as part of the collectivity that is responsible for the decision. In other words, he is not responsible for the decision as an individual, but only as part of the group. Although this occurs not wholly anonymously—for at times, the camera lovingly pans in on individual faces in the crowd—the studio audience nonetheless represents, *for all intentions,* the anonymous audience in front of its television screens at home.

Condemned to partial participation—no-one can know in advance when the cameraman and the director at his or her monitor will turn their attention to the individual—he or she can only, if he doesn't fancy booing himself out of "business," collaborate in the show's success. Especially if the individual—now representative of both audience groups, that in the studio and that in front of the screens—may step into the middle of the stage, as elected one-night master of the studio betting, may join the prominent personalities sitting in the circle of comfortable armchairs there. He is now—for about 120 minutes—one of them, at least he has to be addressed and questioned as though he were, for the duration of the show, so that his presence is not forgotten. The other viewers whose elected representative he is might resent that as a sign of indifference toward "the man in the street." If they looked more closely, however, they would discover that this resentment would be all they have: the choice of detecting either indifference or embarrassed friendly condescension toward their representative.

The system of representation that multiplies and reproduces itself now shows the following picture: For the space of two hours, a de-anonymized viewer represents a partially de-anonymized group of viewers, who in turn represent the anonymous viewers "of the nation." These for their part recruit from among themselves the candidates for election who escape the collective anonymity for a few minutes, finally acting rather than watching and—before once again sinking back into their role of viewer—became eligible for the delegates of their electorate, that is, the viewers.

It is inevitable that both the studio audiences and the candidates film their performances with video recorders—the ones in order to later watch themselves watching, the others in order to watch others watching them. It is an act of documenting a social relevance consisting in having been visible at least once (1) for many others, (2) in the media, and (3) on videotape.

The viewer repeats and reinforces the collectively approved publicity pattern and a basic conviction of his society. It is true for him as viewer/actor, as well as for the prominent performers from politics, sports, (entertainment) culture: Whoever doesn't exist in the media, doesn't exist, or exists merely in a shadow world. In a practical and at the same time symbolic way, this conviction combines in a specific, unifying ritual in the show "Do You Want to Bet?": A prominent guest takes on the bet of one or a group of those everyday people who appear as candidates. It goes without saying that he for his part takes on the obligation, according to the redoubling mechanism, if he loses his bet to undertake something spectacularly charitable, philanthropic, or simply notable. This act can then be inserted into a sequel program as a canned image and documentation; thus we can preserve friendly memories of the person in question regardless of whether he wins or loses. It is hardly surprising that prominent personalities for their part and for a brief period of time, "playfully" slip back into the role of the "man in the street." That fits into the picture, a visible expression of which we had in the guise of the minister-president of the Saarland, who—Harun al Rashid posing as our buddy—dressed up in a journeyman miner's uniform, played in a miners' band before his secret was aired on stage, and then proceeded to take his place in the circle of armchairs appropriate to his class.

Whoever suspects—following a traditional sociological habit of thinking—that the "real existing" difference between "those up there" and "those down there" is consciously concealed (whatever "conscious" may mean in the context of television entertainment programs) by such stagings, is missing the point that there is not much left that needs concealing. Master and servant, prominent personalities and their admirers, are so close in their basic convictions and probably also qualities that the problem is not to conceal existing differences, but that these differences practically no longer exist in this sector of self-staging and external presentation.

The "Rudi-Carrell-Show" lives on this: Here, the audience chooses one of five candidates who is the best stand-in for a so-called original

(Mireille Matthieu—viz. Edith Piaf, Howard Carpendale, etc.). In the form of citing citations,[27] standing in for stand-ins, it is less a question of who resembles which—by now rare indeed—original than of repeating, confirming, and possibly reinforcing patterns of presentation which, themselves collectively approved forms of presentation, are the precondition for actors becoming presidents and for presidents or chancellors becoming sometimes (but rarely) passable actors.

On the level of presentation, the contours blur between accepting the portrayal of a personality (by a stand-in) and the personality as the portraitist, between the princess and the tennis queen. Thus for example in the headline "The Princess Plays with the Tennis Queen."[28] The photograph under this headline shows Princess Di(ana) smiling in embarrassment next to the self-assured Steffi Graf who—the point of this arrangement—gave the Princess her tennis racket after the game; at least a slight variation on tossing one's Adidas sweatband into the crowd.

If the point is neither the election of those who give unusual performances—the inflation of unusual kings of wager makes such elections seem senseless—nor the election of "unmistakable originality" in the face of the ubiquitousness of stand-ins, what then creates the social appeal of elections in television entertainment programs? It can be but one part of the explanation that the elections themselves, making decisions about others, can be enjoyed in relaxed, carefree, and gamelike situations, because it seems to open up whole expanses of freedom and availability. What remains open is the question of *what* is being decided and whether this "what" still has any significance at all.

All Taste Comes from the People

The type of "opinion quiz" shows ("Pro und Contra," "How Would You Decide?"), which I have thus far scarcely touched upon, highlights the content-related point which we shall now, in conclusion, focus on. But there are more than mere trace elements in the short interviews "concerning the person" or concerning "personal interests" in the other entertainment programs, too.

The show "How Would You Decide?" alludes to the fictionality of the decision and background for the decision by using the subjunctive in its title, and at least demands opinions from the audience as decision bearers, opinions formally dressed up as reasons. "Pro and Contra," on the other hand, takes up an already mentioned pattern, albeit in slightly modified form. Prominent personalities (politicians, journalists, television moderators, experts) appear as protagonists of two opposing yet thoroughly popular and familiar opinions—as standard bearers of familiar stereotypes. Since the goal is to draw some of the opponent's supporters over to one's own side in the course of the broadcast, everything initially seems to be heading for a contest of arguments. On the other hand, arguments on the side of stereotypes usually have the stereotypes' quality, that is, they divide the thematic stereotypes into subgroups of stereotypes. So, the persuasiveness of the speakers is hardly nurtured by the arguments, but rather by the protagonists' rhetoric and the "impression management": by the art of performance displayed according to the situation.

The repertoire of stylistic devices for successful performances at a given time in history has changed but little since its analysis and propagation in Tertullian's antique rhetoric. However, at certain times different levels of presentation have stepped into the foreground. Where for a while it was "polished speech," the succession of pointedly formulated arguments, the bathos of one's own publicly staged righteousness or of a collective moral, for some time now it has become hard to overlook that make-up of mawkishness that is accompanied rhetorically by such expressions as "that really somehow moved me a lot, touched me, horrified me, left me speechless." While formerly, the presentation of feelings had to be performed with an appropriately stylized pattern of gestures and facial expressions, now it is already enough to present a purely linguistic marking of emotions like "mourning," "fear," and that ubiquitous "being moved" that will not go away.

Thus, a gradual transformation is now taking place from the mere opinion mannequin to the mannequin of attitudes and feelings. No matter how different the opinions propagated may be, some of their adherents will yet unite in their *common liking* of the performance and the publicly staged empathizing.

Schütz still found, in his essay on the "well-informed citizen," that "socially approved knowledge...draws its power and approval from the authority of the persons representing and conveying it [the knowledge] (parents, scholars, sages, priests, etc.)"[29] and that, in accordance, in the public-political discussion "only the person *who* is recognized as expert or well-informed citizen is *valued* as such"[30] (emphasis added). In this context, he could define the socially accepted knowledge as "the origin of public opinion" and equally as "the source of prestige."[31] At the same time, he described how the increasing attention to and effect of opinion polls (the U.S. in the year 1946!) made a new trend visible that was undermining those old structures. For after all, in opinion polls it is not experts or well-informed citizens who make preliminary political decisions by suggesting tendencies, but rather, the "people in the street," those who do not expose themselves, who make preliminary decisions about their exponents and vice-versa. The so-called opinion leaders borrow their opinions from those whose opinions are led. The opinion of the man in the street "which is the public opinion as one understands it today, becomes more and more socially acceptable, to the detriment of the informed opinion, and thus forces itself upon the better-informed member of the community as an imposed relevance" (Schütz, 1946).[32]

The monthly (German) national quiz called "How Would You Vote if Parliamentary Elections Were Held Today?" is thus structurally more than a mere recording of the trends in public opinion. Implicitly, it makes it appear as though there were incessant elections: the opinion poll borrows characteristics from elections and conversely, the election that finally really takes place seems merely the temporarily last installment in a serial opinion poll—the one as irrelevant and without consequences as the other.

Since political elections are not only accompanied by the show elections and their patterns, but are, in terms of the presentational devices in the public staging of persons, in part co-formed and also framed—not only on election nights—by entertainment programs and shows, the political elections on Sundays and their little brothers and sisters, the elections in entertainment programs, begin to resemble each other so closely that they merge and blend into one single family, one total figure: voting as *one* of the many entertaining activities in the vast field of leisure-time behavior.

As a result, some, but not all, contents of socially accepted knowledge tend to start shifting. A desire for information about the *opinions* of others is superimposed on the desire for information about events, plans, and actions. Not the events are of interest, but rather, the opinions about the events, and not even the opinions themselves, but rather, the public presentation of an opinion with the stamp of authenticity lent by the presented, legitimizing emotion. It is thus no longer sufficient for the presenters to surf on the crest of the opinion wave. They must also be qualified in the practice of staging emotions.

But the public, repeated, and ever newly to-be-staged presentation of feelings was and is the job of actors, who thereby—this is the special aesthetic quality of their profession—submit, not exclusively but largely, to the audience's *judgment based on taste.*

And with this, my argumentation comes to a close. The decisions handed down in the entertainment programs' elections have taken on, almost exclusively, the character of judgments based on taste. These voting habits are transferred to a large extent to the sphere of political elections, along with their practices of presentation and staging. The structural similarity of the action patterns followed by prominent personalities and their audiences—the electing-each-other, watching, observing, and imitating—is complemented by a decision-making criterion that unites both groups and is accepted by both as well. That criterion consists of having a taste for the public presentation and for the mutual examination and coordination of tastes in the media. On this side of economic and political structures and events, a public sphere is established that subjects the traditional theater of public presentation to the genres and means of depiction of a media-defined aesthetic.

In the reciprocity of the behavior of public actors on the one hand and the "man in the street" on the other, the viewer-as-decision maker in television show and opinion poll experiences himself, *in individual instances,* as sovereign in taste and thus—enjoying himself and redeemed in individual instances for his habitual invisibility—as an equal among equals. It seems to be the case that not "emotions and passions"[33] themselves guide the public political audience, as Schütz assumed, but rather, the media-supported *taste for the presentation of emotions and passions* and therewith a thus-far ignored sector of socially approved knowledge: the knowledge of taste.

The change in the theater of political/public life and its practices of presentation described by Sennett (1983) has now, after the legitimation through the presented *authenticity of the emotion,* found its way to a new decision-making criterion for judging public action and its presentation: the criterion of taste and its genres. In their specific way, media-produced and over-formed genres thereby support the societal task not only in constructing images of world and society, but also in collective self-presentation, self-observation, and self-enjoyment!

Functionally, these constructions remain—in spite of all changes—within the traditional framework of the social production of knowledge and images which Xenophanes of Kolophon (570–474/470 B.C.) is said to have described thus: If cattle could create images of the Gods, then they would create images that resemble cattle. So if the "man in the street," that is, all of us in his role, want to create social models, what do we think they will look like?

Notes

1. Schütz, Alfred (1972), *Der gut informierte Bürger,* in Schütz, A., *Gesammelte Aufsätze II, Studien zur soziologischen Theorie,* Den Haag, 85–101.
2. Ibid., 87.
3. See Habermas, Jürgen (1985), *Die Neue Unübersichtlichkeit, Kleine Politische Schriften V,* Frankfurt, and Beck, Ulrich (1986), *Risikogesellschaft. Auf dem Weg in eine andere Moderne,* Frankfurt.
4. Schütz, Alfred (1972), *Der gut informierte Bürger,* in Schütz, A., *Gesammelte Aufsätze II,* op. cit., 85.
5. On the problem of socially imposed relevancies see A. Schütz, op. cit, 95.
6. Ibid., 95.
7. Ibid., 95.
8. Ibid., 87 ff.
9. Ibid., 87.
10. Ibid., 87.
11. Ibid., 87 f.
12. My co-workers Thomas Lau and Andreas Voß collected some quite astonishing material. I owe them both for the taped audiovidual material and for quite a few unsuccessful battles against drowsiness while "evaluating" the material.
13. Schütz, Alfred (1972), *Don Quixote und das Problem der Realität,* in Schütz, A., *Gesammelte Aufsätze II,* op. cit., 103.
14. See Soeffner, Hans-Georg (1988), *Kulturmythos und kulturelle Realität(en),* in Soeffner, H.-G. (ed.) (1988), *Kultur und Alltag, Soziale Welt,* Sonderband 6, 3–20.
15. For the still displeasing state of the research, see Deutsche Forschungsgemeinschaft (ed.) (1986), *Medienwirkungsforschung in der Bundesrepublik Deutschland, Teil I Berichte und Empfehlungen; Teil II Dokumentation.* Katalog der Studien. Enquête der Senatskommission für Medienwirkungsforschung unter dem Vorsitz von Wilfried Schulz und der Mitarbeit von Joe Groebel, Weinheim.
16. See Kreuzer, Helmut (1982), *Sachwörterbuch des Fernsehens,* Göttingen, 67.
17. See among others Oevermann, Ulrich (1979), *Exemplarische Analyse eines Ausschnitts aus einem Protokoll einer Fernsehsendung "Dalli Dalli,"* MS, Frankfurt.
18. Goffman, Erving (1977), *Rahmen-Analyse. Ein Versuch über die Organisation von Alltagserfahrungen,* Frankfurt, 42.
19. Eibl-Eibesfeld, Irenäus (1970), *Liebe und Haß. Zur Naturgeschichte elementarer Verhaltensweisen,* Munich (12, 1985), 85.
20. See Noelle-Neumann, Elisabeth, and Reumann, Karl (1971), *Nachrichtenwesen,* in Noelle-Neumann, E., and Schulz, W. (eds.) (1971), *Publizistik,* Frankfurt, 195 ff.

21. In this context see the discussion on the "iconography of power" in television news broadcasts, among others in Helmut Kreuzer (ed.), *Sachwörterbuch des Fernsehens*, op. cit., 150.
22. Ibid.
23. One of the few successful structural analyses of the genre "information" is to be found in Angela Keppler (1985), *Präsentation und Information. Zur politischen Berichterstattung im Fernsehen*, Tübingen.
24. Hans Ulrich Gumbrecht refers to this state of affairs ("*Variation ohne Veränderung/ohne Geschichte*") in his article "'*Ihr Fenster zur Welt' oder Wie aus dem Medium 'Fernsehen' die 'Fernsehwirklichkeit wurde,*'" in Soeffner, H.-G. (ed.) (1988), *Kultur und Alltag*, op. cit., 234–50.
25. See Luckmann, Thomas (1986), *Grundformen der gesellschaftlichen Vermittlung des Wissens: Kommunikative Gattungen*, in Neidhardt, F., Lepsius, M. R., and Weiss, J. (eds.) (1986), *Kultur und Gesellschaft*, Sonderheft 27 of the *Kölner Zeitschrift für Soziologie und Sozialpsychologie*, Opladen, 191–211; and Bergmann, Jörg (1987), *Klatsch. Zur Sozialform der diskreten Indiskretion*, Berlin, esp. 35 ff.
26. Halbwachs, Maurice (1967), *Das kollektive Gedächtnis*, Frankfurt (1985), 155.
27. See among others Baudrillard, Jean (1978), *Kool Killer oder der Aufstand der Zeichen*, Berlin.
28. *Bonner Generalanzeiger*, 11 June 1988.
29. Schütz, Alfred (1972), *Der gut informierte Bürger*, in Schütz, A., *Gesammelte Aufsätze II*, op. cit., 100.
30. Ibid.
31. Ibid.
32. Ibid., 101.
33. Ibid., 87f.

6

Borrowed Charisma—Populist Stagings

In the usage of the modern media they are practically treated as siblings: the charismatic and the populist. As soon as a new face stands out recognizably in the crowd of familiar politicians and delegates, one starts searching for potential charismatic strains in the person. To be charismatic nowadays apparently means to be eligible (or already prognostically elected).

As a result, there often comes about a hidden, at times titillating, often uncanny alliance between the so-called personalities of public life and their audience. The latter, for the greater part condemned to spending its life firmly in nonpublic life, spends a large proportion of its (supposedly) political actions approving or disapproving of the performances by the public actors. While the audience searches for charismatic sheen or the flair of the extraordinary in the socially "distinguished" persons (i.e., those who are to be distinguished or are striving toward becoming distinguished), the latter strive to decorate themselves with the traits expected from them.

One tends to attribute if not the character of the unique, then at least that of the rare to what is unusual. But in conspicuous contradiction to this uniqueness is the sheer multitude of those who consider themselves to be participating in "public life." Since they are denied scarcity and inimitability, the only thing left many "public" persons is to distinguish themselves strenuously from the multitude of others *on this side* of the unusual, insofar as they are more concerned with their popularity than with fulfilling the tasks and obligations of their office.[1]

For this kind of procedure of distinguishing oneself, human societies have always had the matching costumes, techniques, backdrops, and "pre-typified" situations at the ready—with the variations appropriate to the historical and cultural settings. These repertoires are often fed, especially in the public ceremonial arena, by attributes that appear to be surrounded by a charismatic aura because they were formerly "used" by charismatic persons or connected with them in some way. They are usually ritualized patterns of action embedded by tradition in the public knowledge of public representation and its forms—specific forms of presentation for the unusual and the noneveryday.[2]

Unlike in strictly hierarchically ordered societies in which the few elevated social positions with their arrangements, action patterns, ceremonies, and situations are largely prescribed and determined structurally, modern, "democratically" organized societies give room—also structurally—to populism. On the flat roof of an ever-broadening social "pyramid" a battle ensues—sometimes for the smallest elevations. The paradoxical interplay of "ideologically" and legally postulated equality on the one hand, and the claim on the other hand that only the best in a given society are eligible as representatives of the people, seems to allow no more than the smallest elevations, where it is no longer controlled by the political rationale of the "well-informed citizen,"[3] namely, the pragmatically consensually restrained "extraordinary."

Even for official charisma there is limited space here. It is restricted to some small number of positions that derive from and are secured by long tradition.[4] Personal charisma, though, is (and always was) at "cross-purposes" to any form of society and state: It proves itself in times of crisis and presumably derives from whatever constitutes a threat to order (see below).[5] Not so populism; it lives and thrives in practically any social field, and blooms all the more profusely the more it borrows (or lends itself) the appearance of charisma.

As someone who is used to dancing at very different balls and is at home in fundamentally different situations, the populist is a social chameleon. Like Grimmelshausen's "Baldander," he has to be "now big, now small, now rich, now poor, now high, now low, now happy, now sad, now mean, now kind, and all in all now thus and now different."[6] But as adaptable and blurred populists are as individuals, one can nonetheless differentiate within their group between various types of actors, who in turn have recourse to various patterns of action and presentation: to excerpts and parts of that repertoire that society holds ready for their emulation.

In the following, I shall concentrate on two forms of presentation or elements of figuration that share a common symbolic type of action. In so doing, my aim is to (re)construct ideal types, albeit not (primarily) "personal types." Rather, my focus is on "typical," ritual ceremonial presentational devices which some actors evidently consider of great significance for "political acting" and the concomitant practice of performance: in the hope of having chosen, from society's jewel-box or perhaps its box of precious ornaments, those insignia that elevate the trivial to the special and earn it the rating "valuable."

Two Scenes
I

For the past seventy-two years, veterans of World War I have been meeting annually at the soldiers' cemetery in Verdun in memory of the fallen soldiers. After the Second World War, this cemetery became a place both for the French and the Germans where not only veterans met, but also statesmen and political representatives of both nations, to combine the memory of the victims of both wars with gestures of reconciliation and later of friendship as well. To the military ceremonies of laying down wreaths, lowering flags, and parading at the "grave of the unknown soldier" were added political declarations and appeals. The predictability, repetition, and length of the ceremonial gradually made of the soldiers' cemetery at Verdun a ritually designated place, a prominent place for memorial figures and declamations, for admonitions and vows. The grave of the unknown soldier as a symbolic form of collective emotion, this memorial which is seen as a symbol of technically perfect wars of mass destruction becomes, in public opinion, a cult place for the simple, "unknown" soldier, not (or no longer) recognizable as an individual. Yet by so doing, the cult anonymizes not only the victim(s) but also the perpetrators: the perpetrators are no longer Ares or Mars, but "the" war. The symbolic superelevation of the "unknown soldier" and of the ritually offered veneration accorded him in the form of wreaths suggest that any one of us could be in that grave. But characteristically enough, there is no grave of the "unknown civilian." Women and children are excluded.

Moreover, anonymizing the victim has the effect that the "any one of us" turns into a "none of us." The sadness presented and probably at times really felt is not directed at a person or persons. The "admonishment" is directed at everyone and thus ultimately at no one directly and personally. Ritually formed staging of emotions in collective memorial celebrations is, simultaneously, a domestication of emotions. The venerated "unknown soldier," that faceless creature, can become a common denominator across national borders and a collective symbol as well, because it addresses perfectly the horror of war, at the same time depersonalizing it and removing it from immediately comprehensible experience; because it harmonizes, in the symbol of the anonymous and the responding ritual procedure, the catastrophe of which it purports to be warning us; because it accords the former enemies an (anonymizing) commonality which is without conflict precisely because it doesn't occupy a place in the *personal* (*not* anonymous) relationships between people.

Detached from the surviving veterans' self-elevation and self-healing that are also implicit in the ritual, the political and economic "rapprochement" of the two so-called traditional enemies France and Germany took place. What had been begun by the "Europeans of the first hour" (Schumann, Monet) was given a political foundation by De Gaulle and Adenauer. Successive political leaders reinforced the new bond, in spite of occasional "irritations" in the relationship between the two countries. The fundamental work was done, a firm foundation for the collaboration between the two countries laid, the relationship between the nations, according to opinion polls, surprisingly unequivocal and marked by at least mutually professed goodwill.

In this situation, the ceremonially arranged meeting between the French president François Mitterand and the German chancellor Helmut Kohl at the cemetery of Verdun was brought about after many common "summits," personal meetings, and mutual reassurances of friendship. It is this meeting at Verdun which I shall now address.

What was "captured" in the photographs often appeared in the text (captions) as "hand holding" by the two statesmen. The press in both countries [not only the "Canard Enchainé" and the "TITANIC" (satirical press) but also the "serious" press] mocked this gesture. The readers were amused, and this in view of pictures taken at the soldiers' cemetery in Verdun, that cemetery weighted with tradition, pictures that showed a coffin draped with the flags of both countries.

The coffin stands between two wreaths, which the representatives of the two former enemy countries have just laid down. In befitting distance from the coffin and the wreaths, there are a respectable number of addi-

Kohl and Mitterand commemorate the dead of two world wars on the battlefield of Verdun

tional representatives of the two countries, standing in straight rows, the military men giving a military ceremonial salute, the male civilians bare headed, hats in hands.

This symbolically dense scene, almost overladen with accents of significance, signalizes (at least in the ritual) that the metaphorically buried enmity of the two nations has been overcome, and at the same time signalizes the mourning for the joint sacrifices and victims, and the "friendship" of the French and Germans that grew out of (and in spite of) war and death. It is one of those scenes in which the power of symbolism is very vividly drawn: how contradictions are developed and at the same time harmonized, how borders between the everyday and the noneveryday are crossed, how full attention is demanded from all participants' senses, and arguments excluded—how the senses are united in a collective perception and reaction.[7]

Between the rows of representatives and veterans from the two countries and the coffin, much closer to the former than the latter and conspicuous in the unoccupied space, are the two whose intentionally arranged pose lets the rest of the significance-laden framework recede into the background. It is—in spite of the familiarity of the elements—a figure of expression that can hardly be copied, inconsistent in spite of all advance planning, with a generous admixture of unintentional comedy, but also a touch of involuntary innocence in spite of the identifiable tactical calculation aimed at media effectiveness.

There they are, then, each one of them locked into the unmistakable personal demeanor that they appropriated themselves and subsequently reinforced by the media. Serious and collected, his eyes fixed on something apparently significant (and invisible to the viewer) beyond the chancellor, is the French president. His right arm hangs straight down alongside his body, his hand clenched in a fist. His left arm is stretched out away from his body at an acute angle. His left hand almost disappears in Helmut Kohl's noticeable larger one. Kohl's fingers engulf those of his partner; they have the "hand of the friend" firmly in hand. Kohl's right arm, of which these fingers are the extension points, like Mitterand's, at an acute angle away from his body, albeit a slightly bent angle. But while Kohl's right shoulder slopes downward a bit, Mitterand's left shoulder is fractionally raised, following the exigencies of their unequal height.

The physically taller and more massive chancellor is directing his gaze from behind his glasses at the president—his head bent to the side and downward a little, facing the shorter Mitterand. Kohl's facial expression is a peculiar combination between a smile and a (suggestion of a) contented grin. His left arm points straight down alongside his body, his left hand clenched in a loose fist.

The harmony of their clothing—dark overcoat, dark suit underneath, along with the customary white shirt and striped tie (broad stripes for Mitterand, narrower ones for Kohl—compare the size of the stripes to their respective physical size)—is only a bit marred by the fact that the German chancellor is standing with his legs slightly apart, while the French president looks to be a bit knock-kneed because of his trousers that are too long and thus bunched up, although his feet are also placed about a foot apart.

Disturbance, disharmony, and comedy to a great extent originate in the composition of unmatching, rather contradictory elements, quite apart from the overpowering impression created by the difference in size between the two actors. The chancellor, who smiles contentedly at his partner while standing in front of coffin and wreaths, "fits" just as little to the serious look of the president, who is avoiding the eyes of the smiling German, as the friendly handshake fits to the clenched presidential fist and the suggested chancellerian fist formed by their respective free and thus uncontrolled hands. And, as though this composition weren't ill-fitting enough, its ill-fittedness increases painfully yet again through the central element and leitmotif of the total arrangement: the hand holding.

That two statesmen stand *next to each other* and hold one another by the hand instead of shaking hands in a "friendly" manner while facing one another is in itself unusual enough. Such a gesture is organized, if at all, in rare—and rarely comedy-free cases—by third parties. I call to mind Heinrich Lübke's memorable, but fortunately not decisive intertwining of Johnson's and De Gaulle's presidential hands. In our cultural circles, we find hand holding among bridal couples, lovers young and old, parents and children, children among themselves—particularly when they are being lined up by kindergarten or nursery-school teachers—and among girl friends. In rare cases, it happens while the participants are standing still, but usually it is while they are strolling or walking together. And their arms are not extended away from their bodies; their bodies are, in keeping with the closeness expressed in the act of holding hands, close together. They are brought closer by arms and hands. Outside of such twosomes, there is "collective" hand holding, which indeed does simultaneously create closeness and distance: in "human chains," demonstrations, at Church congresses, and the like—within the framework of a communal ritual.

But to Kohl and Mitterand, neither the one nor the other symbolic or action context applies. Yes, it *is* a demonstration, but is it also a twosome between the two men? Of course, something collective is meant to be presented and also expressed representatively for two collectives, but surely a two-linked human chain or two-headed community is not being implied here? Friendship and closeness are meant to be signaled, but is that shown in a demonstrative distance by extending one's arms away from one's body? By holding hands on one side and making a fist on the other?

Whoever thought up this particular Franco-German arrangement did indeed choose a number of quite common elements and patterns out of the prop box of public-ritual representational devices, but then didn't bother to ask, in composing them into a whole, whether they actually fit together. Thus a collection of (seeming) contradictions is brought about, a dissonance that suggests involuntary comedy even in the most innocent interpretation. "Objectively," almost the exact opposite of what was intended is expressed. There is a distance where closeness was intended. Demonstrative hand holding and simultaneous—slightly concealed—clenched fists imbue the glowing accord of friendship with disturbing extraneous noises. The contented smile (or implicit grin) on one of the actors' faces makes it seem clear that the earnestness of the ritual and of the symbolic context (coffin, wreaths, flags) is being ignored, or that the ceremony is being regarded as a show. The Frenchman's serious demeanor and avoidance of his neighbor's eyes show that he knows the laws inherent to the symbols and rituals in which he is moving, but that precisely for this reason he cannot accept the "interaction proposition" to smile contentedly with his partner in full view of the coffin (and of the camera people with their ever-ready cameras behind it). In short, one has to be master of the rituals if one doesn't want to be mastered by them; one has to know their meaning if one wants to mean something with their help. Whether one likes it or not, the meaning of rituals and symbols uses those who think they can use them at random. Either one is a very good actor indeed or else a perfect teammate. There are no halfway solutions here.

II

November, 1989—In the formerly German, now Polish Kreisau, after long discussions about the "proper place," there is a meeting between the Polish minister-president Tadeusz Mazowiecki and the German chancellor Helmut Kohl. The meeting is announced as a meeting of reconciliation between their two countries. After the reconciliation in the West, the reconciliation in the East is now reportedly to be given a visible expression as well.[8] Here, too, the political negotiations are accompanied by ceremonylike arrangement and special meetings: tailored to the media and their broadcasting methods.

The place where the two politicians meet, Kreisau in the former Silesia, is also a symbol of resistance against Hitler: the *"Kreisauer Kreis"* ("Kreisau circle"). So one is in a frequently disputed area, but seemingly on neutralized ground. The first impression of the picture evokes precisely this neutralization theme, the—as is evidently believed—fitting pitch and mood that lets the old be forgotten and renders the new possible. The photograph shows the two men embracing under a statue of Saint Hedwig, who seems to be giving her sacrally superelevated approval—representative of others as symbolic backdrop—as she stands on her pedestal in the background, a mild and friendly expression on her face.

Those responsible for the photograph are Dieter Bauer, Sven Simon, and Sepp Spiegl, all three successful press photographers and documentarists. The photograph in question is one of a series on the preparations for and the course of the ceremonial reconciliation arrangement. Three pictures from this series (the one described is the middle picture) were published in the magazine "Stern."[9] On all three photographs, the legs of the politicians have been "cut off." Depending on the angle of the camera, the amputation occurred at a higher or a lower point. Only one figure in the picture remains unscathed: Saint Hedwig. Although she is in the background, she is unharmed. Apparently the photographer considered it important to leave this "personified" symbol, this symbolic third person, intact. Our description follows the photographer's view, so it begins with St. Hedwig.

Saint Hedwig, an important saint in the former Silesia, has been depicted variously: "In nun's garb with duke's crown and coat as founder...of the Trebnitz (monastery); often praying before a crucifix...or administering to and caring for the poor and ill, or barefoot with shoes in hand."[10] The one on the photograph seems to be one of the most familiar depictions: Saint Hedwig as "duchess with model of a church,[11]" as wife of the sovereign, as church founder, and preserver of faith.

It is not unusual for the image of a saint to be symbolically "protecting" or "supporting" a ceremony of reconciliation. Poland (including Silesia) is a Catholic country. Both of the politicians participating in the ceremony are professed Catholics. The saint called upon to protect the ceremony was active in the country where the ceremony of reconciliation is taking place: so far, so fitting.

But Saint Hedwig isn't just any old Silesian saint. She was Duchess of Silesia and Poland, wife of Duke Henry I, to whom she was betrothed in 1186 at the age of twelve. She had six children—and her three sons also ruled Silesia and the surrounding duchies. She lived, according to hagiography, in abstinence after the birth of her children for thirty years, firmly supported by her husband, and in addition, as Franz von Sales Doyé strongly emphasizes, "her efforts on behalf of the improvement and Germanization of Silesia are (also) notable."[12]

The historical background of these efforts was the move to the East by the German Hohenstaufen Emperor Frederic I. Polish throne disputes allowed him to chisel two Silesian duchies away from the Polish kingdom (1163). The settling of German colonialists had already begun under the Polish dukes Boleslav (Duchy of Breslau) and Mieszko (Duchy of Ratibor). Their successor, Hedwig's husband Henry I, intensified those efforts—aided by his wife. In short, Saint Hedwig stands both for a "holy life" and for the integration of the formerly Polish Silesia into the Holy Roman Empire of German Nations. The reconciliation ceremonial is supposed to illustrate symbolically both the end of the enmity and the integrity of Poland's western border. But the Saint Hedwig who was chosen for the meeting is precisely that holy duchess of the Holy Roman Empire of German Nations through whose complicity Poland's western border was infringed upon and shifted eastward.

Whoever chose this specific depiction of St. Hedwig for the arrangement of the reconciliation ceremony brought to light, beyond all subjective intentions, the effective historical framework of meaning that marks the "Silesian question" and the answer implicit in the symbolic arrangement, namely, that it is still open. For the interpretation it is completely irrelevant whether that person did this consciously (cunningly) from his subjective point of view or unconsciously or even unknowingly.

Kohl and Mazowiecki at Kreisav

Below Saint Hedwig's statue, dressed in dark overcoats, we have the Polish minister-president and the German chancellor embracing each other and creating a bell-like shadow that is turned fractionally to the right. The bent back of the German to the right—his height forces him to bend deeper than his partner has to—makes it seem as though he is practically "nestled up against" the statue of the saint, seeming to follow the movement of the folds in her robes. The chancellor's bespectacled head with the carefully parted hair almost wholly obscures the head of his Polish partner, of whom we see only the hairline in back.

Kohl's head rests with his chin on the shoulder of his Polish colleague. His lips are firmly closed, cheek muscles and lines between chin and neckline very pronounced. The neck itself is obscured by the angle of the head. The two men are embracing. Left arm and hand of the physically taller German, slightly bent, lie on the also slightly bent arm of Mazowiecki. The chancellor's partially open hand, little finger splayed out a bit, finds a resting-place below Mazowiecki's shoulder. The pushed-up coat sleeve (caused by the lifting of the arm) reveal watch and white shirt cuff. Mazowiecki's right arm, although also slightly bent, is somewhat straighter than that of Kohl. Nonetheless, the stretched-out fingers of his completely open hand (wedding band on the fourth finger) do not reach all the way to the chancellor's back. They rest below the armpit, a bit behind it, on the left upper side of the chancellor's body.

Even if Mazowiecki would stretch his arm out completely, he could not reach the chancellor's back: the two bodies that strive toward each other and embrace in their upper halves (heads and shoulders) strive apart below. Their feet are apparently so far from each other's that any closer bodily contact is impossible. The taller Kohl is thus forced to bend his back, as described above.

Open and closed, near and distant, simultaneously occurring gestures of contact and avoidance of contact mark the "form" of this embrace: The contradictions are not—as purportedly signalized—"erased"; they lie spread over the reconciliation. The problem that is depicted as solved exemplarily in the gesture of embrace is in fact still open. The individual elements of this gesture of reconciliation are at variance with one another. In this respect Saint Hedwig, conjured up as a patron saint, is objectively in "harmony" with the expression of the rest of the picture. She repeats and reinforces symbolically what the divided gesture expresses: the continuing existence of tensions that the gesture was supposed to present as overcome.

The chosen ceremonial form does not succeed in domesticating the contradictions that lie "outside" of its sphere of validity and power. The symbolic elements chosen do not adapt to the intended framework. The individual rituals become independent from the planned ceremonial rite. They develop an independent form in which what subjectively was supposed to be hidden is shown objectively: Here, the topic is at the same time "reconciliation of distrust" and "distrust of reconciliation."

Unintentional Consequences and Disregarded Intentions

In both cases—the meeting of Mitterand and Kohl at the grave of the unknown soldier in Verdun and the meeting between Mazowiecki and Kohl in Kreisau—the intention of the "arrangers" is unmistakable. It is to drape a ceremony around a political situation or political intention. Ceremonies are solemn actions secured by tradition, uniform repetition, and hence, regulated recognizability. They supply a solid framework for symbolic and ritual elements that are related to one another in prescribed form.[13]

It is true that ceremonies are structurally ambivalent as symbolic forms. But they present the contradictions that they signalize, as everyone from Freud to Cassirer to Eco is agreed, as "removed" contradictions. They purport to be the only possible solution of those contradictions which, they themselves suggest, are insoluble outside of the symbolic.[14]

It takes time before a collectively formed and particularly emphasized event can be reflected in a form secured by tradition. The time is filled with repetition, removal of inconsistencies, cleansing and filing of a symbolic form which in its turn is worked into social knowledge and collective habits by sheer repetition. In short, one cannot simply invent ceremonies or piece them together out of spare parts of assorted rituals.

However, that is precisely what was attempted at the Mitterand-Kohl meeting in Verdun. The media, for whom the spectacle was staged, probably seduced the arrangers into using precisely those stylistic devices that the mass media themselves use in "show business"—photo collages and scenery montages. But what is right for shows, those daily celebrations of the supposedly ever new, ever special, misses its mark in the context of ceremonies. Ceremonies are supposed to emphasize the special as the *noneveryday,* which, although it can be repeated, remains the tried and true old. If one starts pushing show props into ceremonies, one ends up being pushed around oneself.

Of course it is true, rituals and symbols have been "cited" again and again and fitted into hitherto unfamiliar contexts, but acting is not the same as texts. In the latter, ever-shifting strings of citations produce new forms of meaning and argument (in trendy terminology: "discourses") that live on the inner systemics of signs.[15] Acting, on the other hand, takes place on the irreversible chronological line of the course of events. Texts are renewable fodder that can be canceled at any moment—a gravy train for interpreters. Acting, on the other hand, disappears "as a date"[16] in the course of its execution. What remains are results of actions[17] or, insofar as the acting was recorded, records of actions (also photographs). Acting obeys "practical" reason while the line of text and interpretation obeys "reflexive" reason. Acting obeys the necessity (the decision), interpreting obeys the possibility (not having to make any direct decision). Acting documents the course, text and interpretation (as a unity) document the "discourse." Only playing out traces of the "course" against each other in records of the action on the one hand and discursive interpretation of precisely those records on the other hand brings those selection processes to light and also precisely those inconsistencies that are at least not visible in the unity of the action (as a sequence that becomes manageable and summarized retroactively).

The same holds true for the description and interpretation of that arrangement of action and scenery which purports to be the ceremony described. The discrepancy in the basic symbolic form produces, on the formal level, precisely that emptiness and arbitrariness which is expressed in one of its parts, in the presented action, a collage of rituals. The blend of signals of significance, in themselves inconsistent, conjures up a comic element, particularly when it is tucked into a "solemn" framework. Comedians themselves are artists in the targeted use of stylistic devices of inconsistency; populists who piece together a patchwork of significant elements turn out to be rank amateurs.

The celebration, limping in the wake of history, of a long-since accomplished détente and normalization between two nations—the term "friendship" would be too strong, as the ceremony itself illustrates—radiates the same morbid charm as the church wedding of a couple that has co-habited for decades and can no longer recall the first days of courtship. The Mitterand-Kohl photograph is an objective expression of precisely that charm: the discrepancy of the form representing the discrepancy of the action.

It is different in the Mazowiecki-Kohl photograph: Form and expression are not only discrepant because set pieces were pieced together. Rather, they are defined by *one* constitutive, not (yet) wholly solved contradiction that transfuses the whole photograph. To return to the already quoted image: We have to do here with a couple that swears to love and be true, but distrusts their own avowals based on the many years of experience of living with one another.

In this case, one is not piecing together at random. Instead, one is trying to combine what has hitherto been irreconcilable. The ambivalence implicit in the statue of Hedwig—duchess of Silesia *and* Poland— is rescinded symbolically by the statue's insignia. At the same time, they (the insignia) illustrate the perspective under which alone such a cancellation was formerly considered possible. It is only *one* perspective: the German one. On the other hand, the photograph as a whole documents, in its manifestation, two thus far not yet (or only partially) joined perspectives—and the presentation of the gesture originating in them—that are working at cross purposes.

Here, too, the form of presentation brings to bear the objectively given whole historical potential of meaning in the symbolic form as against the subjective protestations (or even views?) of the performers.[18] This "objective" meaning does not hide *"behind"* the presentation: on the contrary, it shows what it is in its pure form *in* the presentation, without any adulteration whatsoever.

Charisma—Pawnshop without a Keeper?

The description of the contradictions in these populist stagings might give the impression that they were simply "mishaps," or that perhaps the actors merely made a few mistakes in their performances, easily avoided if the director had been more capable or the actors more qualified. As though by more careful planning and more talented performances certain ceremonies could start radiating charisma. This is certainly not the case. Populism and charisma are irreconcilable. One can find "mistakes" in *all* populist stagings, insofar as their goal is to cloak themselves in a charismatic aura.

These mistakes are not coincidences; they stem from the structural irreconcilability of populism and charisma. And the preceding analysis accordingly does not claim to lead to a "representative" event encompassing the entire arsenal of types and repertoires of populist behavior, but does claim to do so in regard to the fundamental difference between populism and charisma.

As colorful and multifarious as the phenomenon of populism is, different basic patterns can nonetheless be discerned in the colorful patchwork blanket of attractions with which social popularity tends to surround itself. There are, in almost all "Western" parliaments, the "simple folks"—the "best of us," men and women who fulfil their duties in everyday life—the trusty union man, the honest civil servant, the "thoroughly decent" and rooted "local personality," the "long-serving party soldier." They can all rest assured that "we" agree with them, just as we would agree with ourselves, the multifarious multitude. We are pleased at their success, not so much because of their achievements which, as we know, many others could also have accomplished, but because they seem to signalize that any of us could be in their place when, for example, they become minister of something—if only we had also won in the social lottery like they did.

Then there are the petty bourgeois, who spend their time currying favor, some of them rushing from beer tent to fairground, from there to a talk show, then on to an international soccer match and the "celebratory meeting" of the Carnival clubs in Cologne or Mainz (particularly Carnival-happy German cities); the others, in addition to the above activities, producing achievements modeled in the vein of the *Guinness Book of Records* (swimming across the Rhine in neoprene suits, endurance jogging, parachuting, mountain climbing, etc.) or then, in the purportedly comic variant, bursting compulsively into puns, falling backward in their chairs into the water for the photographers on their "private" holidays, holding those—by now institutionalized—speeches "against the beastly seriousness" in a manner that evokes utter horror with its terrifying jollity.

And finally, there are those to whom one could attribute something like a "demonic" populism: They are capable of visibly transforming the power of populist approval into personal power and thus to either pursue, with the help of "public opinion," those whom they themselves and public opinion declared to be their opponents (McCarthy), or to place themselves at the head of public opinion as "great communicator" (Reagan). In the process, the opinion of the majority is no longer sought *about* something, public opinion has already caught up with everything that could be "opposite" to it. So it carries itself away to wherever without a controlling opposite number. Generally, this type of populism is also said to have charisma: wrongly so, for then what does the carrying along is no longer differentiated from what is carried along.

At the same time, one can see a determining factor in this last group to which both charisma and populism are linked: *The (public) opinion* in which Durkheim saw that primary social phenomenon that "can be understood (as) the source of authority," in which case one would even have to ask "whether authority is not the daughter of opinion."[19] Max Weber, too, defines charisma not only as a "quality of personality that is seen as non-everyday…" but in addition, he links this "quality" to the interplay of "testing" and "recognition by those who are dominated."[20] Both Durkheim and Weber make clear how ambiguous, one-sided, and hence, problematic it is if one, as is common, misinterprets charisma exclusively and quasi-substantially as "quality." Practical action in general as well as "stagings" by charismatic persons (and populists) are correlative factors. They are linked to expectations and approval by others, be it the interaction partners in general or the dominated people or followers. There is no absolute measure outside this interplay of action, testing, expectation, and approval.[21] *Charisma, and to an equal degree populism, are interactively created social products.*[22]

On the one hand, in the case of pure charisma, the noneveryday and the breaking open of the new against the routines of the habitual is experienced (or imagined) in the combined effect of charismatic leader and followers, of testing and approval. And on the other hand, populism (the populist) confirms the habitual in familiar, albeit loudly colored images. While the "personal" charismatic and his followers transform the passivity of the "as usual" into activity aimed at the new (or into a belief in activity itself as the new—even at the cost of destroying the old), and while the professional charismatic strives for the "permanently available" securing of those extraordinary, but now proven activities, the populist moves in the market squares of the everyday as an adherent of already existing or presumed opinions, in the company of other adherents of these opinions.

He and his supporters are particularly drawn to the fairgrounds. There, the everyday assembles in noneveryday colorfulness, the customary assembles in unaccustomed numbers. The everyday dresses up as a party—and in the process collects the entire personnel of the everyday public life. Here, the one who is the way everyone wants to be and presumably also could be, proves himself and receives approval: Populism's aim is to continue driving the social cart in the tracks that have been used over and over again and have been imperceptibly but inexorably worn deeper and deeper. Socially created charisma, though, marks the structural spot for the new.

The pure charismatic in his role as "innovator" is, just like the official charismatic in his role as preserver and perpetuator of the new, specialist for the noneveryday/significant and thus often enough also for the (ad nauseam) serious; the populist on the other hand is a generalist, practiced in cabaret, in dealing with the multifarious everyday patterns and routines. Charismatics have problems or fail because of everyday routines. Populist generalists, however, stumble on the noneveryday/significant and move among it as among alien scenery. Charismatics exaggerate (for their opponents and for "external observers") the serious until it turns round into the ridiculous. Most populists create ridiculousness before things can get serious. Not for nothing do they prefer the light genres, shows, and fairgrounds. There, they are safe (even though we are not safe from them).

The charismatic and his adherents concentrate, in their desire for the unusual and significant, on the few but extraordinary things that constitute the "essential" for them. Only a few "select" albeit overdrawn presentational devices focus the attention on the "fascinosum" and let the everyday be forgotten. This limited yet seemingly forever "new" repertoire that in fact has been handed down over millennia in old motive and symbol sequences can be compiled without great effort. It is effective due not to its abundance but rather to its economy of elements and exaggeration of the means of expression. It constitutes an image with sharp contours and an elevated center. There is no room for "irrelevancies." A trademark of populism, on the other hand, is its patchwork diversity. Diversion is its medium, and the media use it in order to divert. The charismatic has followers—the populist an audience.

"Divertedness," lack of focus, and blurred contours characterize populism as much as the tendency of populist performers toward ceremony and ritual. The latter inevitably grows out of the fear of losing a form which one doesn't in fact possess. Moreover, the range of products of acting and actors, a range determined by mass consumerism and casual use, tries to find support and significance in ritual ceremonial forms. Thus, the irreconcilable is joined together. The effect is as though one were to present a Big Mac on a venerable antique gold tray as eucharistic host in the Cathedral of Aix-la-Chapelle. And it appears as a normal case of populist efforts that "dignity" and "distinctiveness" are bestowed upon the meaningless, that they are lent that form that finds its exemplary expression in the creed system: "formally a caste convention, but materially plebeian."[23] That is ultimately the form that places the demeanor of the present German chancellor in visible contrast to his French and Polish partners.

The brief and to-the-point elaboration of the charismatic "form" occurs in the repetition of the identical ceremonies and rituals from a limited repertoire: Across from the economy in the use of presentational devices stands the wastefulness of the basically invariable stagings. Through repetition, time is "symbolically" brought to a standstill and with that, the communal conviction offered for an unlimited time, a time whose temporal modus however is the present tense of "experiencing." That modus determines the staging's publicity and its repetition. Its trademark is the moment, manifested by the chosen one's (supposedly) "magic" look and touch. In just these specific "manners of approach," the charismatic pierces that distance, drawing the communal ritual and ceremonial around him like a first aural ring.

In all, the charismatic's adherents shape themselves into precisely that aura that they believe they perceive in him. This shaping is done through communal conviction and staging. The "fascinosum" of the charismatic figure in the center turns into an innerworldly anchored form of "numinosum"[24]: A community of convictions and beliefs consecrates itself (and is startled) by creating and preserving an unmistakable center. The "pure" charismatic and his followers demand *mutual* testing and approval in devotion and veneration, fear and shaking, loyalty and allegiance. In illusion and success, delusion and failure, they tread a common path. Accordingly, there is no "divided," only common responsibility here.

In spite of repeated attempts at borrowing from the stock forms of charismatic stagings, populism has nothing in common with charismatic movements either in appearance or in fundamental pattern, apart from the fact that it, too, is an interactively created social product. Populists legitimately fear that popularity wears thin through constant repetition; so they rush from one première to the next. Where the charismatic grinds form into the fitting shape, the populist grinds formlessness flat. He is addicted to the present: up-to-the-minute is his trademark, it is the measure of his market value—and of his "expiration date." For activity is a form of present tense that cannot be offered in any long run. It makes the passage of time particularly evident as the present wears out visibly. Charisma "becomes everyday" (Max Weber) when the unusual, the new, loses its sheen in the course of time (i.e., in the course of being repeatedly recalled into the present). The populist's popularity evaporates when he can no longer think up anything new.

For the charismatic, the ritual distance to his followers is constitutive, and touching individuals unusual—a rare reward for followers. The populist cannot hold and shake enough hands. He loves bathing in that mass he just stepped out of himself. When he tries to surround himself with a ceremonial aura and distance, he is in danger of being recognized for what he is—one of the mass, nothing special. Populism is among other things the trademark of societies without human or ideal centers and/or of societies in which institutions of political and economic decisions on the one hand, and media presentation of politics on the other hand are organized according to the principle of the division of labor, and committed to diverse goals and targets. It signals the wish to preserve a consensus that transcends all conflicts of interest and that—as everyone suspects—has long been lost.

By contrast, the longing for charismatic domination doesn't require preserving or securing the familiar. It aims at renewal by destroying the existing. Its aim is to break open social classification grids and norms.[25] It doesn't stop at "class boundaries" or family ties; it replaces relatives with adherents, tradition with immediacy. Charismatic movements see themselves, at all times, as a respectively new departure from "ossification" and from what is seen as unbearable social solidification. Considered objectively, charismatic rule doesn't merely propagate a break with history. Rather, it appears next to other forms of rule—transcending culture and history—as an elementary collective power of action and interpretation in the social construction of order(s). In the seemingly tightly woven net of historical conditions, "causes," and consequences, of the not predictable yet reconstructibly "effected" developments, charismatic rule is the structural place for something "new," even if it dresses up in the garb of "re-formation."

In the symptomatic striving by populists and their audience for the de facto, no longer discoverable "center" (left center, right center, liberal center, progressive center, etc.), the various interest groups and majorities (who, by comparison with the rest of society, are all minorities) cling to the fiction of a common denominator. The "unity" of the members of that pluralistic society is not supposed to be legitimized by the economic and political functional systems and the ensuing interests, but rather by an idea in which the various lifestyles meet again. Here, each individual is to have the opportunity of discovering himself in the center of society.

The at present dominant idea of the autonomous, "self-fulfilling" individual and the consequent talk of the "individualization of life situations and lifestyles" guarantees this opportunity, but without the individual having any possibility of focus other than himself. Thus the populist is—has presumably always tended to be, but is now with immense perfection—the individual as everyman multiplied by himself in the many others.

Charismatic dominance gives a society an unmistakable center. It not only has the effect of changing structure, but also of developing its own structure. Populism, however, refers to the type of society that in specific historical situations gives a specific organizational form to diverse functional units, interest groups, ethnicities, and religious communities. That organizational form consists of tight interweaving of economic form and state administration on the one hand and on the other, loosening the individual's traditional ties to the state. In this case, populism proves itself as the connecting element within the unconnectedness.

Proving oneself sometimes brings forth the sensational, usually the pleasing, that which the *audience* wants, measured by the standards of being up-to-date and of a curious audience rather than those of extraordinariness and high expectations by one's followers. Thus the proof of a populist is in the value of his entertainment, presentation, and inoffensiveness, and in the—slightly newly clad—affirmation of the familiar as something that is approved. In the populist, as its smallest common multiple, a society highlights what is imposed on its individual members: adaptability to an assumed opinion of others or to whatever one believes others believe to be normal.

In this respect, the populist feels just as little responsible as his audience for the public opinion, an (assimilated) part of which they both are. Both feel not as makers but as "made" in this context—if they're lucky, then as "made men/women." From *this* point of view, it is difficult to make a populist responsible for anything beyond the more or less accepted *presentation* of public opinion. The conscience from which this responsibility emanates is the public's taste.

The structural difference between the charismatic and the populist results from their different ways of approaching normality and everyday life. The populist who is chasing after the current, the "minor" novelty, orients himself, just like his audience, according to what is presumed to be normal. His practice is to affirm the familiar, trying to counter its feared blandness with new spices. But the effort to reaffirm the familiar over and over again points to the possibility that fear of the bland taste of the familiar conceals a deeper-lying fear: the fear, that is, of the ever-possible collapse of the mundane,[26] of everyday certainties crumbling, of routines not holding up, the formerly reliable becoming unreliable, and faith in normality perhaps breaking down abruptly. The compulsive processing of the (purportedly) new according to old patterns shows up populism as a—historically belated—offspring of this fear.

The wish for charismatic domination, charismatic leaders, or movements stems from the same source. Charisma as "fascinosum" is also founded in the knowledge of how basically fragile the "familiar" world is. Yet habits and routines do not prove to the charismatics, "leaders" or adherents, that things would continue as before; for them these are signs that the "great" and the "important" are crumbling, signs that one has turned away from the extraordinary as the "really" essential, that time is slipping away into the everyday. As much as charismatics love rituals and ceremonies in staging the extraordinary, they hate the "minor" rituals of habit, tradition, and custom. As "innovators," they are antiritualists in the face of those rituals[27]: articulators and activists of the new, the unfamiliar, and the change in perception, they are admirers of the illusion that by breaking away from the old, one could once and for all counter the feared breach of trust in a world totally controllable by humans.

Considered in this light, populism and charismatic domination relate to and answer the same insecurity and profound threat that have in all of history been mankind's motives for creating social order and seeking shelter in it. But in acting within this order, they proceed to lose all they once had in common.

Notes

1. See Soeffner, H.-G., *Rituale des Antiritualismus—Materialien für Außeralltägliches,* this volume.
2. See Schütz, Alfred (1972), *Der gut informierte Bürger,* in *Studien zur soziologischen Theorie, Gesammelte Aufsätze II,* Den Haag, 85–101.

3. See Brosch, Joseph (1951), *Charisma und Ämter in der Urkirche*, Bonn, ditto the contribution by Bergmann, Luckmann, Soeffner (1991): *Erscheinungsformen von Charisma—Zwei Päpste*, in Zingerle et al. (eds.) (1991).

4. Max Weber calls charisma *"the* great revolutionary power in traditionally bound epochs." This characterization seems to me an insufficient definition in terms of structural theory as well as in the description of "the social motivation" for action. See *Wirtschaft und Gesellschaft* (5, 1976), 142, 10, 5.

5. Grimmelshausen, H. J. Chr. von (no year), *Der abenteuerliche Simplicissimus*, Sechstes Buch, 9. Kapitel.

6. Soeffner, Hans-Georg (1991), Zur Soziologie des Symbols und des Rituals, in Wegenast and Oelkers (eds.), *Das Symbol. Brücke des Verstehens*, Bern.

7. What the photograph doesn't show, but what characterizes nearly all of Mitterand's public appearances permeates this scene, too: the French president's efforts to fulfill the demands of office *and* of the concomitant charisma, or, as they say in France, to "be more gaullist than DeGaulle." In other words, the meeting between Kohl and Mitterand is a meeting between a populist and a professional charismatic. Thus, the already existing dissonance is enhanced by yet another discordant note.

8. Here, too, I have consciously omitted a detailed characterization of the historical and political "surroundings" of the meeting at Kreisau. Here, too, my priority lies with the gestures and expressions captured in the photograph: *They* and *their* traditions are to be described and verbalized, the structure of their composition analyzed and interpreted according to *their* meaning. In short, the focal point is inner structure, references of meaning within the picture, and historical-symbolic allusions of the (photographical) document, and not the revelation of a particular action situation outside the picture and its "context."

9. *Stern*, no. 11, year 43, 8–14 March 1990, 34 and 35.

10. Franz von Sales Doyé, *Heilige und Selige der römisch-katholischen Kirche. Deren Erkennungszeichen, Patronate und lebensgeschichtliche Bemerkungen*. Two Volumes. Volume I, Leipzig 1629, 488.

11. Ibid.; see also the clothing: duke's crown and duke's garb.

12. Ibid.

13. See Hahn, Alois (1977), *Kultische und säkulare Riten und Zeremonien in soziologischer Sicht*, in *Anthropologie des Kults*, Freiburg, 51–81.

14. Soeffner, Hans-Georg (1991), *Zur Soziologie des Symbols und des Rituals*, in Wegenast and Oelkers (eds.), *Das Symbol. Brücke des Verstehens*, Bern.

15. For a representative example see Derrida, Jacques (1967, 1976), *Die Schrift und die Differenz*, Frankfurt; Lyotard, J.-F. (1983), *Le Différend*, Paris. Concerning the relation of "discourse theory" and sociology see Giesen, Bernhard (1990), *Entzauberte Soziologie*, Lecture at the Soziologentag in Frankfurt 1990.

16. See Bergmann, Jörg (1985), *Flüchtigkeit und methodische Fixierung sozialer Wirklichkeit*, in Bonß, W., and Hartmann, H. (eds.), *Entzauberte Wissenschaft, Soziale Welt*. Sonderband 3, 299 ff.

17. See the difference as emphasized by Luckmann between "acting" and "action." Schütz, Alfred, and Luckmann, Thomas (1984), *Strukturen der Lebenswelt*, Vol. 2, Frankfurt, 84 ff.

18. "Rational choice" theoreticians—even, unfortunately, the more reflective among them—in principle ignore this difference between subjectively intended purpose of action and the objectively attained goal of the action, revealed by the "reflex-

ive" reason's interpretation (see above). See for instance Esser, Hartmut (1990), "Habits," "Frames" und "Rational Choice": Die Reichweite von Theorien der rationalen Wahl (am Beispiel der Erklärung des Befragtenverhaltens), in Zeitschrift für Soziologie, Jg. 19, Heft 4, 231 ff.

19. Durkheim, Emile (1912/1981), Die elementaren Formen des religiösen Lebens, Frankfurt, p. 287. Here Durkheim also discusses the ties of science to precisely that public opinion the battle with and control of which he considers a major duty on the part of science.

20. Weber, Max (1972), Wirtschaft und Gesellschaft, Tübingen, 140.

21. It is to a large part the "dominated" ones themselves who decide on what should or should not be recognized as their "welfare," the measure Max Weber (op. cit., ibid.) speaks of.

22. The broader concept of interaction used here includes both "direct," face-to-face interaction and indirect (mediated) interaction.

23. Allert, Tilmann (1990), It never rains in southern California. Polen im Herbst, in Merkur, Heft 495: 391. In his article Allert refers, in quoting Max Weber, to the historical perpetuation of a demeanor that has left behind its specific caste and thereby seems even more obtrusive than before.

24. See Otto, Rudolf (1963), Das Heilige, Munich, esp. 5–55.

25. As so often, I am indebted to Thomas Luckmann in this article, too. In this case, he urged me to work out more precisely and distinctly the structural difference between "charisma" and "populism."

26. See Schütz, A., and Luckmann, Th. (1984), Strukturen der Lebenswelt, Vol. 2, Frankfurt, esp. 139–77.

27. See Soeffner, H.-G., Rituale des Antiritualismus—Materialien für das Außergewöhnliche, this volume.

Bibliography

Adam, Adolf. 1962. *Die Herkunft des Wortes vom menschlichen Willen als Reittier Gottes*, LuJ, 25–34.

Alciatus, Andreas. 1531. *Andreae Alciati Emblematvm Libellvs*. Paris.

Allert, Tilmann. 1990. It never rains in southern California. Polen im Herbst. In *Merkur*, Heft 495/1990, 381–98.

Apel, Karl-Otto. 1970. Einführung: Peirces Denkweg vom Pragmatismus zum Pragmatizismus. In Peirce, Band 2, 11–211; In Karl-Otto Apel: *Der Denkweg von Charles S. Peirce. Eine Einführung in den amerikanischen Pragmatismus*. Frankfurt a.M. 1975.

Apel, Karl-Otto (ed.). 1976. *Sprachpragmatik und Philosophie*. Frankfurt a.M.

Baczko, Bronislaw. 1970. *Rousseau: Einsamkeit und Gemeinschaft*. Wien/ Frankfurt a.M./Zürich.

Balthasar, Hans U. (ed.). 1961. *Die großen Ordensregeln*. Einsiedeln/Zürich/ Köln.

Bateson, Gregory. 1981a. *Ökologie des Geistes*. Frankfurt a.M.

———. 1981b. *Eine Theorie des Spiels und der Phantasie*. In Bateson, 1981a, 241–61.

Baudrillard, Jean. 1978. *Kool Killer oder der Aufstand der Zeichen*. Berlin.

Beck, Ulrich. 1982. *Jenseits von Stand und Klasse?* In Kreckel, R. (ed.), 1982. *Soziale Ungleichheiten*. Göttingen.

———. 1984. *Perspektiven einer kulturellen Evolution der Arbeit*. In *MitAB*, *1*:1984.

———. 1986. *Risikogesellschaft. Auf dem Weg in eine andere Moderne*. Frankfurt a.M.

———. 1988. *Gegengifte: die organisierte Unverantwortlichkeit*. Frankfurt a.M.

———. 1991. *Politik in der Risikogesellschaft*. Frankfurt a.M.

Benedict, Ruth. 1946. *The Chrysanthemum and the Sword. Patterns of Japanese Culture*. Boston/New York.

———. 1955. *Urformen der Kultur*. Hamburg.

———. 1982. *Race: Science and Politics*. Rev. ed., Westport, Conn.

Berger, Peter L. 1980. *Der Zwang zur Häresie: Religion in der pluralistischen Gesellschaft*. Frankfurt a.M.

Berger, Peter L., and Luckmann, Thomas. 1969. *Die gesellschaftliche Konstruktion der Wirklichkeit. Eine Theorie der Wissenssoziologie.* Aus dem Amerikanischen übers. von Monika Plessner. Mit einer Einleitung z. dt. Ausgabe von Helmuth Plessner. Frankfurt a.M.

Berger, Peter L., Brigitte Berger, and Hansfried Kellner. 1975. *Das Unbehagen in der Modernität.* Frankfurt a.M.

Bergmann, Jörg. 1981. *Ethnomethodologische Konversationsanalyse.* In Peter Schröder und Hugo Steger (eds.). 1981. *Dialogforschung.* = Jahrbuch 1980 des Instituts für Deutsche Sprache. Düsseldorf, 9–51.

———. 1985. *Flüchtigkeit und methodische Fixierung sozialer Wirklichkeit.* In Bonß/Hartmann (eds.). 1985. *Entzauberte Wissenschaft.* Göttingen, 299–320.

———. 1987. *Klatsch. Zur Sozialform der diskreten Indiskretion.* Berlin.

Bergmann, Jörg, Thomas Luckmann, and Hans-Georg Soeffner. 1991. *Erscheinungsformen von Charisma—Zwei Päpste.* In Arnold Zingerle, et al. (eds.). 1991. *Charisma—Theorie, Politik, Religion.* Stuttgart.

Bierce, Ambrose. 1986. *Des Teufels Wörterbuch. 1881–1906.* Zürich.

Boccaccio, Giovanni. 1492. *Der Decamerone.* Zürich, 1957.

Boff, Leonardo. 1972. *Die Kirche als Sakrament im Horizont der Welterfahrung. Versuch einer Legitimation und einer struktur-funktionalistischen Grundlegung der Kirche im Anschluß an das II. Vatikanische Konzil.* Paderborn.

Bohler, Johannes. 1921. *Klosterleben im deutschen Mittelalter.*

Bornkamm, E. 1979. *Martin Luther in der Mitte seines Lebens.* Göttingen.

Bourdieu, Pierre. 1979. *Entwurf einer Theorie der Praxis auf der ethnologischen Grundlage der kabylischen Gesellschaft.* Frankfurt a.M.

Brecht, Bertolt. 1926/1939. *Marxistische Studien.* In Bertolt Brecht: *Gesammelte Werke in 20 Bänden.* Band 20. *Schriften zur Politik und Gesellschaft.* Frankfurt a.M. 1967, 45–123.

———. 1967. *Die Dreigroschenoper.* In *Gesammelte Werke in 20 Bänden,* Bd. 2, *Stücke 2.* Frankfurt a.M.

Brosch, Joseph. 1951. *Charisma und Ämter in der Urkirche.* Bonn.

Buck, Günther. 1981. *Von der Texthermeneutik zur Handlungshermeneutik;* in: Fuhrmann, Manfred/Jauß, Hans-Robert/Pannenberg, Wolfhart. 1981, 525–535.

Bühler, Karl. 1934. *Sprachtheorie. Die Darstellungsfunktion der Sprache.* 2. Auflage. Mit einem Vorwort von Friedrich Kainz. Stuttgart 1965.

Bultmann, Rudolf. 1954. *Zum Problem der Entmythologisierung.* In Bultmann, Rudolf. 1954. *Glauben und Verstehen. Gesammelte Aufsätze. Vierter Band.* Tübingen, 128–37.

———. 1956. *Adam, wo bist du?* In Bultmann, Rudolf: *Gesammelte Aufsätze. Zweiter Band.* Tübingen.

Cassirer, Ernst. 1953. *Philosophie der symbolischen Formen*. 3 Bände. 2. Auflage. Darmstadt.

Castiglione, Baldesar. 1528. *Il Libro del Cortegiano, 1986: Das Buch vom Hofmann*. Munich.

Cicourel, Aaron V. 1970. *Methode und Messung in der Soziologie*. Frankfurt a.M.

Clausen, Lars. *Fürst Pückler auf dem Höhepunkt der Krise*. In Matthes, Joachim (ed.). 1981. *Lebenswelt und soziale Probleme*. Verhandlungen des 20. Deutschen Soziologentages zu Bremen 1980. New York/Frankfurt a.M., 383–96.

Crooke, W. 1961. *Kissing*. In Hastings, J. (ed.). 1961. *Encyclopedia of Religion and Ethics*. New York: 739.

Derrida, Jacques. 1967. *L'écriture et la différence*. Paris.

———. 1970. *L'ordre du discours*. Paris.

Deutsche Forschungsgemeinschaft (ed.). 1986. *Medienwirkungsforschung in der Bundesrepublik Deutschland. Teil I: Berichte und Empfehlungen. Teil II: Dokumentation*. Katalog der Studien. Enquête der Senatskommission für Medienwirkungsforschung unter dem Vorsitz von Wilfried Schulz und der Mitarbeit von Jo Groebel. Weinheim.

Dilthey, Wilhelm. 1900. *Die Entstehung der Hermeneutik*. In Dilthey, Wilhelm: *Gesammelte Schriften*. Leipzig/Berlin 1914–1936. Fortgeführt Stuttgart/Göttingen 1962 ff. Band 5, 317–31.

———. 1958. *Entwürfe zur Kritik der historischen Vernunft*. In Gadamer/Boehm. (1976), 189–220.

Douglas, Mary. 1974. *Ritual, Tabu und Körpersymbolik. Sozialanthropologische Studien in Industriegesellschaft und Stammeskultur*. Frankfurt a.M.

Douglas, Mary, and Wildavsky, Aaron. 1983. *Risk and Culture. An Essay on the Selection of Technological and Environmental Dangers*. Berkeley/Los Angeles/London.

Durkheim, Emile. 1912. *Die elementaren Formen des religiösen Lebens*. Frankfurt a.M. 1981.

Duster, Troy. 1990. *Backdoors to Eugenics*. New York/London.

Eibl-Eibesfeld, Irenäus. 1970. *Liebe und Haß. Zur Naturgeschichte elementarer Verhaltensweisen*. 12. Aufl. München 1985.

———. 1980. *Grundriß der vergleichenden Verhaltensforschung*. 6. Aufl. München.

———. 1984. *Die Biologie des menschlichen Verhaltens. Grundriß der Humanethologie*. München.

Eliade, Mircea (ed.). 1987. *The Encyclopedia of Religion*. New York/London.

Erikson, Erik H. 1958. *Young Man Luther*. New York.

Esser, Hartmut. 1990. *Habits, Frames und Rational Choice—Die Reichweite von Theorien der rationalen Wahl. am Beispiel der Erklärung des Befragten-*

verhaltens. In *Kölner Zeitschrift für Soziologie und Sozialpsychologie,* Jg. 19, Heft 4/1990, 231–47.

—————. 1991. *Der Doppelpaß als soziales System.* In *Kölner Zeitschrift für Soziologie und Sozialpsychologie,* Jg. 20, 2/1991, 152–66.

Evans-Pritchard, Edward E. 1978. *Hexerei, Orakel und Magie bei den Zande.* Frankfurt a.M.

Fagerhaugh, Shizoko Y., and Strauss, Anselm. 1977. *Politics of Pain Management: Staff-Patient Interaction.* Menlo Park, Calif.

Firth, Raymond. 1930/31. *Totemism in Polynesia, Oceania.* Vol. I, No.3 + 4.

Fishman, Joshua A., et al. 1971. *Bilingualism in the Barrio.* Bloomington, Ind.

Foreville, Raymonde. 1970. *Lateran I-IV. Geschichte der ökumenischen Konzilien.* Edited by G. Dumeige and H. Bacht. Bd. IV. Mainz.

Frank, Manfred. 1977. *Das individuelle Allgemeine. Textstrukturierung und Textinterpretation nach Schleiermacher.* Frankfurt a.M.

—————. 1983. *Was ist Neostrukturalismus?* Frankfurt a.M.

Freud, Sigmund. 1910. *Über den Gegensinn der Urworte.* In Sigmund Freud: *Studienausgabe.* Edited by Alexander Mitscherlich, et al. Bd. 4. Frankfurt a.M. 1970, 227–34.

—————. 1920. *Psychologie des Unbewußten. Jenseits des Lustprinzips. Studienausgabe.* Band 3. Frankfurt a.M. 1975, 213—72.

—————. 1974. *Studienausgabe.* Edited by Alexander Mitscherlich, et al. Band 9. Frankfurt a.M.

Friedenthal, Richard. 1983. *Luther, sein Leben und seine Zeit.* Frankfurt a.M.

Frost, Robert. 1958. *Complete Poems.* New York.

Fuhrmann, Manfred, Hans Robert Jauß, and Wolfhart, Pannenberg (eds.). 1981. *Text und Applikation. Theologie, Jurisprudenz und Literaturwissenschaft im hermeneutischen Gespräch.* München.

Gadamer, Hans-Georg. 1972. *Wahrheit und Methode. Grundzüge einer philosophischen Hermeneutik.* 2. erw. Auflage. Tübingen.

Gadamer, Hans-Georg, and Gottfried Boehm (eds.). 1976. Seminar: *Philosophische Hermeneutik.* Frankfurt a.M.

————— (eds.). 1978. Seminar: *Die Hermeneutik und die Wissenschaften.* Frankfurt a.M.

Galling, Kurt (ed.). 1957–1965. *Religion in Geschichte und Gegenwart. Handwörterbuch für Theologie und Religionswissenschaft,* 6 Bde. Bd. 4.3. Völlig neu bearbeitete Aufl. Tübingen.

Geertz, Clifford. 1987. *Dichte Beschreibung. Beiträge zum Verstehen kultureller Systeme.* Übersetzt von Brigitte Luchesi und Rolf Bindemann. Frankfurt a.M.

—————. 1990. *Die künstlichen Wilden. Der Anthropologe als Schriftsteller.* Aus dem Amerikanischen von Martin Pfeiffer. München.

Gehlen, Arnold. 1961. *Anthropologische Forschung.* Hamburg.

————. 1963. *Studien zur Anthropologie und Soziologie.* Neuwied und Berlin.

————. 1973. *Urmensch und Spätkultur.* 3. Aufl. Frankfurt a.M.

————. 1978. *Der Mensch. Seine Natur und seine Stellung in der Welt.* 12. Aufl. Wiesbaden.

Gerhardt, Uta. 1986. *Verstehende Strukturanalyse: Die Konstruktion von Idealtypen als Analyseschritt bei der Auswertung qualitativer Forschungsmaterialien.* In Soeffner, Hans-Georg (ed.). 1986. Sozialstruktur und soziale Typik. Frankfurt a.M./New York.

Giovio, Paolo. 1555. *Dialogo dell'imprese militari et amorose de monsignor Paolo Giovio vescouo di Nucera.* Roma.

Giesen, Bernhard. 1991. *Die Entdinglichung des Sozialen: eine evolutionstheoretische Perspektive auf die Postmoderne.* Frankfurt a.M.

Girtler, Roland. 1984. *Interaktion und Kommunikation großstädtischer Vagabunden Wiens.* In Soeffner, Hans-Georg (1984), 215–42.

Goffman, Erving. 1971. *Interaktionsrituale. Über Verhalten in direkter Kommunikation.* Frankfurt a.M.

————. 1977. *Rahmen-Analyse. Ein Versuch über die Organisation von Alltagserfahrungen.* Frankfurt a.M.

————. 1983. *Wir alle spielen Theater. Die Selbstdarstellung im Alltag.* Vorwort von Ralf Dahrendorf. 4. Aufl. München.

Goody, Jack (ed.). 1981. *Literalität in traditionalen Gesellschaften.* Frankfurt a.M.

Goody, Jack, and Ian Watt. 1981. *Konsequenzen der Literalität.* In Goody, Jack. 1981: 45–104.

Grathoff, Richard. 1978. *Alltag und Lebenswelt als Gegenstand der phänomenologischen Sozialtheorie.* In Hammerich, Kurt/Klein, Michael. 1978: 67–85.

————. 1979. *Über Typik und Normalität im alltäglichen Milieu.* In Sprondel, Walter Michael, and Grathoff, Richard (eds.). 1979. *Alfred Schütz und die Idee des Alltags in den Sozialwissenschaften.* Stuttgart, 89–107.

————. 1989. *Milieu und Lebenswelt.* Frankfurt a.M.

Grimm, Jakob u. Wilhelm. 1956. *Deutsches Wörterbuch.* Edited by the Deutsche Akademie der Wissenschaften zu Berlin. 15 Bde. Bearbeitet von M. Heyne, H. Seedorf, H. Teuchert. Leipzig.

Gumbrecht, Hans Ulrich. 1988. *»>Ihr Fenster zur Welt< oder Wie aus dem Medium >Fernsehen< die >Fernsehwirklichkeit< wurde«.* In Soeffner, Hans-Georg (ed.). 1988. *Kultur und Alltag. Soziale Welt,* Sonderband 6, 234–50.

————. 1990. *Eine Geschichte der spanischen Literatur.* 2 Bde. Frankfurt a.M.

Gumbrecht, Hans Ulrich, and Karl-Ludwig Pfeiffer (eds.). 1988. *Materialität der Kommunikation.* Frankfurt a.M.

Gurwitsch, Aron. 1977. *Die mitmenschlichen Begegnungen in der Milieuwelt.* Edited and with an introduction by A. Metraux. Berlin/New York.

Habermas, Jürgen. 1970. *Zur Logik der Sozialwissenschaften.* Frankfurt a.M.

—————. 1973. *Der Universalitätsanspruch der Hermeneutik.* In Habermas, Jürgen, *Kultur und* Kritik. *Verstreute Aufsätze.* Frankfurt a.M., 264–301.

—————. 1981. *Theorie des kommunikativen Handelns.* Bd. I: *Handlungsrationalität und gesellschaftliche Rationalisierung.* Bd. 2: *Zur Kritik der funktionalistischen Vernunft.* Frankfurt a.M.

Hahn, Alois. 1977. *Kultische und säkulare Riten und Zeremonien in soziologischer Sicht.* In Hahn, Alois. 1977. *Anthropologie des Kults.* Freiburg/Basel/Wien.

—————. 1981. *Zur Soziologie der Beichte und anderer Formen institutionalisierter Bekenntnisse: Selbstthematisierung und Zivilisationsprozeß.* In *Kölner Zeitschrift für Soziologie und Sozialpsychologie* 34: 408–34.

—————. 1984. *Religiöse Wurzeln des Zivilisationsprozesses.* In Braun/Hahn (eds.). 1984. *Kultur im Zeitalter der Sozialwissenschaften.* Friedrich Tenbruck zum 65. Geburtstag. Berlin.

Hahn, Alois, and Volker Kapp (eds.). 1987. *Selbstthematisierung und Selbstzeugnis: Bekenntnis und Geständnis.* Frankfurt a.M.

Halbwachs, Maurice. 1925. *Das Gedächtnis und seine sozialen Bedingungen.* Frankfurt a.M. 1985.

—————. 1967. *Das kollektive Gedächtnis.* Frankfurt a.M. 1985.

Haller, Max, Hans-Joachim Hoffmann-Nowotny, and Wolfgang Zapf (eds.). 1989. *Kultur und Gesellschaft.* Verhandlungen des 24. Deutschen Soziologentages, des II. Österreichischen Soziologentages und des 8. Kongresses der Schweizerischen Gesellschaft für Soziologie in Zürich 1989. Frankfurt a.M./New York.

Hammerich, Kurt, and Michael Klein (eds.). 1978. *Materialien zur Soziologie des Alltags.* In *Kölner Zeitschrift für Soziologie und Sozialpsychologie,* Sonderheft. 1978. Opladen.

Havelock, Eric A. 1963. *Preface to Plato.* Cambridge, Mass.: Harvard University Press.

Hegel, Georg Wilhelm Friedrich: *Werke in 20 Bänden.* Auf der Grundlage der Werke von 1832–1845 neu edierte Ausgabe. Redaktion Eva Moldenhauer und Karl Markus Michel. Frankfurt a.M. 1970.

Heidegger, Martin. 1927. *Sein und Zeit.* 9. unv. Auflage. Tübingen 1960.

Heider, Fritz. 1969. *Soziale Wahrnehmung und phänomenale Kausalität;* in: Irle, Martin. 1969, 26–56.

Heller, Agnes. 1970. *Alltag und Geschichte: Zur sozialistischen Gesellschaftslehre.* Neuwied/Berlin.

—————. 1978. *Das Alltagsleben. Versuch einer Erklärung der individuellen Reproduktion.* Frankfurt a.M.

Henscheid, Eckhard. 1980. *Ein scharmanter Bauer*. Frankfurt a.M.

Hermann, Ferdinand (ed.). 1960. Symbolik der Religionen. Band VI. *Symbolik der katholischen Kirche*. Stuttgart.

———— (ed.). 1967. *Symbolik der Religionen*. Band X. *Kultsymbolik des Protestantismus*. Stuttgart.

Hildebrandt, Hans-Hagen. 1985. *Ich-Fiktion im Spiegel. Bruchstücke aus der Geschichte der Subjektfiguration*. Ms. Habilitationsschrift, Essen.

Hildenbrand, Bruno. 1984. *Methodik und Einzelfallstudie*. Studienmaterialien der FernUniversität. Hagen.

Hitzler, Ronald. 1988. *Sinnwelten: ein Beitrag zum Verstehen von Kultur*. Opladen.

————. 1991. *Der banale Proteus. Eine >postmoderne< Metapher?* In Kuzmics, Helmut/Mörth, Ingo (eds.). 1991. *Der unendliche Prozeß der Zivilisation*. Frankfurt a.M./New York.

Hitzler, Ronald, and Anne Honer. 1988. *Der lebensweltliche Forschungsansatz*. In *Neue Praxis*, 18. Jg., 6/1988, 496–501.

Hörning, Karl H., et al. 1990. *Zeitpioniere: flexible Arbeitszeiten—neuer Lebensstil*. Frankfurt a.M.

Hoffmann, Hilmar. 1982. *Das Taubenbuch*. Frankfurt a.M.

Hoffmann-Nowotny, Hans-Joachim. 1979. *Migration: Ein Beitrag zu einer soziologischen Erklärung*. Stuttgart.

————. 1988. *Ehe und Familie in der modernen Gesellschaft*. In *Aus Politik und Zeitgeschichte*, 13/1988, 3–13.

Honer, Anne. 1989. *Einige Probleme lebensweltlicher Ethnographie*. In *Zeitschrift für Soziologie*, 4/1989, 297–312.

Horowitz, Irving Louis. 1991. *Daydreams and Nightmares*. University Press of Mississippi.

Husserl, Edmund. 1936. *Die Krisis der europäischen Wissenschaften und die transzendentale Phänomenologie. Eine Einleitung in die phänomenologische Philosophie*. Edited by Walter Biemel. 2. Auflage. =Husserliana, Edmund Husserl, Ges. Werke, Band V. Den Haag, 1969.

Irle, Martin (ed.). 1969. *Texte aus der experimentellen Sozialpsychologie*. Edited and with an introduction by Martin Irle in collaboration with Mario von Cranach and Hermann Vetter. Neuwied/Berlin.

Iser, Wolfgang. 1972. *Der implizite Leser. Kommunikationsformen des Romans von Bunyan bis Beckett*. München.

James, William. 1893. *The Principles of Psychology*. Reprint New York, 1951.

Jandl, Ernst. 1980. *der gelbe hund. gedichte*. Neuwied.

Jauß, Hans Robert. 1981. *Zur Abgrenzung und Bestimmung einer literarischen Hermeneutik*. In Fuhrmann, Manfred, Robert Hans Jauß, and Wolfhart Pannenberg. 1981, 459–81.

Jaspers, Karl. 1932. *Philosophie*. Berlin, 1948.

————. 1971. *Psychologie der Weltanschauungen*. 6. Aufl. Berlin.

Kant, Immanuel. 1785. *Grundlegung zur Metaphysik der Sitten.* = Immanuel Kant, *Werke in 10 Bänden,* edited by Wilhelm Weischede, Bd. 6. *Schriften zur Ethik und Religionsphilosophie I.* Darmstadt 1968, 7–121.

————. 1907. Kant's Gesammelte Schriften. Edited by the Königlich Preußische Akademie der Wissenschaften. Erste Abteilung. Berlin, 1907.

Kellner, Hansfried, and Frank Heuberger. 1988. *Zur Rationalität der >Postmoderne< und ihrer Träger.* In Soeffner, Hans-Georg (ed.). 1988. *Soziale Welt,* Sonderband 6: *Kultur und Alltag.* Göttingen, 325–90.

Keppler, Angela. 1985. *Präsentation und Information. Zur politischen Berichterstattung im Fernsehen.* Tübingen.

Kierkegaard, Sören. 1959a. *Die Krankheit zum Tode.* Translated by G. Jungblut. Hamburg.

————. 1959b. *Die Tagebücher. Gesammelte Werke.* Selected, reorganized and translated by H. Gerdes. Düsseldorf/Köln.

————. 1964. Werke. 5 Bände, Bd. V: *Philosophische Brocken*; in neuer Übertragung und mit Kommentar von Lieselotte Richter. Reinbek bei Hamburg.

Klein, Stefan. 1981. *Reportagen aus dem Ruhrgebiet.* Frankfurt a.M.

Knigge, Adolph Frh. v. 1977. *Über den Umgang mit Menschen.* Edited by Gerd Ueding. Unv. Aufl. Frankfurt a.M.

Knilli, Friedrich. 1976. *Talk-Show: Das Kabinett des Dr. Biolek.* In *Medium 6*, Heft 12, 1976, 8–23.

Knoch, W. 1983. *Die Einsetzung der Sakramente durch Christus. Eine Untersuchung zur Sakramententheologie der Frühscholastik von Anselm von Laon bis zu Wilhelm von Auxerre. Beiträge zur Geschichte der Philosophie und Theologie des Mittelalters.* Neue Folge, Bd. 42. Münster.

Knorr-Cetina, Karin. 1984. *Die Fabrikation von Erkenntnis. Zur Anthropologie der Naturwissenschaften.* Frankfurt a.M.

————. 1989. *Spielarten des Konstruktivismus.* In *Soziale Welt I,* 1989, 86–96.

König, René. 1962. *Die Beobachtung.* In König, René (ed.). 1962. *Handbuch der empirischen Sozialforschung.* Band 2. Stuttgart, 1–65.

Koselleck, Reinhart. 1972. *Geschichte, Historie.* In Brunner, Otto, Werner Conze, and Reinhart Koselleck, (eds.). 1972. *Geschichtliche Grundbegriffe.* Stuttgart, 593–717.

Kracauer, Siegfried. 1963. *Das Ornament der Masse.* Essays. Frankfurt a.M.

Kreuzer, Helmut. 1982. *Sachwörterbuch des Fernsehens.* Göttingen.

Kuhn, Thomas S. 1976. *Die Struktur wissenschaftlicher Revolutionen.* Zweite revidierte und um das Postskriptum von 1969 ergänzte Auflage. Frankfurt a.M.

Labov, William. 1972. *Sociolinguistic Patterns*. Philadelphia.

Langer, Susanne K. 1965. *Philosophie auf neuem Wege. Das Symbol im Denken, im Ritus und in der Kunst*. Frankfurt a.M.

Lau, Thomas. 1991. *Die Heiligen Narren. Punk 1976–1986*. Berlin.

Lau Thomas, and Andreas Voß. 1988. *Die Spende—eine Odyssee im religiösen Kosmos*. In Soeffner, Hans-Georg. 1988. *Kultur und Alltag. Soziale Welt*. Sonderband 6, Göttingen, 285–97.

Leach, Edmund. ed.). 1973. *Mythos und Totemismus. Beiträge zur Kritik der strukturalen Analyse*. Frankfurt a.M.

Leach, Edmund. 1978. *Kultur und Kommunikation. Zur Logik symbolischer Zusammenhänge*. Translated by Eberhard Bubser. Frankfurt a.M.

Lefebvre, Henri. 1972. *Das Alltagsleben in der modernen Welt*. Frankfurt a.M.

———. 1974. *Kritik des Alltagslebens*. 3 Bände. München.

Lepsius, Rainer M. 1990. *Interessen, Ideen und Institutionen*. Opladen.

Lévi-Strauss, Claude. 1962. *Das Ende des Totemismus*. Frankfurt a.M. 1965.

———. 1967. *Strukturale Anthropologie*. Frankfurt a.M.

———. 1974. *Traurige Tropen*. Translated by Suzanne Heintz. Köln.

———. 1978. *Mythologica I: Das Rohe und das Gekochte*. Translated by Eva Moldenhauer. Frankfurt a.M.

Loewenich, Walther V. 1983. *Martin Luther. Der Mann und das Werk*. München.

Lohse, Bernhard. 1962. *Mönchtum und Reformation*. München.

Luckmann, Thomas. 1963. *Das Problem der Religion in der modernen Gesellschaft*. Freiburg.

———. 1979. *Soziologie der Sprache*. In König, René (ed.). 1979. *Handbuch der empirischen Sozialforschung*, Band 13. Zweite völlig neubearbeitete Auflage. Stuttgart, 1–116.

———. 1980. *Lebenswelt und Gesellschaft*. Paderborn.

———. 1981. *Zum hermeneutischen Problem der Handlungswissenschaften*. In Fuhrmann, Manfred, Hans Robert Jauß, and Wolfhart Pannenberg (1981): 513–23.

———. 1985. *Riten als Bewältigung lebensweltlicher Grenzen*; in: *Schweizerische Zeitschrift für Soziologie*, 3/1985, 535–550.

———. 1986. *Grundformen der gesellschaftlichen Vermittlung des Wissens: Kommunikative Gattungen*. In Neidhardt, Friedhelm, Rainer M. Lepsius, and Johannes Weiss (eds.). 1986. *Kultur und Gesellschaft*. Sonderheft 27 der KZfSS. Opladen, 191–211.

———. 1989. *Kultur und Kommunikation*. In Haller, Max, Hans-Joachim Hoffmann-Nowotny, and Wolfgang Zapf (eds.). 1989. *Kultur und Gesellschaft*. Verhandlungen des 24. Deutschen Soziologentages, des 11.

Österreichischen Soziologentages und des 8. Kongresses der Schweizerischen Gesellschaft für Soziologie in Zürich 1988. Frankfurt a.m./New York, 33–45.

Lüning, Hildegard. (no year) *Der Papst in Mexiko*. Düsseldorf.

Luhmann, Niklas. 1986. *Die Richtigkeit soziologischer Theorien*. In *Merkur I*, 1986, 36–49.

———. 1989. *Gesellschaftsstruktur und Semantik. Studien zur Wissenssoziologie der modernen Gesellschaft*. Band 3. Frankfurt a.M.

Luhmann, Niklas, and Peter Fuchs. 1989. *Reden und Schweigen*. Frankfurt a.M.

Lukács, Georg. 1963. *Die Eigenart des Ästhetischen*. I. Halbband. = Georg Lukács: *Werke*. Band II). Neuwied/Berlin.

Luther, Martin. 1983a. *Studienausgabe*. Bd. 3.

———. 1983b. *De servo arbitrio*. In Borcherdt, H. H., and G. Merz (eds.). *Ausgewählte Werke*. München.

Lyotard, Jean François. 1983. *Le Différend*. Paris.

Malinowski, Bronislaw. 1944. *Eine wissenschaftliche Theorie der Kultur und andere Aufsätze*. Frankfurt a.M. 1975.

———. 1948. *Magie, Wissenschaft und Religion*. Und andere Schriften. Frankfurt a.M. 1973.

———. 1986. *Ein Tagebuch im strikten Sinn des Wortes. Neuguinea 1914–1918*. Mit einem Vorwort von Valetta Malinowski und einer Einleitung von Raymond Firth. Frankfurt a.M.

Marquard, Odo. 1981. *Die Frage nach der Frage, auf die die Hermeneutik eine Antwort ist*. In Marquard, Odo (1981). *Abschied vom Prinzipiellen*. Stuttgart, 117–46.

Marx, Karl, and Friedrich Engels. 1956 ff. *Werke*. Edited by Institut für Marxismus-Leninismus beim ZK der SED. Berlin. DDR.

Mauss, Marcel. 1950. *Die Gabe. Form und Funktion des Austausches in archaischen Gesellschaften*. In Mauss, Marcel, *Soziologie und Anthropologie*. Band 2. München 1975, 9–14.

Mauthner, Fritz. 1910. *Wörterbuch der Philosophie. Neue Beiträge zu einer Kritik der Sprache*. Nachdruck der 1. Auflage. Zürich 1986.

Mayer, Karl-Ulrich. 1990. *Generationsdynamik und Innovation in der Grundlagenforschung*. In Max-Planck-Gesellschaft. Berichte und Mitteilungen 3/90.

Mead, George Herbert. 1934. *Geist, Identität und Gesellschaft aus der Sicht des Sozialbehaviorismus*. Mit einer Einleitung von Charles W. Morris. Frankfurt a.M. 1969.

———. 1969a. *Philosophie der Sozialität. Aufsätze zur Erkenntnisanthropologie*. Edited by Hansfried Kellner. Frankfurt a.M.

————. 1969b. *Sozialpsychologie.* Edited and with an introduction by Anselm Strauss. Neuwied/Berlin.

Merleau-Ponty, Maurice. 1966. *Phänomenologie der Wahrnehmung.* Berlin.

————. 1973. *Vorlesungen I.* Berlin/New York.

Mertens, Veronika. 1983. *Mi-parti als Zeichen. Zur Bedeutung von geteiltem Kleid und geteilter Gestalt in der Ständetracht in literarischen und bildnerischen Quellen sowie im Fastnachtsbrauch vom Mittelalter bis zur Gegenwart.* Remscheid.

Merton, Robert K. 1975. *Social Theory and Social Structure.* Glencoe.

Meyer, Hubert, Klaus Wolf, and Jürgen Czekalla. 1983. *Kriminalistisches Lehrbuch der Polizei Hilden.* Hilden.

Moeller, Berndt, and K. Stackmann. 1981. *Luder—Luther—Eleutherius. Erwägungen zu Luthers Namen. Nachrichten der Akademie der Wissenschaften in Göttingen* I. Philosophisch-Historische Klasse 7.

Montaigne, Michel E. de. 1530. *Essais.* Frankfurt a.M. 1976.

Müller-Doohm, Stefan. 1990. *Vom Positivismusstreit zur Hermeneutikdebatte—Die Aktualität des interpretativen Paradigmas.* In *Kultur-Analysen,* 2. Jg. 1990, Heft 3, 292–307.

Müller-Salget, Klaus. 1984. *Erzählungen für das Volk. Evangelische Pfarrer als Volksschriftsteller im Deutschland des 19. Jahrhunderts.* Berlin.

Musil, Robert. 1952. *Der Mann ohne Eigenschaften.* = Gesammelte Werke. Edited by Adolf Frisé. Bd. 1–2. Reinbek bei Hamburg 1978.

Neidhardt, Friedhelm. 1985. *Einige Ideen zu einer allgemeinen Theorie sozialer Bewegungen.* In Hradil, S. (ed.). 1985. *Sozialstrukturen im Umbruch.* Karl Martin Bolte zum 60. Geburtstag. Opladen, 182–98.

Neidhardt, Friedhelm, Rainer M. Lepsius, and Johannes Weiss (eds.). 1986. *Kultur und Gesellschaft.* Sonderheft 27 der *KZfSS.* Opladen.

Nietzsche, Friedrich. 1980. *Werke in sechs Bänden.* Edited by Karl Schlechta. München.

Nixdorf, Heide, and Heidi Müller. 1983. *Weiße Westen—Rote Roben. Katalog zur Sonderausstellung der staatlichen Museen Preußischer Kulturbesitz,* Museum für Völkerkunde, Abt. Europa, und Museum für Deutsche Volkskunde. Berlin.

Noelle-Neumann, Elisabeth, and Karl Reumann. 1971. *Nachrichtenwesen.* In Noelle-Neumann, E., and W. Schulz (eds.). 1971. *Publizistik.* Frankfurt a.M., 187–99.

Oevermann, Ulrich. 1973. *Zur Analyse der Struktur von sozialen Deutungsmustern.* Ms. Frankfurt a.M.

————. 1979a. *Sozialisationstheorie. Ansätze zu einer soziologischen Sozialisationstheorie und ihre Konsequenzen für die allgemeine soziologische Analyse.* In Lüschen, Günter (ed.). Deutsche Soziologie seit

1945. Entwicklungslinien und Praxisbezug. = *Kölner Zeitschrift für Soziologie und Sozialpsychologie,* Sonderheft 1979. Opladen, 143–68.

————. 1979b. *Exemplarische Analyse eines Ausschnitts aus einem Protokoll einer Fernsehsendung >Dalli Dalli<.* Ms. Frankfurt a.M.

————. 1983. *Versozialwissenschaftlichung der Identitätsformation und Verweigerung von Lebenspraxis: Eine aktuelle Variante der Dialektik der Aufklärung.* Ms. Frankfurt a.M.

Oevermann, Ulrich, et al. 1976. *Beobachtungen zur Struktur der sozial-isatorischen Interaktion. Theoretische und methodologische Fragen der Interaktionsforschung.* In Auwärter, Manfred, Edit Kirsch, and Klaus Schröter (eds.). 1976. *Seminar: Kommunikation, Interaktion, Identität.* Frankfurt a.M., 371–403.

————. 1979. *Die Methodologie einer >objektiven Hermeneutik< und ihre allgemeine forschungslogische Bedeutung in den Sozialwissenschaften.* In Soeffner, Hans-Georg. (1979): 352–433.

Otto, Rudolf. 1963. *Das Heilige.* München.

Paulsen, Friedrich. 1919. *Geschichte des gelehrten Unterrichts auf den deutschen Schulen und Universitäten vom Ausgang des Mittelalters bis zur Gegenwart.* 2 Bände. Edited by Lehmann, Rudolf. 3., erw. Auflage. Berlin.

Peirce, Charles S. 1970. *Schriften.* Band 2. *Vom Pragmatismus zum Pragmatizismus.* Edited by Karl-Otto Apel. Frankfurt a.M.

Platon. 1977/1978. *Sämtliche Werke.* In der Übersetzung von Friedrich Schleiermacher, mit der Stephanus-Numerierung. Edited by Walter F. Otto, Ernesto Grasso, Gert Plamböck. Band I. Hamburg.

Plessner, Helmuth. 1929. *Die Stufen des Organischen und der Mensch.* 3. Aufl. Berlin/New York 1975.

————. 1959. *Die verspätete Nation. Über die politische Verführbarkeit bürgerlichen Geistes.* = Gesammelte Schriften VI). Frankfurt a.M. 1982.

————. 1970. *Philosophische Anthropologie. Lachen und Weinen. Das Lächeln. Anthropologie der Sinne.* Edited by Günter Dux. Frankfurt a.M.

Plutarch. 1947. *Kinderzucht.* Griechisch-deutsche Ausgabe. Erlangen.

Pope, Alexander. 1734. *An Essay on Man.* Edited with an introduction by Frank Brady. Indianapolis 1965.

Popper, Karl. 1963. *Conjectures and Refutations. The Growth of Scientific Knowledge.* London.

————. 1972. *Objektive Erkenntnis. Ein evolutionärer Entwurf.* 2. Auflage. Hamburg 1974.

Pseudo-Augustin. 1632. *Hypomnesticon contra Pelagianos et Caelestianos 3,* II, 20. MPL 45.

Radcliffe-Brown, Alfred Reginald. 1952. *Structure and Function in Primitive Society.* London.

Reichertz, Jo. 1986. *Probleme qualitativer Sozialforschung. Zur Entstehungs-
geschichte der Objektiven Hermeneutik.* Frankfurt a.M./New York.
———. 1991. *Zur Produktion von Aufklärung.* Stuttgart.
Ricoeur, Paul. 1972. *Der Text als Modell. Hermeneutisches Verstehen.* In
Bühl, W. L. (ed.). *Verstehende Soziologie 1972*, 252–83.
Sales-Doyé, Franz v. 1929. *Heilige und Selige der römisch-katholischen
Kirche.* Leipzig.
San Francisco Chronicle. 19 September 1987: A10, A12.
Schätzler, C. v. 1860. *Die Lehre von der Wirklichkeit der Sakramente—Ex
opere operato—in ihrer Entwicklung innerhalb der Scholastik und ihrer
Bedeutung für die christliche Heilslehre.* München.
Scheler, Max. 1923. *Wesen und Formen der Sympathie. Die deutsche
Philosophie der Gegenwart.* Edited by Frings, Manfred S. 6. durchgesehene
Auflage von >Phänomenologie und Theorie des Sympathiegefühls<,
Deutsche Philosophie der Gegenwart. 2. durchgesehene Auflage. Bern u.a.
1973.
———. 1926. *Die Wissensformen und die Gesellschaft. Probleme einer
Soziologie des Wissens.* Erkenntnis und Arbeit. Eine Studie über Wert und
Grenzen des pragmatischen Prinzips in der Erkenntnis der Welt. Universität
und Volkshochschule Leipzig.
———. 1947. *Die Stellung des Menschen im Kosmos.* München.
———. 1957. *Vorbilder und Führer.* In Scheler, Max, *Schriften aus dem
Nachlaß.* Bd. I: *Zur Ethik und Erkenntnislehre.* 2. Auflage. Bern.
Schiller, Friedrich v. 1787. *Was heißt und zu welchem Ende studiert man
Universalgeschichte?* Eine akademische Antrittsrede. In Schillers Werke.
Nationalausgabe. Begründet von Julius Petersen. Hg. im Auftrag der
Nationalen Forschungs- und Gedenkstätten der klassischen deutschen
Literatur in Weimar. Goethe- und Schiller-Archiv und des Schiller-
Nationalmuseums in Marbach von Lieselotte Blumenthal und Benno von
Wiese. Siebzehnter Band. *Historische Schriften.* Erster Teil. Edited by Karl-
Heinz Hahn. Weimar 1970, 359–76.
Schmaus, Michael, et al. (eds.). 1989. *Handbuch der Dogmengeschichte.
Sakramente—Eschatologie.* Faszikel I a: Die Lehre von den Sakramenten
im allgemeinen von der Schrift bis zur Scholastik. Bd. IV. Freiburg/Basel/
Wien.
Schütz, Alfred. 1932. *Der sinnhafte Aufbau der sozialen Welt.* Frankfurt a.M.
1974.
———. 1971/1972. *Gesammelte Aufsätze. 3 Bände.* Den Haag.
———. 1985. *Briefwechsel 1939–1959.* Edited by Richard Grathoff. München
1985.
Schütz, Alfred, and Thomas Luckmann. 1979/1984. *Strukturen der
Lebenswelt.* Band I 1979, Band 2 1984. Frankfurt a.M.

Schulz, Walter. 1972. *Philosophie in der veränderten Welt.* Pfullingen.
Scott, Marvin B., and Stanford M. Lyman. 1976. *Praktische Erklärungen.* In Auwärter, Manfred, Edit Kirsch, and Klaus Schröter (eds.). 1976. *Seminar: Kommunikation, Interaktion, Identität.* Frankfurt a.M., 73–114.
Searle, John R. 1969. *Speech Acts.* Cambridge, 1969.
Sennett, Richard. 1983. *Verfall und Ende des öffentlichen Lebens. Die Tyrannei der Intimität.* Frankfurt a.M.
———. 1991. Civitas. *Die Großstadt und die Kultur des Unterschieds. Aus dem Amerikanischen von Reinhard Kaiser.* Frankfurt a.M.
Simmel, Georg. 1977. *Philosophie des Geldes.* 7. Auflage, unveränderter Nachdruck der 1958 erschienenen 6. Auflage. Berlin.
Soeffner, Hans-Georg. 1974. *Der geplante Mythos. Untersuchungen zur Struktur und Wirkungsgeschichte der Utopie.* Hamburg.
———. 1979. *Interaktion und Interpretation. Überlegungen zu Prämissen des Interpretierens in Sozial- und Literaturwissenschaft.* In Soeffner, Hans-Georg. 1979. 328–51.
———. 1983. >*Typus und Individualität*< oder >*Typen der Individualität*<? *Entdeckungsreisen in das Land, in dem man zu Hause ist.* In Wenzel, Horst (ed.). 1983. *Typus und Individualität im Mittelalter.* München, 11–44.
———. 1989. *Auslegung des Alltags—Der Alltag der Auslegung: Zur wissenssoziologischen Konzeption einer sozialwissenschaftlichen Hermeneutik.* Frankfurt a.M.
———. 1991. *Zur Soziologie des Symbols und des Rituals.* In Wegenast/ Oelkers (eds.). 1991. *Das Symbol. Brücke des Verstehens.* Bern.
Soeffner, Hans-Georg (ed.). 1979. *Interpretative Verfahren in den Sozial- und Textwissenschaften.* Stuttgart.
———. (ed.). 1982. *Beiträge zu einer empirischen Sprachsoziologie.* Tübingen.
———. (ed.). 1984. *Beiträge zu einer Soziologie der Interaktion.* Frankfurt a.M.
———. (ed.). 1986. *Sozialstruktur und soziale Typik.* Frankfurt a.M./New York.
———. (ed.). 1988. *Kultur und Alltag. Soziale Welt,* Sonderband 6, Göttingen.
Srubar, Ilja. 1981. *Max Scheler: Eine wissenssoziologischer Alternative.* In Stehr, Nico and Volker Meja (eds.). 1981. *Wissenssoziologie.* = *KfZSS,* Sonderheft. 1981. Opladen, 343–59.
———. 1988. *Kosmion. Die Genese der pragmatischen Lebenswelttheorie von Alfred Schütz und ihr anthropologischer Hintergrund.* Frankfurt a.M.
Starobinski, Jean. 1971. *Jean-Jacques Rousseau. La transparente et l'obstacle: suivi de 7 essais sur Rousseau.* Paris.
Stegmüller, Wolfgang. 1969. *Hauptströmungen der Gegenwartsphilosophie. Eine kritische Einführung.* 4. erweiterte Auflage. Stuttgart.
Strauss, Anselm. 1968. *Spiegel und Masken. Die Suche nach Identität.* Frankfurt a.M.

————. 1976. *Images of the American Cities*. San Francisco.

————. 1978. *Negotiations. Varieties, Contexts, Processes and Social Order*. San Francisco.

————. 1984. *Qualitative Analysis in Social Research*. Grounded Theory Methodology. Studienmaterial der FernUniversität. Hagen.

Strauss, Anselm, et al. 1985. *Social Organization of Medical Work*. Chicago/London.

————. 1991. *Creating Sociological Awareness. Collective Images and symbolic Representations*. New Brunswick/London.

Szondi, Peter. 1975. *Einführung in die literarische Hermeneutik*. Edited by Jean Bollack and Helen Stierlin. Frankfurt a.M.

Tarski, Alfred. 1956. *Logic, Semantics, Mathematics*. Oxford.

Thomas, William Isaac and Florian Znaniecki. 1918. *The Polish Peasant in Europe and America*. Boston.

Thompson, Edward P. 1967. *Time, Work-Discipline and Industrial Capitalism*. In *Past and Present 38*, 56–97.

Volkart, Edmund Howell (ed.). 1951. *Social Behaviour and Personality. Contributions of W. I. Thomas to Theory and Social Research*. New York.

Voß, Andreas. 1993. *Betteln und Spenden—eine soziologische Studie über Rituale freiwilliger Armenunterstützung, ihre historischen und aktuellen Formen sowie ihrer sozialen Leistungen*. Berlin.

Watzlawick, Paul, Janet H. Beavin and Don D. Jackson. 1969. *Menschliche Kommunikation*. Bern.

Weber, Max. 1917. *Der Sinn der >Wertfreiheit< der soziologischen und ökonomischen Wissenschaften*. In Weber, Max, *Gesammelte Aufsätze zur Wissenschaftslehre*. Edited by Johannes Winckelmann. 4. erneut durchgesehene Auflage. Tübingen 1973, 489–540.

————. 1919. *Politik als Beruf*. In Weber, Max. 1971: 505–60.

————. 1971. *Gesammelte Politische Schriften*. Edited by Johannes Winckelmann. 3. erneut vermehrte Auflage. Tübingen.

————. 1972a. *Wirtschaft und Gesellschaft. Grundriss der verstehenden Soziologie*, 5. revidierte Auflage. Edited by Johannes Winckelmann. Tübingen.

————. 1972b. *Gesammelte Aufsätze zur Religionssoziologie I*. Tübingen.

Wenzel, Horst (ed.). 1983. *Typus und Individualität im Mittelalter*. München.

————. 1985. *Exemplarisches Rittertum und Individualitätsgeschichte. Zur Doppelstruktur der >Geschichten und Taten Wilwolts von Schaumburg. 1446–1519<*. In Gerhard, C., et al. (eds.). 1985. *Geschichtsbewußtsein in der deutschen Literatur des Mittelalters*. Tübinger Colloquium 1983. Tübingen.

Weymann, Ansgar (ed.). 1989. *Handlungsspielräume: Untersuchungen zur Individualisierung und Institutionalisierung von Lebensläufen in der Moderne*. Stuttgart.

Whitehead, Alfred N. 1938. *Verstehen*. In Gadamer, Hans-Georg, and Gottfried Boehm. 1978, 63–82.

Woll-Schumacher, Irene. 1971. *Gesellschaftsstruktur und Rolle der Frau. Das Beispiel der Irokesen*. Berlin.

Wundt, Wilhelm. 1921. *Völkerpsychologie. Eine Untersuchung der Entwicklungsgesetze von Sprache, Mythos und Sitte*. Stuttgart.

Wuttke, Adolf. 1900. *Der deutsche Volksglaube*. Berlin.

Zapf, Wolfgang. 1987. *Individualisierung und Sicherheit: Untersuchung zur Lebensqualität in der Bundesrepublik Deutschland*. München.

Zweig, Stefan. 1945. *Legenden*. Frankfurt a.M. 1972.

Name Index

Aaron, xii
Abel, 7
Abelard, 44–45n. 23
Adam: and Eve, 18; the old, 4, 24–25, 30. *See also* Luther, Martin
Adenauer, Konrad, 138
Adonis, 102
Akbar the Great, 99
Albers, Hans, 98–104
Allert, Tillman, 156n. 23
Anfortas, 103
Aphrodite/Venus, 101
Astarte, 98, 101
Atargatis, 101
Augustine, Saint, 8–9, 43n. 5

Bach, Johann Sebastian, 102
Bach, Vivi, 102
Bauer, Dieter, 142
Belafonte, Harry, 60
Bierce, Ambrose, 85
Bocaccio, Giovanni, xvi, xvii
Boleslav, Duke of Silesia, 143
Bora, Katharina von, 21
Brecht, Bertolt, 103
Brutus, 98
Bultmann, Rudolf, 10, 14

Cain, 7
Calvin, John, *see Calvinism*
Carpendale, Howard, 128
Cassirer, Ernst, 145
Castiglione, Baldassare, ix
Cher Ami, 101

David, 6, 7
de Gaulle, Charles, 138, 140
Diana, Princess, 128
Dietrich, Marlene, 94n. 22
Dilthey, Wilhelm, xiii
Dire Straits, 81

Djozer (pharoah of Egypt)
Douglas, Mary, 71
Doye, Franz von Sales, 143
Drayton, Michael, 107
Duke of Braunschweig, 57
Durkheim, Emile, 110–11, 149, 156n. 19

Eastwood, Clint, 91
Eco, Umberto, 145
Elstner, Frank, 120
Eleutherius, Luther's use of, 3–4

Firth, Raymond, 111, 112
Francis, Saint, 59
Frederick the Great, 57
Freud, Sigmund, 9, 38, 40–41, 145

Gadamer, Hans-Goerg, xiii
Gehlen, Arnold, 73, 75, 92
Geyer, Florian, 57
God, 4–46, 81, 112; punks' conception of, 62, 67, 83; representative of, *see* John Paul II, Pope
Goethe, Johann von, xv
Gottschalk, Thomas, 120
Graf, Steffi, 128
Greco, Juliette, 57
Gunther, Count of Schwarzburg, 57

Habermas, Jurgen, viii
Hahn, Alois, 44n. 21
Halbwachs, Maurice, 60
Hedwig, Saint, 142–45
Hegel, Georg Wilhelm Friedrich, 67, 115
Henry, Duke of Silesia, 143
Hieronymous, 13
Hitler, Adolph, 57, 142
Hoffmann, Hilmer, 98–110 passim, 115n. 4
Hyde, Mr., 26

173

Subject Index

American Indians, 55; Iroquois, 55–56, 59
anti-ritualism, 71–94
autobiography, 1, 10–15, 23

Calvinism, 6; compared to Lutheranism, 32, 36–38; traditions of, 37
Catholic Church, 18–20, 31, 79, 102; and confession, 20; and psychotherapy, 64; teachings of, and Pope John Paul II, 85–91
Central Europe, viii, 1, 56, 72, 76
ceremonial milieu, 60
chapter on offences, *see* offence chapter
charisma, 67, 76, 81–83, 87, 89, 135–56; definitions, 149, 155n. 4; personal, 136, 149; stagings, 151
Christianity, 10; early community, 67; concept of God in, 41; liberated Christian, 30; mythology in, 12–13, 102–3; traditions of, 4, 35, 39
classes, vii–ix, 23, 77, 127, 152; educated, 124
clothing, ix, 50–59, 140; black, history of, 56–57; punks wearing of, 54–55, 56–59; peace movement, 77
collective symbol, 90, 92, 96–97, 110–14, 138; meaning of, 97
communal soul, 81–83
confession, 16–20, 22, 39; as public control, 20; widespread phenomenon of, 18
conversion, 9, 30; negative, 6; punks and, 60–63; symbolic, 4–7
curriculum vitae, collective, 10–15

Deus absconditus (revealed God), 28–42
Deus praedicatus (concealed God), 28–42

Diet at Worms, 14, 18, 27

ego, 14, 21–22, 26, 38–39, 42
Enlightenment, 35–36, 40, 66, 84
ethics of belief, 37

faith, 1–48, 64, 73, 80, 85–86, 154; basis for, 29; leap of, 31, 33
fascinosum, 150, 151, 154

Germany, 15, 72, 138; number of pigeon breeders in, 104
Green party, 54, 56
group milieu, 60
group soul, 78
Guinness Book of Records, 123

habits of conduct, xi
hermeneutics, xii–xiv
hierarchies, viii, 72
Holy Ghost, 39–40, 102
human chain, 78–79, 94nn. 12, 14; 141
Humanistic Circle, 3

identification, 109–110; figure, 5
individual-orietation, 66
individualization, vii, 9, 13, 14, 15, 153
inner action, 36, 37, 42
inner world, 35–37, 80; disciplining, 22
interwovenness, xiv
invisible religion, 41, 58
isolation, viii, 1–2, 17–19, 21–23, 30, 34, 58; external, 7; structural, 1

Judaism, orthodox, 11; traditions of, 39, 102. *See also* Christian traditions and Judeo-Christian tradition
Judeo-Christian tradition, 7, 39, 40–41, 87

175